Praise for *A Thing of Beauty*

'Fiennes is a brilliant and generous guide through Greece. He weaves the ancient world and the modern together with intelligence and elegance... There's a wry Sebaldian humour at work here... *A Thing of Beauty* is a must-read.'

Alex Preston, *Observer*

'This book is a lament for a poisoned planet... He goes in search of the numinous but relishes the bathos of modernity... not so much a travelogue as an excursion into the psyche of Anthropocene man.'

Literary Review

'A highly personal travelogue...with the historical and modern-day detail that late British travel writer Jan Morris might bring to the task.'

Booklist, starred review

'In *A Thing of Beauty*, myths are not presented as dust-covered artefacts but vibrant, living, often frightening things that, like Greek gods, still affect and manipulate our lives. The quest that Peter Fiennes undertakes is of urgent relevance in this time of environmental change. Startling, informative and often very funny.'

Nick Hunt, author of *Outlandish*

'Self-deprecating, funny, deeply knowledgeable about Greek mythology, yet simultaneously confronting the challenges that face our world head-on, Fiennes is a most delightful travelling companion.'

Katharine Norbury, author of *The Fish Ladder*

T0001017

Also by Peter Fiennes

Footnotes: A Journey Round Britain in the Company of Great Writers
Oak and Ash and Thorn: The Ancient Woods and
New Forests of Britain
To War with God: The Army Chaplain Who Lost His Faith

A THING
OF BEAUTY

Travels in Mythical & Modern Greece

Peter Fiennes

ONEWORLD

A Oneworld Book

First published by Oneworld Publications in 2021
This paperback edition published 2022

Copyright © Peter Fiennes 2021

The moral right of Peter Fiennes to be identified as the
Author of this work has been asserted by him in accordance
with the Copyright, Designs, and Patents Act 1988

ISBN 978-0-86154-435-6
eISBN 978-0-86154-062-4

Illustrations © David Wardle

Typeset by Hewer Text UK Ltd, Edinburgh
Printed and bound in Great Britain by Clays Ltd, Elcograf S.p.A.

Oneworld Publications
10 Bloomsbury Street
London WC1B 3SR
England

Stay up to date with the latest books,
special offers, and exclusive content from
Oneworld with our newsletter

Sign up on our website
oneworld-publications.com

MIX
Paper from
responsible sources
FSC® C018072

For Anna, of course

'A thing of beauty is a joy for ever.'
JOHN KEATS, 'ENDYMION'

Contents

Preface

'Big book, big evil.'

CALLIMACHUS

There is a simple idea behind *A Thing of Beauty*. I hoped to travel around Greece visiting the sites of some of the most remarkable ancient myths, to see if any of them (the stories and the places where they emerged) are in any way relevant to our now apparently distant lives. The myths were never just tales for children, even if that is what they have become, and I wanted to know if we could draw on some ancient wisdom, or even perhaps turn it to our use. Of course it helped that my route took me to the most exquisite beaches in the world, through ancient oak and pine forests to architectural wonders, and up lonely mountains in search of sacred springs, satyrs and nymphs. It helped that I have an unquenchable appetite for Greek salad.

But what can I say? I was spurred on by Keats's wild claim that 'a thing of beauty is a joy for ever'. Far from beauty being resilient or untouchable, and impervious to our worst excesses, it more often seems that there is almost nothing on our fierce, fragile planet that is not under assault, or off balance, or on the way out. Greece is no different from anywhere else, although perhaps it is easier to see here what it is that we all have to lose.

I was especially anxious to know whether the myths had anything to say about our escalating environmental crises. The fires that rage (in Greece, Siberia, California and beyond), the convulsing climate, the mass extinctions. Surely, I thought, the ancient Greeks, who seemed to know so much about everything, would have addressed this looming ecological doom . . . or at least have suggested ways to be more philosophical about it. I dug deep into the myths, looking for resonances, searching for anything that could help. And I asked: if these people had possessed our technologies, was there any code, or anything about their beliefs, that would have restrained them from taking and using whatever they wanted? It seemed like an urgent question.

The year in which I ended up making this journey was especially turbulent (although any ancient Greek could have told us that it is sheer hubris to presume we know what is coming next) and my plans were inevitably disrupted. Probably because of this, and the anxiety and fear in the air, I became preoccupied with the myth of Pandora. Above all I wanted to know what happened to Hope when the jar was opened and all the evils of the world were released and only she remained (or maybe in fact she didn't). There are so many versions of every story, and it was a sneaking relief to find that it would be hard for me to be 'wrong' about any of it.

I went looking for hope (or Hope). I asked everyone I met – taxi drivers, conservationists, hoteliers, dancing activists, an Arcadian shepherd – and interviewed many others. I even consulted the Oracle at Delphi. Where can I find hope? I wondered, worming the question into every conversation. Their answers (and mine) are in *A Thing of Beauty*.

So the book became about hope, and the search for beauty. It is rooted in the past, but because myths are slippery (and are never still) it is concerned with the present. And even the future, I suppose. What else are oracles for? I have retold some of the stories, mainly because they are so extraordinary it was hard not to, but also because I think we all overestimate how well we know them. There are, as I say, many versions.

I have tried hard to make sure that *A Thing of Beauty* is not off-puttingly 'classical'. Greece is a wondrously beautiful land and its history and myths and the relics of the ancient world are life-giving. But there is too often a closed-room fug of elitism permeating 'the classics', and I was eager to throw open the windows. The stories are exhilarating – and of course they still have something to say to us. Even so there is also something undeniably alien about ancient Greece. The world the myths describe is genuinely strange, and we cannot assume that the people who told these stories thought the same way that we do.

I am aware that the names, even if you half-learned them at home or at school, can be bewildering. All those people beginning with 'A' – Achilles, Actaeon, Artemis – it is easy to baulk at the sight of them. But trust me, I felt the same way, and I have lowered us gently into this bath. As Ovid once wrote, it is no crime to get lost in a dark wood . . . but at least I have provided a glossary. And I have started just a few steps back in time, with Lord Byron, because he was obsessed with Greece, and died there, and because he believed that his life was entwined with an oak tree that he planted at his home in Nottinghamshire when he was ten years old. An old Greek idea. He thought he would wither if his tree did the same, just like a woodland nymph, although they would never have made their way this far into the chilly north.

I also discovered the second-century CE writer Pausanias, who wrote the gigantic and compelling *Guide to Greece*. I spent much of my working life writing and editing and planning guidebooks, and he is the forerunner of us all. So along with Byron (who had a copy in his luggage on his first trip to Greece) I clung tight to Pausanias, who writes with vivid clarity about the sights that are still there (and the many that are not). He was living at a time when the world was losing its faith, and about to embrace a new one, and (let alone for anything else) I am glad I read him for that.

Above all, Pausanias could have told us (any Greek could) that everything hangs in the balance. It is easy to despair when the news can seem so unrelentingly awful. But all I can tell you is that I went looking for beauty and hope, and I found them both.

Peter Fiennes, London, 2021

ONE

Half Empty

'I am afraid that this sounds flippant, but I don't mean it to be so.'

LETTER FROM LORD BYRON TO
THOMAS MOORE, 8 MARCH 1822

I hope that this is right.

The remnants of a dead oak tree are propped up on the lawns at the front of Newstead Abbey in Nottinghamshire. The tree was planted in the autumn of 1798 by George Gordon Byron, who was just ten years old at the time, and trying to absorb what it meant to be the future sixth Baron Byron of Rochdale – or 'Lord Byron' as the world would come to know him. He had not grown up expecting to be a Baron, and lord of a vast estate, at least not for the first six years of his life. But the previous son and heir had been cut in half by a cannonball in Corsica four years earlier; and Byron's great-uncle, the 'Wicked' fifth Lord Byron, had died of rage in May, aged seventy-eight, worn out, they said, by orgies and satanism, having driven away (or murdered) his wife and taken up with the housekeeper and been forced into selling everything he could lay his hands on, which included the many beautiful and ancient trees in Newstead's once lush woodlands, but also most of the contents (portraits, furniture, jewellery) of the defunct and derelict house and abbey. And young George's father, 'Mad' Jack Byron, could not become the next Baron because he had already expired, probably of tuberculosis, perhaps taking his own life, seven years earlier in France, where he had been living in enthusiastic incest with his sister.

There was something, people said, about the Byrons, some stain in the family, an original sin that tainted every successive generation. A very Greek idea. But this is why little George had travelled down from Scotland to Nottinghamshire, where he had been living frugally with his mother, and why he was now destined to spend his life as the sixth Baron Byron of Rochdale, lord of a bankrupt estate and inheritor of the family curse. Or so we're told.

It was soon after he arrived at Newstead, in September 1798, that George planted the sapling that lingers as a bleached husk on the front lawn. It is a ridiculous place for an oak tree. Right up close to the house, blocking the view of the lake, a child's idea of where a tree should live, with no thought for the future, or how an oak can grow. The man who bought the estate from Lord Byron, and paid off his debts, wanted to have it chopped down, until he was stopped by a gardener, who told him that this was the tree that the poet had cherished.

Perhaps it was an acorn, not a sapling, that Byron planted. In any case, it's the kind of thing a mother would allow, who needed to bring a smile to her little boy's face, hoping to hold his hand as he limped around the overgrown and forlorn gardens in the autumn rain, the house with half a roof, the woods tormented and felled. Or maybe it was the servant who was with him that day who helped him plant the tree, May Gray, who was fired not long afterwards for reasons that we may have to come back to. There is so much we will never know, although stories cling to Byron like feathers to hot tar. Many of them generated by him.

We do know that Byron nursed the idea that his fate was umbilically linked to this tree. 'As it fares,' he said, 'so will fare my fortunes.' He was shocked when he returned to Newstead as a nineteen-year-old student in 1807 and found his oak tree stunted and choked with weeds. The house and the estate had been rented for the past nine years to a man who could not have cared less about its upkeep, and Byron (presumably a nightmarish land-lord) had no money to spend on repairs. He fretted about the tree and wondered what its scrawny state might say about his own prospects. And this is also an ancient Greek idea, the belief that a tree and a spirit can be entwined for life. Not only Greek, of course, but it was them who said it best, and with simple poetic grace, what we all once knew, but have since forgotten, that an animating force radiates from trees, or shifts deep within them, and sometimes even moves among us. Perhaps not every tree. There must have been some whose spirits chose not to emerge, or were prevented from doing so, but instead lingered in the roots and branches and whispered through the living leaves. In those days there was an infinite plenitude of trees.

The greatest of the trees, the tall pines and heavy oaks of the wildest and most remote mountains, were born with their spirits already on the move, and yet conjoined, in a life-long two-step of pleasure and joy. These were the nymphs, known as dryads, that sang and danced in the meadows and glades, and hunted and hid, and took the hairy-legged satyrs to their caves for days and nights of loving, and also often those gods of the wild, Hermes and Pan. They were beautiful, and they lived far longer than any of us can imagine. Aphrodite, goddess of love and laughter, chose the nymphs to raise her son, at least for the first five years of his life. There was a time when people would never have dared or even wanted to take an axe to these ancient mountain oaks and pines, because as soon as the tree fell then their nymph too would die, vanishing into the ether like a severed daemon. They did live long, but they were not immortal.

Presumably these thoughts were on the adult Byron's mind as he brooded about his tree, although being Byron he appears to have cast himself into the role of a nymph. He was an incessant, life-long self-dramatiser, a chameleon in his deeds and poetry, and ever ready for a tumble with the nearest nymph or indeed shaggy-shanked satyr. When he was ten years old, and seeing his new home and gardens for the first time, knowing that this derelict but undeniably romantic estate was now his, he visited the strip of woodland that lies just behind the sunken gardens and the abbey. It was known as the 'Devil's Wood' by the locals, who were unsettled by the two leering, more than life-size statues of an androgynous faun and Pan, the god of wild places, that had been placed there by Byron's predecessor, the 'Wicked' Lord. Of course (thinking about it) we don't know if these statues are 'more than life-size', because all the living fauns and mountain gods are long gone, even if their bronze effigies are still there in the Newstead woods, exuding playful menace.

The knowledge that he was now lord of all this (the stately home with its ruined abbey, the servants, the statues, the hundreds of acres) sunk deep into the child Byron's psyche on that first walk around the grounds, although, strangely, he never seems to have felt entirely comfortable with the idea. Well, he swithered, let's say, between gorging on his new life and agonising spasms of self-loathing. As soon as he had got his hands properly on Newstead Abbey, aged twenty, he did everything that family tradition demanded: he drank to oblivion (downing claret by the pint from a monk's skull he'd unearthed in the grounds); he started a menagerie (including a bear that he had kept in a tower at Cambridge when the authorities told him he couldn't have a dog); he shot (mostly indoors – tearing chunks out of the Great Hall with his inebriated friends); he preyed on the maids; and he moved a handsome young man, Robert Rushton, into the bedroom next to his own.

Much of this, if not the sex, was for show: he took his responsibilities as an old-style aristocrat extremely seriously (laws being for lesser folk) and he was proud and self-conscious, vain, brilliant, and indeed beautiful, and he suffered to excess from that excruciating English fear of being laughed at for being too middle class. When he was young and had been sent away to school, he would cringe every time his mother visited. She was not at all aristocratic (even if she had once been rich), and she was loud and large, and hungry for his love, and he suffered humiliatingly in front of his new snobbish friends. 'Byron,' said one, 'your mother's a fool' . . . and he found himself agreeing.

So that is one reason why Byron affected a disdain for the social mores. He had a fear of seeming to care. Never give your enemies a target. For many years he flung away money as though it burned, and racked up huge debts, and refused to pay the tradespeople who turned up (presumptuously!) asking for their bills to be settled, and he would never take any royalties for his wildly successful poetry. Only the publishers got rich. That last bit changed eventually, but he had his excuses ready. 'What I get by my brains I shall spend on my bollocks,' he announced, and not, God forbid, on rent or food or the simple staples of life.

That's another thing about Byron: we could disappear forever into the technicolour complexities of his life – and he knew it too. But I have to remember that we are here for Greece, where Byron died of a fever aged just thirty-six, fighting (or on the brink of fighting) for the freedom of the Greeks from the Ottoman Turks and less than twenty years after he had turned up as a teenager to moon over his neglected oak tree.

There was always something that kept Byron on the outside of the social world he occupied with such apparent ease and entitlement. His pride, for starters. He was also surprisingly shy. He was too clever and sensitive not to see through the absurdity of things. Most immediately, what lit the fuse that led to him leaving mainstream English society for good in April 1816 was the rather urgent matter of the incest with his half-sister, Augusta. But beyond all that, if you linger beneath these statues of the faun and Pan in the old lord's 'Devil's Wood', you'll be reminded that what also kept Byron on the outside, alienated and aloof, angry and defensive, but always on the attack, was his deformed clubfoot.

I should quickly add that it was Byron himself who called his right leg and foot a 'deformity'. Most likely, he was born with spinal dysraphism and not, as he thought, and everyone said, a 'clubfoot'. It didn't really matter, because he was tortured in his childhood by quack surgeons who strapped him into savage metal correctives, and by the teasing of bullies at school and even, at times, by the taunts of his own mother. His father ('Mad Jack') left home when his son was three, by which time Byron had still not walked, his father assuming he never would. By the time he was in the full swing of childhood, he was painfully aware of his heavy limp. He became a powerful swimmer, and rode everywhere he could, and boxed and fenced with manic intensity, and when he arrived at parties he would almost gallop into the centre of the crowd and then stop dead, legs planted, unmoving. He was, everyone agreed, so very beautiful. And he would have known it, although standing here aged ten under these restless statues, rather chubby, listing on his good leg, he must have gazed in horror at the great cloven hooves of these hairy, alien, mocking monsters. The very devils, whose misshapen feet and goatish legs parodied and mimicked his own. And him, a child, the family curse incarnate.

After Byron's death in Missolonghi in Greece on 19 April 1824, his entirely unreliable friend and hanger-on, Edward Trelawny – his 'jackal', as the world knew him – travelled from Athens, where he had been living after having transferred his allegiance to a rival Greek faction, to see and pay homage to Byron's corpse, although (who knows?) perhaps he just wanted to fight over the scraps. But this is what he wrote:

> I uncovered the Pilgrim's [Byron's] feet and was answered – the great mystery was solved. Both his feet were clubbed and his legs withered to the knee – the form and features of an Apollo, with the feet and legs of a sylvan satyr.

Byron was steeped in the classics. It was just about the only thing the British upper classes learned at school, even if Byron said he preferred literature and history. He would have known about the lame, limping god, Hephaestus, the god of industry, fire and anvils, of metalwork and the sparks that fly. Hephaestus who was the son of Hera, the queen of the gods. He also – like Byron – didn't have a father. He married Aphrodite (the laughing goddess of love), and she cheated on him from time to time with taller, stronger, less lame gods and mortals, although 'cheated' is not the right word to describe what a goddess may choose to do.

Hephaestus himself had taken an axe and split open Zeus' skull, when it was time for the goddess Athena to be born. And out she had sprung, fully formed, spear and shield in hand. And then later (we don't know when, because time has no meaning here) Hephaestus had limped after the beautiful but chaste goddess and tried to make love to her and she had swatted him away, but in his excitement he had spattered her thigh with his semen – ridiculous, lame, incontinent god – and she had wiped herself down with a cloth and flung it to the ground, and that is how one of the first kings of Athens was born, half snake and half human, arising from the earth where Hephaestus' sodden and embarrassing scrap of cloth had been tossed.

Stories. Byron, aged ten, would have known that one; it was only later that schoolteachers and clergymen would make a more determined attempt to censor and eviscerate these ancient tales. The real point, for Byron, was that Hephaestus, the limping god, was a figure of crude ridicule because of his deformed foot. It is there in the first book of *The Iliad*, when he tries to defuse the tension between Zeus and Hera by serving drinks for the gods and goddesses, and they all laugh as he lurches across the room. I often think that every one of us is linked or drawn to one particular god or goddess (because even if the nature of these immortals is unfixed and slippery, their essence holds true) and for Byron there are some obvious choices – beautiful, aloof lovers; musicians and poets; reckless drinkers – but it was also Hephaestus who echoed and rippled through Byron's short life.

I went to see Byron's oak on a late summer's day in the first year of Covid, with the sun still hot and high in the sky. The tree (or what is left of it) is now no more than a long, bleached stump, twisted and fallen, like a man hunted to exhaustion and at bay, a couple of severed branches raised to ward off the final blows. It is zombie grey and propped up above the earth into which it appears to be longing to sink, and it is impossible not to think of Byron, dying in Missolonghi in Greece, many hundreds of miles from this place, no longer strong enough to tell the doctors that he did not want to be bled, or leeched, even as they held cups to his veins and drained his life away. The tree outlived him by at least a century, which may have disappointed him, but it still died early for an oak.

Some remnant of Byron lingers in the air where his dead oak now lies. At the far side of the tree a bald, bearded man is sprawled out on the close-cropped grass, holding forth to a younger woman about the poet. The words 'Clairmont' and 'Lady Caroline' and 'Shelley' and 'mad' and 'bear' and 'bad' and all the rest of it come bouncing over the dead trunk, and I watch as the man hitches his already surprisingly tight shorts even higher up his meaty thighs to drive home a point about Byron's notebooks with an alarming swivel and thrust of his pelvis along the green sward. The woman appears to be saying nothing – what's to say? – but is as transfixed as I am. And also, just down the hill from them, there's another picnicking couple, and this time it's the woman talking ('Bosun' and 'vampires' and 'cantos' and 'Greece') but I can't catch her words so clearly. She has a long floral dress and a tumble of dark hair and her companion is listening intently, propped on one elbow, nodding in the shifting sunlight under the dappled branch of a copper beech tree, his chestnut hair pulled and tethered into a luxuriantly glossy bun. He looks (there's no getting away from this) Byronic.

And also, about a dozen paces from Byron's dead tree, close to where the tight-shorted man is still talking, there is a vibrant young oak that was planted in 1988 as a way of showing that time has not stood still in Newstead Abbey. The new tree, on this late September day, is brimming over with acorns, while its leaves are just starting to shift from a deep to a thinner, yellowing green. Judging by the quantity of nuts, it looks like this must be a Mast Year, those years when trees seem to synchronise their behaviour in order to produce a deluge of food all at the same time. It happens every five to seven years (it is hard to predict when) and people think that the trees are attempting to control their predators through starvation, and then overwhelm them with food, so that some of the seed, at least, will survive to grow. Just like Byron and his fellow Romantics, I'd say, with their prolific outpouring of lyric and long-form poetry. The critics never stood a chance. Not that Byron would have wanted to be lumped in with the others: as far as he was concerned, Wordsworth was 'Words-words' or 'Turdsworth' and Keats's poetry was 'a sort of mental masturbation . . . a Bedlam vision produced by raw pork and opium'.

Anyway, Byron didn't get to see his oak tree grow. He was sent away to school and then headed for Cambridge University, where his studies were occasionally poetic but mostly priapic (and determinedly bisexual). This was at a time when a conviction for homosexuality could carry the death penalty, and Byron and his friends agreed a code for describing their casual meetings and deeper affairs, which included the word 'hyacinths' for young male lovers, after the man who was loved and then accidentally killed by the god Apollo. The god (who was blazingly beautiful) had stolen Hyacinthus away from Zephyrus, the god of the West Wind; and soon afterwards Zephyrus got his revenge by diverting a discus thrown by Apollo into Hyacinthus' face, killing him outright. In his grief, Apollo turned Hyacinthus into a flower, and in this form he comes to life again every spring, bringing immortality, of sorts. You are meant to be able to see the words *ai ai* ('alas! alas!') etched by Apollo on the flower's radiant petals, but don't go looking for them on those big blowsy hyacinths we give each other at Christmas. It's most likely the corn lily you're after, growing wild in Greece.

It is striking, once you think to look for it, how much of ancient Greece infuses the poetry and the lives of Byron, Shelley and Keats. Not so much the earlier generation of poets – Coleridge was sunk in a German metaphysical morass – but Greece, at the time of Byron's first visit to Newstead Abbey, was at last emerging from centuries of western European ignorance, hostility and neglect. It was still a hard place in which to travel, an integral if volatile part of the Ottoman Empire, but those French and British travellers that did get there (braving the suspicions of the Ottoman authorities and the very real danger of death from disease, shipwreck and brigands) were soon reporting the staggering fact that the ancient cities of Athens, Corinth and Sparta and the sacred sanctuaries of Delos, Delphi and Eleusis, not to mention Thebes and Arcadia and Thermopylae and probably even Troy itself, for heaven's sake, the places that every school child had read about in Pindar, Euripides, Plato and Homer, they were *all still there*. A mind-bending thought. The city of Athens, with its Acropolis and perfectly proportioned temples, where Socrates once taught in the marketplace and where theatre and debate and philosophy and democracy and indeed the very foundations of European architecture, thought, art and literature were supposedly born – *that* was all still there. With just a few thousand modern Athenians (no more than would fill a large village) living in their shadows.

Sure, these places were often in ruins, or semi-ruined, or about-to-be-ruined, but there was an awful lot of stuff to be found, just lying around, neglected and ignored and ready, let's be honest, to be packed up and carted off to Paris, London and the chateaux and stately homes of the antiquities-crazed nobility. As James Stuart and Nicholas Revett reported so nonchalantly when they reached Delphi in 1762:

> We discovered some remains of the temple of Apollo
> at Delphos, a wall of large stones filled with inscrip-
> tions, rather too large to take away.

And when I visited Delphi not long after my trip to Newstead Abbey, that wall they describe of large and exquisitely carved stones, expertly slotted together in polygonal blocks, is still there, exactly where it should be, aligned to the curve in the hill, drawing the visitor round and up to the temple of Apollo. And it is still filled with inscriptions, dating back many hundreds of years. So it is rather sobering to discover that the only reason it is not in Wiltshire or Cambridge or the British Museum in London is because Stuart and Revett lacked the machinery or perhaps just the mules to get it down the mountain and into a ship.

As the world well knows, Lord Elgin had no such difficulty in chiselling the statuary from the Parthenon, although eye-witness accounts speak of severe collateral damage, with shards of ancient marble bouncing off the scaffolding and shattering to the ground. Byron, who rode into Athens on Christmas Day in 1809, not long after Elgin had left with his loot, raged at the barbarism of what this 'cold . . . barren', hard-hearted man had done. There is a famous passage denouncing Elgin in the second canto of *Childe Harold*, the poem that made Byron an overnight sensation in 1811. Not that Elgin seems to have cared, especially once he'd sold the marbles in 1816 to the British government for £35,000.

Byron made two trips to Greece. The first, from 1809 to 1811, was taken with his friend John Cam Hobhouse and servant William Fletcher. Hobhouse left in July 1810 and Byron sent Fletcher home soon afterwards, most likely so he could get better acquainted with a multitude of Greek youths. Fletcher had been scandalised by the sight of Byron's young Greek lover,

Eustathius, ready to accompany them on a horse with his
'ambrosial curls hanging down his amiable back', wrote Byron.
That was bad enough for Fletcher, but the boy was also shield-
ing his silky skin from the sun with 'a *parasol*'. In any case, as
Byron told his mother in early 1811, he'd had to send his servant
back to England, because:

> the perpetual lamentations after beef & beer, the
> stupid bigoted contempt for every thing foreign, and
> insurmountable incapacity of acquiring even a few
> words of any language, rendered him like all other
> English servants, an incumbrance.

Byron liked to tease. The next time he left for Greece, in July
1823, after twelve tumultuous years, when he'd already become
one of the most famous men in Europe – for his lean, rhythmic,
lyrical, coruscating poetry, of course, but also the incessant,
escalating scandals – and fearing perhaps that he was going
there to die (possibly even hoping he would), the long-suffering,
beer-loving, xenophobic William Fletcher was once more in
tow. In the period between his first and second trips, and in the
years that followed his death, Byron managed to transform a
British interest in Greece into an obsession. The archaeological
discoveries made in the eighteenth and nineteenth centuries
revolutionised the way that Britain looked and thought – for the
second time. And as for the Greeks themselves, well, David
Constantine has this rather dampening take in his book *In the
Footsteps of the Gods*:

The modern Greeks have always had a hard time of it satisfying the largely inappropriate hopes of Western enthusiasts, particularly those from English public schools.

Byron didn't make many changes to Newstead Abbey in the few, brief periods when he lived there. He spent a lot of money he didn't have on soft furnishings. He blew holes in the Great Hall. For a few months in 1811, soon after the death of his mother, he installed a trio of young maids ('nymphs' he called them, troublingly). In the hard January of 1814, he was thrilled to be snowed in with his half-sister, Augusta, who was pregnant (very likely with Byron's child) and he turned twenty-six. It is easy to forget how young he was, although for years he had been convinced that the best of his life was behind him.

And he built a mighty monument to his dearly beloved dog, Boatswain, who had died of rabies in 1808, and inscribed it with these lovely words, which were denounced by just about everyone who read them for their supposedly inappropriate sentiments.

Near this Spot
are deposited the Remains of one
who possessed Beauty without Vanity,
Strength without Insolence,
Courage without Ferosity,
and all the virtues of Man without his Vices.

As he goes on to write, he only ever had one friend, and that was good old Boatswain. Perhaps it was this that upset his human friends the most.

Byron was a shape-shifter. He contained multitudes. To put it in terms an ancient Greek would understand, he was Protean. He flitted behind layers of irony and anger and passion, but at heart he meant everything he said or wrote at the time he said or wrote it.

> And feeling, in a poet, is the source
> Of others' feeling; but they are such liars,
> And take all colours – like the hands of dyers.

He swore he would never be separated from his ancestral home, but when his creditors pressed, he couldn't wait to sell it. And then when it was, he wrote this moving poem to Augusta, on his last visit to Newstead.

> I did remind you of our own dear lake
> By the old hall, *which may be mine no more* . . .
> I feel almost at times as I have felt
> In happy childhood; trees, and flowers, and brooks.
> Which do remember me of where I dwelt
> Ere my young mind was sacrificed to books.

On a September day over two hundred years after Byron wrote those lines, I wandered with my wife Anna to the edge of his 'dear lake'. There were benches, but very few people to sit on them in this year of abstinence and absences. A single cloud was floating high in the blue-rinsed English sky. Byron once took issue with Wordsworth, who had written that the skies of Greece were 'variegated' and its plains were 'fertile', when any damn fool would have known that the rivers are dry for half the year, the plains are parched and barren and the skies 'for months & months' are 'darkly – deeply – beautifully blue'. He was often spoiling for a fight.

We sat on a bench in front of the Japanese garden, with its damp brick pathways and busy streams. Mature beech trees and willows and limes stood at the fringes of the lake (did Byron know any of them?), their first autumn leaves adrift or clinging to the reeds, and in front of us there was a softly undulating mat of luminescent waterlilies, some of them still in bloom. We watched a fat bee wriggle into one. A swan eased by, followed by a solitary mallard, working harder, and after that a coot came bustling over, ploughing through the flat dark waters like an eager Labrador, its forehead flashing white in the sunshine. The Japanese anemones were flowering pink and the leaves on the acers were turning liquid shades of purple and crimson among the tall stands of bamboo.

There is much that Byron would not recognise about this place, but we have come a long way in the years since Pliny the Elder was surprised to find a new variety of plane tree in his native Italy:

> Who is there that will not, with good reason, be
> surprised to learn that a tree has been introduced

among us from a foreign clime for nothing but its shade?

Two thousand years ago, when the Roman Empire stretched out its claws and raked in the bounty of the world, Pliny was amazed to come across a plane tree so far from its own land. And now here we are, in the grounds of Newstead Abbey, surrounded by Grecian statues, Roman columns, urns, fountains and follies, palms, acers, rhododendrons and the shriek of peacocks. The drumbeat of trade and plunder. A once fragmentary, local planet, stitched together, or hammered into shape, and most certainly not always with love. Around about the time that the child Byron was planting his oak, everything in the world began to move faster. Trees, plants and animals (dead and alive), the fish in the seas, mountains of coal and ore, oceans of oil, whole forests, even rivers, the rocks and the earth, all of it on the move. Us too. Faster. Populations of people, uprooted, along with everything we've ever made or wanted, spreading and shunted and coerced across the planet. Our ideas, too, about what is right, and true, and beautiful. Multiplying and dying. The poetry and the poison.

But Byron's lake is so placid in the early autumn sun. Why did he ever leave? The Greeks thought that restless travel was a sign of madness. Look at Oedipus, pursued by the Furies, and Odysseus, fighting to get back to Ithaca. It wasn't just madness, but punishment and torment, to be on the move and away from home. This place was Byron's walled garden, his paradise, his rural Arcadia, shut away from the world, rioting with his friends, blissfully snowed in with his half-sister – and yet he left, over and again, and he kept on leaving until, in the end, he sold up and never came back.

There is no wall that can keep out the world. Byron knew it, and so he ran. I am as good as anyone at hiding from what I don't want to hear, but the news is relentless and loud and frightening, and the last months have been especially grim, with some things quietened and intermittently on hold, but with fear in the air, for jobs and lives. If I had to make a list of what was most urgent, I wouldn't know where to start. The pandemic? Or the falling and flaming forests? Polar bears on their dwindling ice cap? Methane and peat? Poisoned rivers and dragged-out seas ... bleached corals and floating shoals of fish. The news pounds in and out. The Chinese paddlefish. Palm oil and soy. Orangutans and shark fins. A world overheating and already ablaze, from California to Australia and Siberia to the Amazon. Charred and burning koalas. Oil spills, plastics and dying sea birds. Albatrosses with severed beaks. Factory farms. The spreading deserts. Hurricanes. Floods. Diesel. Neonicotinoids. Microplastics. The Sumatran rhino and Spix's macaw. Extinct. And all the associated human horrors, of war, disease, crop failure, slavery, murder and flight. We think we can't bear to hear any more of this, but what is coming is worse.

I had come to the gardens of Newstead Abbey in the autumn of the first year of Covid because I didn't want to believe that is true. That everything is getting worse, I mean. I would rather think that it is my age, or disposition, or history, that is making it all seem so bleak. Maybe I just need to get out more, although the horrors are real, and they congeal around us. But are they all that there is? And what are any of us meant to do? I thought that the ancient Greeks might have an answer – they seem to have an answer for just about everything else – but then of course I couldn't get to Greece (where I wanted to dig deep into their myths, in the actual places where they were set, which surely would shed a light on things), so instead I ended up here, in Newstead Abbey in Nottinghamshire, all because of Lord Byron, who died in Greece, but who had also planted a tree that he was convinced was interwoven with his life, just like a mountain nymph's.

I never imagined I would enrol Lord Byron as a spirit guide, to help me negotiate an onslaught of ecological angst. Despite his label as a 'Romantic' poet, he never seemed that interested in wild nature and he was scathing about Wordsworth, Southey and Coleridge's pantheism.

> I hate these talkers one and all, body and soul. They are a set of the most despicable imposters – that is my opinion of them. They know nothing of the world; and what is poetry, but the reflection of the world?

OK, Byron is quoted on a sign at the entrance to the Newstead car park – 'I love not man the less, but nature more' – but what he really seemed to love was getting up late in the afternoon, going for a gallop, loosing off some firearms, scooping up a lovely young thing and carousing till dawn and beyond. I realise there is more to it than that: he did after all write reams of life-giving poetry. But I thought I could just hold his hand, and he'd lead me to the threshold of Greece, and then wave me on my way. It turns out his grip is stronger than I expected.

The fact is, what I am really looking for is some hope. Or Hope. It is a tired word, I know, its meaning eroded, pawed over, leeched and bled, trotted out in songs and speeches and reached for too easily by facile priests and politicians. Remember Bill Clinton, squeezing out a tear, his throat a-quiver with sincerity. 'I still believe in a place called Hope.' Well, sure you do, Bill, and is that what you were trying to find in the blind spot of the White House corridors, out of the protective reach of the CCTV? Our cynicism has festered and grown.

Byron left his rural home to move to London with his new wife, Annabella Milbanke, at the end of 1814, and not much more than one year later, on 23 April 1816, after a miserable marriage, he abandoned England for good. Both Annabella and he agreed that he behaved abominably – unfaithful, sullen and cruel – although as he often wrote to prying friends and enemies, who are we to presume we know the truth? Annabella went back to her parents, taking their young daughter Augusta with her, and refused to answer his letters, while Byron headed for the continent with Fletcher. I think the bear stayed in Newstead. I don't know to what extent Byron was fleeing in chaos, or what hope he had for the future: but his friendship with the Shelleys, and much of his best poetry, including the peerless *Don Juan*, were still ahead of him. A myth was growing. He was only twenty-eight; and eight years later he'd be dead in Greece. I am following him there (I am happy to report that I made it back), but unlike Byron I believe I already know what I would like to find.

Some hope.

TWO

Dream On

'May your sleep be soft and your dreams of me.'

LORD BYRON, JOURNAL, 28 SEPTEMBER 1816

I am speeding to the centre of Athens from Eleftherios Venizelos International Airport in the back of a large beige taxi. It has the kind of suspension that makes me think of old-fashioned fairground rides and 1970s American movies: long, low-slung cars jouncing dustily down potholed southern roads, Marlboro soft-packs and waterbeds. Anna and our son, Alex, are in another car, just ahead or sometimes behind my own. We may well be in a race. You can tell an awful lot about a city from the taxis that greet you at the airport, and I have already fallen in love with Athens.

Anna and Alex are here for a few days to help with research, which is great, of course, and indeed Alex has just emerged from a Classics degree, so will surely be invaluable, but I am worried about the time (and the siren call of the beaches). It is October, I had hoped to be here in March, the weeks are short, and I am already fretting about whether I'll be able to get to Tiryns. The taxi driver was once married to a Dutch woman and lived in the Netherlands for seventeen years, so he speaks immaculate English with Greek swagger and a smudgy Dutch schlur. He is shouting about motorbikes.

'They are scho schtoopid,' he yells, 'they never wear a fucking helmet. What do they expect? A man was killed here last week. Right here!' He turns round to sweep his arm to the right, the little finger of his left hand poised loosely on the wheel. He looks a lot like Wild Bill Hickok, long white hair swept back into a ponytail, the tips of a fine nicotined moustache emerging from his surgical mask. The eyes of a man who has gazed on the prairie. 'They think they are going to live forever.'

We are racing past Athens University, underpasses at our sides, the car swinging easily. We are in the tunnels, excavated for the Olympic Games. Wild Bill is talking about Polish men, and their heart attacks – 'me, I don't make schtressh, because nothing changes' – and then he shouts, 'And here. Here! This is where the motorbike hit Angela Merkel's convoy.'

'Angela Merkel?' I say. Can this be right?

'He flew through the air for 150, maybe 200 metres. Came out of there, going 150kph. No fucking helmet.'

'But . . . *Angela Merkel*? Was she hit?'

'They never learn,' says Bill, cruising into the downtown, riding loose in the saddle, a happy smile on his face. 'Look at them. *Slow down!* And here – you see this? – this nightclub? Here! On the left. The man who owned it was killed last week. So was his friend. No helmets.'

Wild Bill is ready to retire, he tells me, and would have done if the economy hadn't collapsed. And now this Covid.

His car is old and he needs a new one because of the green rules that are coming in next year, but he can't afford it. He hates Toyotas. 'It is time I schtop all this,' he says, 'too much schtressh.'

'It has been a very bad year,' I agree, not for the last time over the next few weeks, 'but do you have HOPE for the future?' I have decided I am going to try and work this question, about hope, into every conversation I have.

'Hope?' says Bill, turning round, the mask slipping, looking now like a middle-aged Nietzsche. '*Hope?* Without hope I would kill myself.'

DREAM #1

Another thing I have decided to do while I am in Greece is record my dreams. I know – please don't go – but dreams mattered to the ancient Greeks. They were warnings and prophecies, possibilities, parodies and misdirections. If you knew what you were seeing, you could tap into the future, or get an answer to a question. So far as I know, no ancient Greek would ever just ignore a dream, or let it sift away. They believed that the future was more or less fixed, and even the gods would not try to alter fate – or not often – and this meant that dreams could contain a message about what was to come. Zeus, the father of the gods, liked to listen to the beautiful Muses singing about the past, present and future. Time never stopped moving forwards, but unlike us Zeus had very little to fear from what might be coming next. Well, he knew that one day he would be overthrown by the child of Metis (Intelligence), and that is why he ate her.

Anyway, on the night before I left for Athens, this was the dream. I was standing in a small gloomy antechamber with ancient, damp, vaulted walls, and the room opened on one side into a sunlit, sand-strewn amphitheatre. I could only see part of it, but I could hear a crowd, fully engaged in some contest. A minotaur, I reckoned. Just then a velociraptor pushed its head into the opening and smacked its jaws hungrily. I sprang for a metal-runged ladder, leading up a dark shaft, and the thing leaped after me, its claws scrabbling on the brickwork. I moved fast, but I could feel it close behind. There was a heavy metal hatch at the top of the shaft, and I pushed it open, the velociraptor's rank breath on my heels, my legs squirming. Up through the hatch and I was in a shopping centre, with people drinking tea at white wrought-iron tables and my mother (who died in the year 2001) trying on clothes somewhere in the recesses of a small boutique. But try as I might, I could not get the hatch closed on the raging and flailing dinosaur.

I am sure everything is going to be just fine.

We have decided to spend a couple of days in Athens. I have been keeping an eye on the calendar, and on the first night I discovered that it was time to celebrate Hekate's 'Deipnon'. The Deipnon: the end of the lunar month, when everything is on the turn; the time of darkness, before a filament of moon reappears. And Hekate: the goddess of the night, of cross-roads and new beginnings, of ghosts, graveyards and hell-hounds, the torch-bearer who watches over horsemen and those who travel by sea. She is worshipped by witches. I go to place an offering (it should be an egg, if I can find one, to symbolise fresh starts) on the small balcony outside our hotel window, but I am distracted and then transfixed by the sight of the floodlit Parthenon, high above us on its hill to the left, exactly as promised by the hotel's website, and so I forget to leave anything to the dread goddess Hekate. Athens is on fire with electricity, the darkness at bay and pushed into corners, and that night I dreamed (#2) of a soft grey mouse held limply and without interest in the mouth of a cat. The horror of it woke me up. The human city is dark and silent and all the dogs are barking.

The next day, the National Archaeological Museum was open, but only part of it, and so Anna and I followed a spool of waist-high plastic tape, reminiscent of a police incident, into a roomful of Mycenaean jewellery and pots and dozens of those heavy-hipped, earthbound, early Cycladic figures that got Robert Graves and others so excited about the Great Goddess and the time, or so they believed, when this part of the world was a matriarchy. We gazed at them for an eternity, these marble shapes with their Modigliani heads, because they are compel-ling, and five thousand years old, but also because we have both independently (and mistakenly) come to the conclusion that this is the only room open today. The guards are staring at their smartphones. We are the only people here.

There are also the Mycenaean artefacts to keep us gripped. Pride of place is given to the discoveries of the controversial German archaeologist, Heinrich Schliemann, the man who found Homer's Troy (or said he did, and that was exciting enough), and who in 1876 dug up the ancient city of Mycenae, Homer's 'city of gold', and unearthed a huge trove of golden treasure. Mycenae was the most important mainland Greek city of the past, long before Athens and Sparta and the rest of them. It was a real place, the centre of a wealthy empire – but also a city of myth, founded by Perseus, built by Cyclopes, visited by Heracles, and home to Agamemnon, High King of the Greeks in the Trojan War, and Clytemnestra, his wife and murderer. Schliemann went at it with pickaxe and dynamite, to the despair of future generations of archaeologists, and what he found astounded the world. Bronze armour and weapons; painted ceramic heads; drinking vessels of rock crystal and clay; vases and pots decorated with fighting men, lions, sphinxes, leopards and dancing birds; silver and gold necklaces; gemstones; ostrich eggs . . .

Schliemann, the peerless publicist, fired off a telegram to King George of Greece, reeling off a list of mythical people:

> With great joy I announce to Your Majesty that I have discovered the tombs . . . of Agamemnon, Cassandra, Eurymedon and their companions, all slain at a banquet by Clytemnestra and her lover Aegisthos.

Best of all was the death mask of Agamemnon himself, a sheet of pristine gold hammered into the shape of a dead king's face. Eyes gummed shut, a gothic moustache, sharp nose and the knowing smile of a tyrant. Schliemann had another telegram ready. 'I have gazed on the face of Agamemnon', he trumpeted to a Greek newspaper, and it was only after Schliemann's death that more rigorous archaeologists were able to point out that this mask must have predated Agamemnon (assuming there was such a man) by about three hundred years. Some have even said that the mask is a fake, created by Schliemann, or a local artist, and indeed if you stare at it for long enough (as I did on that silent afternoon in the National Archaeological Museum), you do find yourself wondering why no one has yet pointed out that the 'Mask of Agamemnon' is an almost exact likeness of the young Heinrich Schliemann. Still, if nothing else, Schliemann made archaeology fun, and ancient Greece too.

Anna and I were surprised to discover, just as the museum was about to close, that there were dozens more rooms to explore, all of which we had assumed were sealed off by the *faux* police tape. Now there was almost no time left, and for some reason I had decided that what I wanted to see more than anything was the painted room from Thera, an island just north of Crete (more commonly known as Santorini) that had been buried by a volcanic eruption 3,500 years ago. So we raced past the bronze statue of a naked Zeus (some say it's Poseidon), standing with his left arm upflung, his right arm poised to throw a thunderbolt, radiating living power, and staring at the wall with empty black eye sockets – which would once have been filled with painted ivory or precious stones. He looks implacable. I wanted to linger in his shadow and watch him strike, but here was Aphrodite, the smiling goddess of erotic love, also naked, her left hand being dragged away from her pubis by the diminutive but muscular god Pan, with his goaty horns and cloven hooves, a look of imploring devilment on his face. She's about to slap him away with her sandal, or maybe toss it over her shoulder. No time for that either.

The tall marble relief from Eleusis did stop me. Perhaps, compared to those sparkling Olympian statues, it might seem flat and static, but it is authentically holy. It shows the moment when the goddess Demeter gave wheat to humanity (standing in front of her in the form of the boy Triptolemus). Demeter's daughter, Persephone, is close behind the boy, looking down on him, scrutinising him, perhaps blessing him. What the god gives, the god can take away. Demeter, goddess of corn and fertility, goddess of the ever-renewing earth, is holding a sceptre or maybe a torch in her left hand; in the other she passes ears of wheat to the boy, who has his hand raised to receive this world-changing gift. The seriousness of the moment is etched into their faces. She is lifting a curse . . . and the times of famine are over.

This marble relief was once hung on the wall of the temple at Eleusis, the most holy of places in a land which had shrines, temples and sacred springs in every valley, forest, meadow, city, village and mountaintop. But Eleusis was the holiest of them all, where for thousands of years untold numbers of people went to experience the Mysteries, a week-long initiation that explained . . . well, what? Everything? Not one of the initiates – and the list of people who made the pilgrimage and submitted to the ceremony includes everyone from Socrates to Cicero – not one of them ever talked about it. Perhaps we prefer it that way.

We do know that this was inscribed on the temple wall:

> For mortals death is to be feared no more: rather, it is
> a blessing.

So, I need to get to Eleusis . . . but in the meantime there are guards jangling keys at me and I scamper up the stairs after Anna and discover that the ludicrous riches of this museum have barely begun, because here are the black and red clay pots, vases and urns, with their fighting men and boars at bay and Heracles with the Hydra, and Heracles with the stinking birds, and the minotaurs and Gorgons, sphinxes, and men and women dancing and offering sacrifice, the fragrant smoke curling up to the heavens, and bulls and bears and lions – many lions – and all those satyrs and lovely nymphs. We know them too well, or we think we do, but then again 'what men or gods are these? What wild ecstasy?' And Keats's dubious lines are flowing behind us,

> 'Beauty is truth, truth beauty,' – that is all
> Ye know on earth, and all ye need to know

as we reach the rooms of the Theran treasures.

There is beauty here, whatever that is. The Greeks were not the only ones who thought they could define it – in their architecture and their art they sometimes agreed that there was a formula, a way to measure beauty, although that was only ever part of the story – but what is *here*, in this room within a room (three 3,500-year-old painted walls from Thera, that somehow survived all this time, through earthquakes and volcanoes and looting), what is here has electricity and power, poise and tenderness, and heart-aching fragility. Perhaps they have this effect only because we know that they have survived so much and for so long, but there is surely more to it than that. It is just three walls – someone's bedroom, maybe, or nursery or, who knows? a shrine – showing some tall rocky hills topped by outsized, flowering crimson lilies. The hills are washed with wide, vertical stripes, painted yellow, red and grey and decorated with shapes that are rocks but are also other things – faces, trees, animals – that slip away when you try and focus on them. In the faded sky above the hills are six red-cheeked swallows, and one couple is tumbling together, twisting and curling in an intimate dance, and another pair is airborne, chest-to-chest, about to brush beaks, and the two single swallows are soaring, backs arched, racing to heaven for the unfettered joy of it. They call it the 'Spring Room', I suppose because it says all you need to know about what it can mean to be released from the prison of winter.

And if you spend time with the rest of the art in the Theran rooms you will see that what these people have done is blend their human world and the world outside them so that there is no longer any boundary between the two. Perhaps they did not recognise that such a boundary existed, or they believed that they could dissolve it. Here, everything flows and is on the move. Dolphins, goats, people, birds, trees and rivers. Flowers and lions. Rocky shorelines and forests. Mingled and separate. Crocuses and lilies. A bird vase with human nipples. The sensuous curve of the pots. A place of endless change and metamorphoses. Fluid and supple. Mortal and immortal. Spirits all around. I am told the Greeks had no word for religion, because why would you even need one when everything about you is self-evidently holy.

This world that you will discover in the Theran rooms of the National Archaeological Museum of Athens. It is beautiful.

How long did a nymph live, assuming that her tree was not destroyed? I have come alone to the Hill of the Nymphs on Filopappou Hill in west Athens, and I can't help wondering if there are any nymphs here, still alive today. It is hard to imagine, what with the noise of the traffic and the grit and the centuries of human busyness. Nymphs were generally not keen on human contact, although humans could become obsessed with nymphs. Nympholepsy, it was called, and the most famous example was a man called Archedemos from the volcanic island of Thera (with its ecstatic wall paintings), who decorated a cave just south of Athens with his cravings, perhaps hoping that nymphs would come and settle in its watery shades. Of course, to us the idea of 'nymphs' is mostly a male fantasy. Our most famous modern nympholept was creepy Humbert Humbert in Nabokov's *Lolita*. And the Victorians filled their rooms (or more likely Victorian men filled their cigar-laden studies) with pictures of nymphs emerging shyly (and decorously semi-naked) from forests and streams. Nymphs ran from the gods, Zeus and Apollo, and were carried off and assaulted, or transformed. But the nymphs of ancient Greece were also powerful and dangerous, magical beings who were best avoided but also, and above all, placated with offerings and prayer.

How long did nymphs live? Well, the ocean nymphs may be a separate case, but the nymphs of the trees lived ten times longer than a phoenix, which itself outlives nine generations of ravens, and *they* live three times longer than a stag, and the stag lives four times longer than a 'chattering crow' – and the 'chattering crow', you may be surprised to hear, lives long enough to see nine generations of 'aged men' laid into the ground, before it too expires. So, it is probably roughly correct that a nymph's earthly life stretches to around 680,400 years (bearing in mind that maths is not my strong point). A long time. And for that reason it may also be the case – depending of course on when they were born – that there are still nymphs treading their lovely dance in the mountains of Greece, albeit not in the hills around Athens, which were brutally deforested, even in Plato's time.

Despite their connection with trees, the most likely place to find a nymph was always a cave. Springs and rivers too, but caves were best. There were very few solitary nymphs. They danced and sang together and followed in the footsteps of the great goddesses, Artemis, who hunted in the wild places, and smiling Aphrodite. As for the Hill of the Nymphs, I think they are long gone.

Across and up the slopes, following the winding stony
paths in front of the prison where Socrates was held in the
nights before the people of Athens had him executed, is a
shrine to the Muses. (This is a hill full of history.) There are
olive and tall cypress trees on the hillside, and umbrella pines
and myrtle, some of them old and heavy, and the paths are
narrow and the sky up above is a cloudless crystal blue
streaked with one solitary, Covid-era, jet plane plume.
Through the gaps in the trees, across the valley and just about
level with where I am standing, the Parthenon is sitting with
geometric certainty on top of its Acropolis. I am at the Muses'
shrine and remembering that they are also nymphs. There
may have been three Muses originally, but now there are
nine, and at some point someone with a busy mind allocated
them all a different area of expertise (poetry, history, dance,
song, etc.), although others were not so sure, and anyway that
seems to be missing the point about Greek myth that I am
only slowly absorbing (because it is hard for us, after centuries
of monotheism): these things were never fixed and there is no
infallible and inflexible book of reference. It is a liberating
thought.

It is Sunday morning and an intricate pattern of church
bells is tolling up the hill. Soon afterwards I hear the priest starting his sermon, which he seems to be conducting from the front
steps of his church through a loudhailer. A tiny old woman with
a stooped back, dressed all in black, comes beetling up the
narrow path, away from the noise, and races past me with a
snappy 'Yassas!' Where do they find all these Greek women, I
wonder, who have been here since I first visited the country in

1977? Why do they never look any different? And what do they think of the changes they have seen? Are they surprised that 'STEVE and MINETTE' have written their names three foot high in blue neon just by this shrine to the Muses? What do they make of us?

Given all this, and more, it is hard to compose myself, but I have come here to make an offering to the Muses, to help me with this book, just like any author should, to ask for inspiration and insight, to pray that I make a true beginning and do not stray from the path. Perhaps they can even put me on the road to Hope. But when I look in my bag, and then my pockets, apart from a few euro coins, all I have to offer is my only pen, which I seem to have picked up at a hotel called Pendley Manor in Tring when I was there for a literary festival in 2019. I will now have no way of making any notes until I get back to the hotel, but I suppose the offering has to be some kind of meaningful sacrifice. So I place this pen on the flat stone slab, which I hope is the altar, and I back away, bowing and wishing, and when I look up with prayer in my mind there is the tiny old Greek woman, standing on an escarpment just above me, outlined by the blazing sun, staring down at my furtive bows with a complicated look in her black eyes.

The road from Athens to Corinth, which follows the southern shore of the famous isthmus, passes through a landscape of straightforward industrial brutality. Many years ago (we don't know when) Theseus cleared this route of robbers and monsters, when he travelled for the first time from Troezen to Athens, on his way to introduce himself to his father, Aegeus, the king of Athens. Towards the end of this blood-drenched journey he arrived at sacred Eleusis and killed the overbearing king, Cercyon, in a wrestling match, and made Cercyon's grandson Hippothoon king instead. (Hippothoon had been raised by wild horses after Cercyon had exposed him as a baby to die on the mountainside.) Some say that Theseus also slept with all of Cercyon's many daughters, but that's the kind of detail that Athenians liked to add about their energetic but tragic local hero. True or not, his journey sounds a whole lot more exhausting than my own, as I whip past the grimy suburbs of Eleusis and then Megara in a rental car, stopping only to pay the tolls. The Gulf of Megara is to the left, where I have been told a last few common dolphins are hanging on in the oily waters, although there's nothing to see, out beyond the infrastructure of the gas and aluminium works and some rusting cargo ships, except for an empty, but beautiful blue sea, with an uplifting sparkle on its placid surface. Taking the long view, I suppose I have Theseus to thank for this friction-less travel.

I will get to holy Eleusis eventually, I tell myself, but I had always planned to start in a place called Sicyon, just outside Corinth. Sicyon was once known as Mecone and it was here that Prometheus and Zeus, the all-seeing King of high Olympia, came to an agreement about which parts of an animal should be offered to the gods, and which retained by people for their own personal consumption. Given how many animals were sacrificed to the gods, and how precious meat could be, this was an important question. But it is a strange story.

Prometheus killed and chopped up an ox and divided it into two, ready for one of those immense feasts that were still held in the days when gods and people mingled freely. In one basket Prometheus put the meat and innards, and covered them with the ox's revoltingly fetid stomach; in another basket he put the bones, and over them he smeared a delicious coating of ox fat (tastes have changed in the last million or so years). He offered first choice to Zeus, as was only right, but Zeus was deceived and chose the basket of bones covered with mouth-watering fat, meaning that ever since that day those are the parts of an animal that we are meant to sacrifice to the immortals, and we are free to keep the steaks and chops and ribs, and the juicy tongues and the brains and the moist, tender entrails and the glistening offal.

Zeus was furious, or he pretended to be furious. But surely if he was 'all-seeing' he would have known what Prometheus was up to? Maybe he really wanted the bones? After all, the Olympian gods and goddesses lived on ambrosial nectar – they didn't actually need the meat. Perhaps he wanted to help humanity. But why go through the charade? These points have been argued over ever since, although Zeus' resentment at Prometheus' trick festered and later – no one knows how much later – that grudge would erupt into rage when Prometheus stole fire from heaven.

This pivotal moment in history, when Zeus was tricked out of the spoils of sacrifice, happened here, in Sicyon. I have arrived at last, having spent an hour lost in the lonely hills, misled or mostly abandoned by the sat nav on my iPhone, which has such a perky way of leading me astray, down goat tracks and riverbeds, that I can't stay cross for long. Anyway, 'she' – the jaunty voice on my phone – is now my only friend, ever since Alex and Anna went back to London leaving me all alone.*

Sicyon is a small village these days; the ancient settlement was much more significant. Driving along dusty streets, past dogs that run and snap at the car wheels, and avoiding the burning gaze of old men who lift their heads from the village taverna's plastic tables, I came to the ruins of a classical amphitheatre, just beyond the ragged edges of the village – and it makes me happy to believe that this is where the sacrifice of the ox took place. Another story about Prometheus is that he was the one, at Zeus' request, who fashioned the first humans out of clay. The Greeks had more than one origin myth – and more than one version of humans to account for – but it is possible that if you are standing in Sicyon, at the site of the ancient amphitheatre, which is currently closed to visitors and blocked by a tall metal fence (there's no one else here, they must have had the foresight to consult the website before they came), if you are here then you could well be standing where our first ancestors were created out of mud. Or so said the people who happened to live here, or hereabouts – other versions are available.

---

* We had originally planned to come to Sicyon first, but were distracted by the beaches around Epidavros Port – you would have been too – and so this journey starts slightly out of order. I'll disentangle it later.

The hills around Sicyon, I have discovered, are thick with clay. Brown, yellow, beige, clays of many colours, gouged out over the centuries, although here by the theatre the dominant tone is red. There is no one about, just me and the cicadas, some yellow and blue butterflies rising from the dry grasses, a dog and a cockerel calling to each other across the valley, and very faintly the intermittent hum of human voices coming from somewhere in the olive grove down below. A fence post is being hammered into dry ground and the sound slaps from the steps of the amphitheatre. There is a locked Portakabin next to the high fence, seemingly a temporary base for the local archaeologists, who must still be working on the theatre and surrounding area. There is so much in Greece not yet found – and not for the first time I find myself envying these archaeologists, with their well-defined tasks and the ever-present possibility of a life-changing, world-shaking discovery. Although I do know it's mostly old pots, and not enough people care.

There is a gravestone in Highgate Cemetery in north London, just up the hill from Karl Marx and George Eliot, close to where my father-in-law is buried, and it reads:

SALLY HUNTER

1958–2015

LAWYER

should have been

a marine biologist

I hope her family don't mind me sharing it, but I often think of Sally and her fifty-seven years (my age today) and what we all wish we had rather done. Archaeology, marine biology, orni-thology, Astronomer Royal . . . the list is long.

The amphitheatre at Sicyon has the feel of an Aztec ruin, high above the Gulf of Corinth, with the sea so blue, and the mountains over the bay, and everything baked to dust by the long, heat-cracked summer. There are tunnels and caves to the side of the tiered seating, and the man-made theatre has blended with the pale gold, red and beige earth from which it has been so recently excavated. This is the earth, I do not forget, from which we were forged. I stoop to take a closer look, and become distracted by a file of ants, working their way through the grit with a burden of seeds and stalks, and when I look up I see a crow not far to the right, perched on a single low stone. The crow is the bird of Apollo, god of prophecy and music, and this one is streaked with grey; and because I haven't had time to check, I wonder if all the crows here are that colour (they're not). I do know that all crows were once white, but Apollo turned them black when one of them went to fetch him a glass of water but stopped to wait for the fruit on a fig tree to ripen, and forgot about the thirsty god's drink. At least, that's one story.

I watch the crow lift and ease itself into the air, and I see it's not a crow at all, but an eagle. The bird of Zeus! No, it's a buzzard. (Should have been an ornithologist . . .) It drifts shak-ily over the olive trees. Byron shot an 'eaglet' not far from here, on his first trip to Greece, just along the coast near Vostitza, and felt a deep shame.

It was only wounded, and I tried to save it, the eye was
so bright; but it pined, and died in a few days; and I
never did since, and never will, attempt the death of
another bird.

It is a pity that the shooters of Greece and Cyprus and the
grouse moors of Britain – where the songbirds and raptors die
in such numbers – have not followed his example.

The eagle-buzzard lands below in the olive grove, and hides
among the branches of a venerable old wild pear tree, under
which someone has made themselves a cosy retreat with a
white plastic picnic table and chair, a lantern hanging from
the lowest branch, a glass and an open bottle of red wine. It
looks so welcoming – I wonder if it's a sign. There's no one
there. Should I go and sit at the table? I have no idea how to
read them, but I am alert to the possibility of auguries in the
flight of birds. The ancient Greeks could find meaning in the
ways that birds flew or flocked or landed, or in the type or
number of birds that were the first to arrive over the horizon.
A stronger impulse, though, is that I wouldn't want to be
discovered at this table, drinking someone else's wine, like a
sozzled Goldilocks. These hills are littered with empty
cartridge shells.

    Another famous story involving Prometheus is the one about
Pandora, which I like to think may also have taken place here in
Sicyon. (Along with every one of these tales, it has more than

one version.) It happened after Prometheus had stolen the fire from heaven, bringing it back in a fennel stalk, and Zeus was intent on revenge. Prometheus had gone away for a while, but he knew that his punishment was imminent, so he warned his brother, Epimetheus ('who from the start turned out a disaster to men who live by bread'), not to accept anything from Zeus. Sure enough, Hermes, messenger of the gods, the trickster and occasional dog-killer (he was a thief and hated their barks), turned up at Epimetheus' door with Pandora, the most beautiful woman anyone, gods or humans, had ever seen. She may even have been the first woman of all, or so Hesiod says, and he wrote down this story before anyone else, so that's what we have.

Hesiod tells us that a man who marries a bad wife 'lives with unrelenting pain in heart and spirit'. He says that all women are descended from Pandora, 'a great affliction to mortals'. He writes that Zeus has created women as 'a bane for mortal men'. Hesiod sounds like he would be happiest in one of the wilder corners of Reddit for isolated and angry men – the Jordan Peterson of prehistory – and I have always assumed he had recently been left by his wife, perhaps for his best friend or even his brother (against whom he seems to bear an enormous grudge) and was sulking on his farm, shaping myths to lodge in our subconscious. Pandora is Eve and she is Helen of Troy and she is Jane Greer in *Build My Gallows High*, luring Robert Mitchum to his doom.

But this is the story we've been left with, that Pandora arrived and was welcomed and married to Epimetheus and one day she was at last overwhelmed by curiosity and opened the jar she had been given by Zeus ('never open it') and all the horrors of the world flew out. Until that time no one had ever been ill or suffered and there was no war or hunger or even any work because the fruits and grains just grew and harvested themselves and people spent their days dancing and making music and when anyone died after many toil-free and happy years they simply keeled over with a blissful smile on their unlined faces and that was it. And now look at us. Murderous, disease-ridden, planet-destroying carnivores. Women, eh?

The first book of Greek myths that I read to myself was *Tales of the Greek Heroes* by Roger Lancelyn Green, and I am still in thrall to its peculiar beauty. He wrote that Prometheus had fashioned people out of red clay in a place called Panopeus, not far to the east of Delphi, and not at Sicyon; and he also said that it was Prometheus who had hidden the jar full of horrors in Pandora's new home, but that she still opened it anyway, and there right at the bottom was a little voice, crying, 'Let me out too! I am Hope!' He doesn't say what happened next. Hesiod wrote that Hope was discovered under the lip of the jar and Pandora slammed down the lid just in time. Other writers, including Geraldine McCaughrean in *The Orchard Book of Greek Myths*, thought that without Hope the world would be unbearable 'so Pandora lifted the lid, and a white flicker, small as a butterfly, flitted out and was blown this way and that by the howling winds.'

Opinions are divided about what happened to Hope. Did she stay in the jar or not? Rather embarrassingly, I have come to Sicyon on the off chance that I might stumble across an old pot and find – tra laa! – our long-lost Hope. (The jar, which was never a 'box' until it was mistranslated by Erasmus, was a *pithos*, which are large and were often used for human burials, which has provoked an endlessly bifurcating wormhole of speculation about the deeper meaning of the myth.) Béatrice Han-Pile on Melvyn Bragg's *In Our Time* summarised it best, when she asked if the jar was 'a Prison' or 'a Pantry' and, perhaps more surprisingly, if Hope was 'a Good' or 'an Evil'.

The first question is whether Hope stayed in the jar, or was released. And if Hope did stay in the jar, then is that jar accessible to us, to be dipped into for sustenance and succour whenever we need it, a little taste of Hope, or is the jar an inaccessible prison? And next: is Hope really a blessing, as Lancelyn Green, Geraldine McCaughrean and Wild Bill Hickok and almost everyone else says? Or is Hope, as Nietzsche wrote, the most exquisite torture of them all? Why, he asked, was Zeus even interested in ameliorating his punishment? That was not his nature. Hope exists to torment us. Hope is false. Hope prolongs the pain. If we could see the world clearly for what it is, without Hope (or hope), we would kill ourselves and be done with it.

That night, alone in my Corinthian hotel, I am visited by Dream #4.

I have done something wrong. Something very bad. Murder even, or some kind of fundamental betrayal. I am with Anna, and the police are here, at our derelict shack out in the bayou, deep in the southern swamplands. They are plain-clothes police, partners, in a beaten-up old car, and they know I have done this thing, just as I know it too (even if I have no clear idea what *it* is). But there is no proof, or not enough, and they are digging around, needling me. 'Come on,' one of them says, the smaller, punchier one, 'you're going to have to come with us.' But I back away, and to my surprise they get into their car and drive off, along the narrow dry track that leads back to civilisation. This should be good news, but it is not enough, because I am still carrying the guilt of this terrible thing I know I have done. And then I look up and perhaps I am relieved because in the distance I can see the police car and it is coming back down along the track, throwing up a dust cloud, a slow, lurching, inevitable return.

The next morning, with the dream clinging like a poisoned cloak and impossible to ignore, I sent a question to the Oracle at Delphi. I had been thinking hard about how best to phrase it, because we all know that you must never leave any room for ambiguity. I also had it ready in ancient Greek.

Ποῦ ἐστιν ἡ τῆς Πανδώρας ἐλπίς

Or, to put it in plain English:

Where is Pandora's Hope?

THREE

Hope Springs Eternal

'And they lived like gods without sorrow of hearts,
remote and free from toil and grief.'

HESIOD, *WORKS AND DAYS*

It is only a handful of miles from Sicyon to Corinth. On the way, as the second-century traveller and guidebook writer Pausanias once wrote with refreshing lack of research, you could see 'the memorial of Lykos the Messenian, whoever he was'. Nowadays there is no longer even the remnant of any memorial, so I suppose Lykos from Messenia is lost to us forever, along with almost everyone else who has ever lived.

I have been using Pausanias' book, *Guide to Greece*, translated and weightily annotated by Peter Levi, as the main source and reference for my travels so far. It may be old ... but in the seventeenth and eighteenth centuries, when the British, Germans and French were rediscovering Greece, they used this ancient guidebook to track down lost temples, tombs and even cities, with extraordinary success. When he wants to be, he is painstakingly precise about the location of things; and it is thanks to Pausanias that we know so much about what Greece once looked like, even though he travelled five hundred years

after its glory days and in the aftermath of three centuries of
Roman interference, rebuilding, slaughter and looting. He still
saw wonders that we can only imagine. Byron had a copy in his
luggage.

I have a personal interest in Pausanias because I spent
twenty-five years trying to work out how to produce the perfect
guidebook, and if I had known that he had got there before us,
I would have paid more attention to his *Guide to Greece*. Not that
it is always a light or easy read. He has an unquenchable interest in who founded cities, and he can list their descendants in
arm-chewing detail, down to the twenty-fifth generation. He is
also preoccupied with the tribes and peoples of Greece, and
how they are connected, and whether they fought at Troy (and
with how many ships) and who came home, and every little war,
battle and scrap between every little city – and that is exhausting. He also (from one guidebook obsessive to another) needed
to think more clearly about how to arrange his material, because
even with the help of Peter Levi, who shunted sections around
to try and make sense of Pausanias' wanderings, anyone trying
to use this book as an actual guide is likely to spend more time
in the index than is healthy. And also, I want to know, does the
museum shop at Delphi close early on a Tuesday and will it
accept all major credit cards?

Despite my industry-insider grumblings, Pausanias' book is
a revelation, and not just because it is filled with the most
wondrous details about so many places that we can all still visit.
Pausanias was a believer in the pagan gods, writing 150 years
after the birth of Christ. He is not Homer or Hesiod, who swam
at ease in their sea of faith. Nor is he a restless golden age

Athenian dramatist or philosopher. Pausanias is a typical guide-book writer: clever (brilliant!), educated, eager to inform, and shot through with a rich seam of pedantry. Perhaps he is emblematic of his age. His audience were sophisticated Romans and Greeks, well versed in the arch game-playing of Ovid and Juvenal, and Pausanias is sometimes eager to show that he is not just blindly swallowing the old tales about Zeus' loves and Pan's magic. He lived in a time of rising anxiety, cynicism and turmoil. But even so, Pausanias evokes a world where there really were spirits in the hills and the woodlands and springs, and temples where a goddess would accept your offering and listen to your prayer. It was a world where the gods really had once walked among us, and loved and punished us, even if they did not do so anymore.

I arrived in ancient Corinth in the late afternoon, clutching Pausanias, who is a) happy that 'The Peloponnese is still as continental as nature intended' – he had gazed with satisfaction at the abandoned ruins of Nero's hubristic attempt to build a canal – and b) quick to make the point that 'not one of the Corinthians of antiquity still lives in Corinth; instead there are colonists sent from Rome'. The reason for this is that in the year 146 BCE the Romans had defeated a rebellious Greek army just outside Corinth, the survivors had fled to the city, and the vengeful Roman General Lucius Mummius had torn down the walls and buildings, murdered all the men and shipped off the women and children to Rome as slaves. Pausanias describes how many of the local traditions were then lost and never revived. This was for a while the city of Jason, the leader of the Argonauts, who brought back the golden fleece; and Medea, his queen, who murdered their children, or buried them one by one in the hope that they would become immortal, or perhaps, as Pausanias says, the children were stoned to death by the people of Corinth for having unwittingly brought Medea's gift of a poisoned cloak to Jason's new wife, the Princess Glauke. You can still see the spring into which Glauke flung herself, trying to wash off the burning poison. It is, as we guidebook writers like to say, 'well worth a visit'.

Corinth was the city of Bellerophon, who rode the flying horse Pegasus and killed the Chimaera, the monster with a lion's head, a goat's body and a serpent for a tail. And it was founded by Sisyphus, who outwitted death, if not forever, and was punished by being made to roll a large stone up to the top of a hill, only to watch it roll down again, and again, for eternity. So many myths. Oedipus grew up here, thinking it was his parents' home, before he left for Thebes. It was most famously a city of springs, of nymphs and fountains and rills of flowing water, some of them created by gods, and one of them – the most sacred of them all – made when a woman called Peirene literally dissolved in tears, unable to stop weeping after her son was accidentally killed by the goddess Artemis. Her grief nourished the city. Many small local divinities and acts of worship were forgotten when the people were exterminated in 146 BCE, although how much of the nature of a place is in its rocks and soil and landscape and somehow seeping into the inhabitants, regardless of when they arrived, and vice versa, is something – mercifully – that does not seem to have occurred to Pausanias. Perhaps he hadn't read his Plato.

The Romans rebuilt Corinth, absorbing earlier elements from the city they had wrecked, but the place has been destroyed many times since, undone by war and neglect. There are precisely seven sturdy columns still standing in the temple of Apollo. The sacred Peirene spring is a shamble of marble debris. The forum is a pile of bricks, around which a lone piebald dog with a furtive air is rootling and scratching. He comes over to say hello. It is late in the afternoon and a pin-sized translucent moon has just risen into the blue-velvet sky, and I stop to watch it float upwards between the pock-marked temple columns, with the sun disappearing behind me, its last rays soaking the ruins with ochre and gold. Apollo, who by many accounts became, or merged with, the god of the sun, must be delighted. One of the things I have very quickly learned since I arrived in Greece is how adept the ancient builders were at placing their temples in exactly the right place.

Just outside the small museum, there is an exhibition (or the teaser for an exhibition, or even the remains of an exhibition, it is hard to tell) on the subject of 'Inner Beauty'. About twenty photographs from around the world are on display, perhaps a third of them from Greece, all of them gorgeously shot. There is a blonde man on a Danish beach with a thick sunburned neck. A naked, middle-aged Argentinian man is staring at his dinner while his naked, middle-aged wife or friend or avenging angel examines herself blankly in a half-length mirror. There is a photo of a man watching TV, slumped into a chair, plugged into a drip, smoking and slurping beer (this one's from Belgium); and there's another one of a green vase with a patterned neck, out of which are leaning some tufts of myrtle. A gaunt woman with a blotchy, yellow-stained face stares with frost-eyed longing or despair at the camera. A red admiral butterfly has settled on her cheek.

Inside the museum are examples of what we might more classically describe as 'Beauty', but not much of it, because most of the riches of Corinth were stolen long ago, or spirited away to the National Archaeological Museum of Athens. There is a collection of headless, naked, smooth-skinned, human male torsos, and the heads of horses, and a bust of Zeus or Poseidon looking a lot like Jeff Bridges. There is a somewhat peremptory Roman mosaic of a couple of griffins eating a horse; and two fine naked men, or *Kouroi*, who have the atmosphere of insouciant power that we might well describe as Corinthian. And in the room devoted to the healing powers of the god Asclepius, there is a wall of human feet, ears, organs, noses and penises, of all shapes and sizes (especially the penises), fashioned out of clay and once offered to the god in the hopes that he could help with a number of very specific ailments.

It may be the end of a long day, or my mood, but I do not find anything here especially 'beautiful'. I would rather be in the Spring Room of Thera, or in a clearing in the nearest forest, watching the long, slow pull of a deep-flowing river and the dance of blue dragonflies on its sunlit, reed-filled banks.

Outside again, I notice that one of the posters has a quote from the art critic Jonathan Jones:

> Beauty is the most dangerous idea in art. It's the most dangerous idea in life, too.

Which is just irritating. Where do these people get their certainty? Him and Keats, blethering on about beauty. What does he even mean, 'the most dangerous idea in life'? What about fascism, feudalism, slavery, misogyny, imperialism, the Great Leap Forward, collectivism, racism, eugenics . . . or in fact the idea that we can carry on taking what we want from the earth, for as long as we like, with no consequences? Our irrational faith in endless growth – and the climate breakdown and mass extinctions and genocides that follow. What about them? Is that idea not more dangerous? And Keats. Is it really all we need to know? That 'Beauty' is 'Truth'. How about how to make a fire, or fashion a wheel, or navigate the poisonous bullies of social media?

Oh, I know. It's probably my mood. Best if I get a drink, go to bed, and see what dreams may come.

The ruins of old Corinth are about five kilometres from the modern city, which is down the hill and on the coast in a scoop of a bay, close to the northern entrance of the canal; while up high, far above on a plateau of rock, where the buzzards call and soar, is the ancient acropolis and citadel known as the Acrocorinth. That is where I am heading next, just as soon as I have composed my question to the Oracle at Delphi and finished my seventeenth Greek salad of the trip. It is almost the end of October, but the sun is fierce and there has been no rain of note for many months. Our world is once again on course to endure one of its five hottest years since we started collecting the data, and new records are being made and surpassed at bewildering speed, like bales being tossed backwards by a runaway threshing machine.* Brooding on this grim thought, I am whining up the hill in my small hire car, smacking through potholes, skidding on slews of gravel, chased by a whirligig of dust. The road is narrow and bent and drops like a stone to the right, and I am trying to hover close to the hillside, hoping without any real hope that no one comes around a corner too fast (although that is something you can more or less guarantee in Greece). The scrubby trees on either side of the road are burned and leafless and charcoal black.

It was decided long ago by Briareos, one of the monsters with a hundred hands who had helped Zeus in his wars of succession, that Acrocorinth should belong to the sun god, Helios, while the isthmus would be sacred to Poseidon, the god of the sea. The only other place that is claimed by Helios for his home is the island of Rhodes, another scorched rocky outcrop with blistering views. Human ownership of Acrocorinth has changed many times, which is surprising, given that it looks impregnable, and it is blessed with fresh spring water all the year round (despite being so high), thanks to King Sisyphus, who struck a bargain with the river god Asopus: 'I'll tell you who has abducted your daughter, if you'll give my city a spring that never runs dry.' He was a great one for a bargain, Sisyphus. You'd think that by now he would have been able to negotiate

---

* The results are in and according to NASA, 2020 was the hottest year on record. The UK Met Office had it in second place, just behind a sweltering 2016. The EU's climate observation programme has the two years tied for first place. What a desperate chart.

his way out from under his rock, but apparently not. Anyway, the answer that Sisyphus gave the river god Asopus was Zeus (hardly a surprise, given Zeus' track record) and he got his spring, and 'if you like to believe it,' sniffs Pausanias, that is why 'he pays the penalty of telling in Hades'. Neolithic and prehistoric peoples, Greeks, Romans, Byzantines, Frankish crusaders, Venetians and Ottomans have all settled here at some point, and reinforced the vertiginous walls and towers. And they have all since departed.

I have parked the suffering car at the entrance to the Byzantine-Venetian-Ottoman fortress and have walked, all alone, through the gates and up one of the hairpin paths that leads towards the top of the Acropolis. Should the sun really be this hot in October and so early in the day? That is one question, but a better one might be, did none of these people – ancient Greeks, neolithic farmers and Ottomans – ever suffer from vertigo? The views are bowel-loosening. The kingdom of Helios is hard and cracked, its soil thinned to the rock, feverishly worked over by rabbits and humans, lumped with ruins and outcrops, overgrown by dry tufted grasses parched a light brown, and everywhere strewn with small sharp white stones. There are a few trees, and I sit under the shade of a young olive and watch a man in the far distance walking around the Frankish tower with that bow-legged, cacked-pants shuffle that is familiar to all fellow vertigo sufferers. I decide to skip the Frankish tower. What's in a view anyway?

The news this morning is that 100,000 people in southern California have just been ordered to evacuate their homes, after two more huge wildfires broke out in Orange County. Two firefighters are in hospital. The world is burning, and the sunny blue skies of California have turned scarlet and black. This is what Byron witnessed in the 'year without a summer' of 1816, twelve months after Mount Tambora had erupted in Indonesia, and he was holed up in Switzerland on the shores of Lake Geneva with his friends the Shelleys, and his reluctant lover Claire Clairmont (well, the reluctance was his, or so he claimed) and the irritating Dr Polidori, who had followed him from Britain; and the sun never shone, and the rains fell, and harvests failed across East Asia, Europe, India and North America, and Mary Shelley wrote *Frankenstein* and Byron produced his great apocalyptic poem *Darkness*:

> Forests were set on fire – but hour by hour
> They fell and faded – and the crackling trunks
> Extinguish'd with a crash – and all was black.

Of course, the volcano was unpredicted and devastating, most immediately to the people who lived close to its source, who died in their tens of thousands. The next year endless night and starvation came north. We are better at monitoring the activity of volcanoes these days, but the fires that are burning across the world are wholly predictable and anything but natural. California, Siberia, Australia, Indonesia and beyond are aflame because of out-of-control climate breakdown, ignorant forest management (or lack of any management at all) and fires that are being set deliberately to clear the last of the forests to meet the bottomless pit of our needs. Here in Greece there are 10,000 forest fires every year, some of them deadly (as they all will be soon enough), ninety per cent of them started by arsonists.

The world has burned before. Long ago the god Helios was begged by his son, Phaeton, to let him drive the chariot of the sun. Just once, he pleaded, to prove to his friends that he really was Helios' child, as his mother always said, and eventually the god relented, although he knew that the horses that pulled his chariot were too powerful and wild for any human. And so it proved. Phaeton stood tall, as Eos, the goddess of the dawn, ushered in his journey, but he lost control almost immediately and dropped the reins, the horses felt his weakness and fear and bolted across the heavens – the chariot of the sun, with Phaeton clinging to its sides, flailing behind them – soaring high, scorching the stars, and racing over the earth, where cities and mountaintops and whole nations were incinerated. Volcanoes erupted. Rivers boiled and disappeared into the cracked earth. Libya became a desert. The Ethiopians were burned black. The oceans shrank, sea creatures floated lifeless on the thick surface, and new islands were born as the waters drained away. Eventually, begged by Mother Earth, Zeus killed Phaeton with a single throw of a thunderbolt and Helios dragged his horses back under control. Phaeton's sisters, inconsolable in their grief, weeping for their lost brother, were transformed into poplar trees and their tears mingled with the returning rivers to emerge as amber, which even now is worn by brides on their wedding days. Or so we're told.

The Greeks liked to tell tales that set out the limits to human aspiration. Icarus is the more famous example, the wax on his wings melted by the sun for daring to fly too high. 'Nothing in excess' was written on the wall at holy Delphi. (Mind you, so was 'Make use of experts.') But even though the world they lived in was younger than ours, and emptier of humans, and fecund with other life – there were once lions on the shoreline at Corinth – they knew, even then, what would happen if we reached too far, or took too much.

Not that this knowledge always stopped them, and not even, I am afraid, that often. Plato wrote about the bare hills that surrounded Athens, that were covered in thick forest, rooted in a dense, fertile soil.

> What now remains of the formerly rich land is like the skeleton of a sick man, with all the fat and soft earth having wasted away and only the bare framework remaining.

There were remains of holy sites all over the hills, he wrote, shrines to the nymphs of the springs and streams, and now there was no water and there were no nymphs left for us to worship. Everything was barren, ever since the trees were felled. This is deep ecological wisdom, something that we are only now relearning, slowly (and the news is not travelling nearly fast enough). If you remove the forests, the rains will no longer fall and the springs will run dry.

The Greeks had other stories, though, about people who were compelled to reach beyond ordinary human limits. Had these people not lifted the stone to take the sword, or drained the swamps and diverted the rivers, then the world would still be haunted by monsters and furies. The Greeks worshipped their heroes for stepping over the line and doing what the rest of us could not. Heracles, the greatest of them all, was needed by Zeus to help him fight off giants. Perseus slew the Gorgon. And Prometheus, who was not even human, if he had not done what was expressly forbidden – and been punished by being chained to the Caucasus mountains so that an eagle, or vultures, could feed on his liver every day for evermore – if he had not disobeyed Zeus and taken heaven's fires, then we would all still be grovelling in the mud.

So the Greeks understood that sometimes we have to strive and break things, much as they feared the idea. But they also knew that in their day (perhaps unlike ours) most change was not down to human agency. Volcanoes erupt. Mourning women are turned into trees. Hunters are torn apart by their own hounds. 'It is no crime to lose yourself in a dark wood.' Things happen, and change comes, because of the gods, who are angry with us, or playful, or in fact only doing what they would like to do without reference to us, uninterested in what we think or want. Often enough, we are superfluous, incidental bit players who might liven up their day, or are simply getting in the way. And beyond the gods there is something else, that is out of even their control, and most certainly ours. It is sheer hubris to think otherwise.

It is easy to fall into a reverie on the Acrocorinth, which is so much closer to the sun than anywhere else on earth (the island of Rhodes excepted). I was jolted from my distressing dreams under the young olive tree by the sound of voices far below. There was a family of three children shrieking by the entrance gate, scrambling over the walls and shooting imaginary arrows down from the tower. This place seems to be a natural amphitheatre. I do hate to generalise, and would always want to attach riders and exceptions and explanatory notes, but – my God, Americans are loud. The dad's voice comes roiling beefily up the hill. 'Do you wanna hike to the tippy top, kids?' and I tense (and so seemingly do the rock sparrows and the cicadas), but then, before his children have a chance to reply, he says, 'No, it's too far. Let's go and get an ice cream instead,' and we all relax. And just then a Belgian or French family arrives at my tree, three young children leaping ahead like otters, and the woman says to me as she walks past, 'Is it worth it, getting to the top?' and I reply, 'Oh yes, it's incredible,' never having been there, and off they bound, and even though the juxtaposition of these families is a coincidence, it was not one I was able to resist, and I have since added another dry stone to the rickety cairn of my prejudices.

The hero Bellerophon found the winged horse Pegasus drinking from the sacred spring near the top of the Acrocorinth, and they set off together to slaughter monsters and people. Pegasus sometimes started springs of his own with a blow of his great hoof, such as on Mount Helicon, near to where the Muses live. He was sacred to the people of Corinth, even the ones who arrived after the extermination. And the spring is still here, that is the incredible thing, so high above the earth, its underground walls standing, the way down narrow, squeezing between the stones, just enough room for one person, the water level perhaps a little low at the end of a drought-ridden summer, flecked with stems and seeds, but cool and dark and still here. I would like to drink this sacred water, but it is behind a metal fence and clearly off-limits, and I'm no hero.

Sunlight has followed me down the steps into this underground chamber, and is filtering through two small openings above the far wall. The light is soft and the stones are golden. I have no idea where this water comes from or how deep it goes, but it is beautiful, all of it, the sacred spring and the ancient rocks that hold it in place, the birdsong that falls with the sunlight from on high and glances through the room, and here, the shimmer and glitter on the golden stones and the glow on the surface of the clear black water with its sheen of seeds and dust. Time swallows itself. I can hear the voices of women from outside, although I haven't been here long – have I? – and I thought there was no one about. And it comes to me all of a sudden, I don't know why, but with a burst of fear, that I would rather not be found down here, all alone, perhaps trapped, and so I clamber quickly up the narrow stone steps into the bright sunshine and the burned dry grass and look around in the glare but there is no one to be seen.

Nor is there anyone at the very ('tippy') top of the Acrocorinth, not even a Belgian. I assume this is down to Covid-19 and also possibly the time of year. Everything at the moment is out of kilter and unsettled, but it is a blessing to be able to sit here all alone under a toasting October sun, taking in a view that soars over ancient and modern Corinth, east over the canal and down the isthmus towards Megara and Eleusis, following Theseus' route when he set out to meet his father for the first

time, arriving at the coastline of the island of Salamis, where
the Greeks – or some of the Greeks – fought the Persians at sea;
or north over the nearest curl in the gulf to the hills of Perachora
where Medea buried her children, and beyond to mountainous
Thisvi and Plataea, where the Greek armies finally destroyed
the Persians in the great land battle of 479 BCE. To the south-
east, over a flat plain streaked with roads and buildings and
olive groves, is the misty blue Saronic Gulf (and its last few
common dolphins) and to the south are the hilly roads that lead
to the great theatre of Epidavros and the ancient citadels of
Mycenae, Tiryns and Troezen.

That must be Mount Kyllini to the west, wreathed in clouds,
birthplace of the messenger god Hermes (patron of thieves
and travellers), son of the nymph Maia and Zeus, and also
home to Pan, the cloven-hooved god of the wild who haunted
young Byron. It is where Tiresias was changed into a woman
when he struck two coupling snakes with a stick, and changed
back into a man seven years later for the same offence, or
maybe he tried to avoid them but was transformed anyway,
and was blinded by Hera for saying women enjoy sex more
than men – nine times more, for the record – and he was made
a prophet by Zeus, or perhaps Apollo, and then again maybe it
was Athena who blinded him, but gave him the power to
understand birdsong, and he became the originator of auguries (that is, reading the future in the flight and song of birds)
and he spoke with Odysseus and great King Cadmus of Thebes
and became entangled with Pentheus (who was torn apart by
his own mother) and tragic Oedipus, and so the myths dance
and coil and shed their gorgeous skins and multiply and are

born again. Kyllini is the holy mountain of Arcadia, and it is drenched in myth.

Pausanias wrote that there was a shrine to the goddess Aphrodite when he visited, although I have my doubts that he ever actually made it to the Acrocorinth. He is the sort of man who would have had a lot more to say if he had. I am now sitting on a fallen stone in what is left of this small shrine, which has also been, according to Peter Levi, 'a church, two mosques, a Venetian gun emplacement, and a Turkish house'. The modern Greeks have scraped it all away and left us only the ruins of the shrine to the goddess of love, because the ancient is what is deemed to have the most value (but not the very ancient, otherwise they might have just carried on digging in the hopes of finding a neolithic farmhouse).

Aphrodite was the goddess of love, indeed, but also of:

> the whisperings of girls; smiles; deceptions;
> sweet pleasure, intimacy, and tenderness.

Or so said Hesiod, and we already know about him. She was born when Cronus, the crooked schemer, father of Zeus, cut off Heaven's genitals (his own hated father) with an excruciatingly sharp sickle and flung them out to sea, and Aphrodite materialised in the foam that formed and floated on the ocean's surface as the genitals drifted to the shore of Cythera, in the Peloponnese, and then on to Cyprus, where she is worshipped to this day in the form of branded perfumes and oils and hyperactive tavernas. She did not step from a pearly seashell, as we would all prefer to think, but it does mean that

Aphrodite is an older deity than Zeus. Eros, her little helper, god of irresistible desire, is even older. Her brothers and sisters were formed from the blood of the severed genitals, spraying onto Mother Earth. These were the Giants who were defeated with Heracles' help many years later, and the terrifying Erinyes who punished wrongdoers, and best of all the lovely Meliai, the nymphs whose lives were interwoven with ash trees, although some people say that it was all of the tree nymphs that were born at this moment, out of the blood that gushed from Heaven's genitals, long-lived but mortal sisters to smiling Aphrodite.

The poet Sappho understood Aphrodite better than anyone. She was the 'deathless daughter of Zeus', the 'wile-weaver', invisible as the winds:

> . . . and I too, Full of the vision,
> Saw the white implacable Aphrodite,
> Saw the hair unbound and the feet unsandalled
> Shine as fire of sunset on western waters

Sappho called Zeus the father of Aphrodite, ignoring the genital story. The fact remains that all the immortals were in her power, even him (especially him), except for three goddesses: Artemis, sister of Apollo, who hunts in the wild places and who made Zeus, her father, promise that she would never have to fall in love; Hestia, sacred to the home and the hearth; and Athena, guiding spirit of Athens and other cities, warrior and weaver of wisdom. Apart from these three, no god was immune, not even Aphrodite herself.

I am sitting in the temple of the goddess of love (as a Motown classic must surely once have begun), staring at a cruise ship at anchor in the distant bay, not far from the northern entrance to the Corinth canal. It may well have been there for most of the year, ever since the pandemic first struck, when the virus got loose among the predominantly elderly and close-packed holidaymakers who were whooping it up on the sea-lanes of the oceans. Since then, almost all cruises around the world have been put on hold, and the destinations of these immense floating hotels have simultaneously suffered a crushing fall in tourist dollars, and been gifted a much-needed moment of respite, when fragile ecosystems and the ravaged fabric of historic cities have been given a chance to recover.

Who knew there were so many cruises? It is hard to keep up with the roster of human activities, let alone keep track of which are most destructive. Cruises come high, no doubt, with their clawing anchors and gargantuan quantities of pumped-out carbon and plastics and effluent. There's a crumpled cigarette pack by my foot (we need to talk about this Greek attitude to litter) and it carries the usual upsetting image of someone's ravaged lungs or punctured throat, with a promise that smoking will kill your babies (and everyone else's too). But don't you think we also need these health warnings flashed up on the booking sites for cruise ships – and emblazoned on every ticket that is sold? 'WARNING: taking this voyage will hasten the end of human civilisation', with a picture of a crushed coral reef or Venice disappearing into its lagoon. Perhaps all industries need them. 'WARNING: eating this pork pie will stop your antibiotics from working', illustrated with a photo of an industrialised mega farm and twenty thousand suppurating pigs. 'WARNING: buying this shampoo will empty the oceans', with a picture of a deformed cod. I catch myself staring at the cruise ship with loathing, although of course it represents many hundreds, perhaps thousands, of people's livelihoods, now floating uselessly in the gulf.

What are we supposed to do? When the first lockdown was operating in Britain, there was much easy talk about people finding the time to reconnect with nature (ignoring the grisly economic imperatives), and the idea became current that perhaps people might emerge with new priorities, and the world would be kinder and slower and less rapacious. And then the lockdown ended and we leaped into our cars and headed for the shops and restaurants and the open (coagulating) roads – because we missed it all so much! – while governments around the world floored the accelerator in a desperate race for growth. But I do wonder whether something is now changing. It certainly will, one way or the other. We really cannot buy our way out of this.

Do people know when they are living through a period of profound change? Not just in technology, or governance, or the slaughter and enslavement of an entire population, but an actual moment of disintegration, a time of dissolution, a tearing up of roots. A universal reordering of what was thought to be true. Is that happening now? Every generation thinks it is exceptional, but all the signs are now flashing that we are at a turning point, or perhaps the end of the road.

Paul the Apostle was here in Corinth, about 100 years before Pausanias visited on his tour of the Greek cities and holy sites (which is somehow surprising, but the gods of the classical world had a couple of hundred years left still to run). The Corinthians were the recipients of two of his most famous letters, including the one that contains the passage about 'Love' (or 'Charity' says the King James Bible) that we know from dozens of weddings and funerals ('when I was a man I put away childish things'). They would have read it just down the hill from where I am sitting, wading (if you ask me) through a sticky mess about virgins and the hair-covering of men's wives, before arriving at the crunch: 'And now abideth faith, hope, charity, these three; but the greatest of these is charity.' And if charity is another word for love (the love that puts others first) and if it is to be put before faith ('which moves mountains') and prophesy, and knowledge, and sacrifices to the gods, and the wisdom of 'the Greeks' (about which he is scornful), and the beliefs of 'the Jews' ('for they require a sign'), and ahead of 'hope' (which is nonetheless, and despite Nietzsche and Sisyphus, to be reckoned one of the three great forces for good), then it is love itself – selfless love – which is going to transform the world. And that was a revolutionary thought at the time of Paul and then Pausanias, a dizzying shift in consciousness and a turning away from old beliefs. As of course it still would be.

It was a different kind of love that was once offered by the temple of Aphrodite, where the prostitutes who worked by its columns were of unparalleled beauty, or so said the traveller Strabo not too long before Paul arrived. Centuries later, the temple was torn down, to make way for a church – and then again, for two mosques, a gun emplacement and a house. Sitting here, I am alert to the possibility that there may be something sacred about this site, in the rock itself, carried through the ages. To say it better, I am aware of the fact that some people believe that certain places on this earth are holy, and filled with spirit, although all I can honestly say at this moment is that the view is awe-inspiring. There is a flat wedge of cloud at exactly my height, moving slowly towards me from Mount Kyllini. I remind myself that it is hope I am pursuing, even if love has now entered the frame. And to my surprise I find myself muttering, to Aphrodite of all beings (mercifully there is no one around to hear me), the goddess of smiles, asking her to help me find love. Not for my family or those close to me. I know what love feels like. But it is no good glaring down from lofty heights on cruise ships and raging about the accelerating extinctions and rapid poisoning of the planet. We know it is happening, but we need more than that. If we are lucky enough not to be embroiled in its immediate convulsions, caught up in the first blast of the volcano, then the world needs more than our distant despair or contempt.

I suppose, with Sappho, we could take the long view:

And I say
That many years from now,
In another age,
Someone will remember who we were.

But would it not be better if what they remembered, and felt for us, was gratitude?

Or even love.

FOUR

Dead Dog, Happy Dog

'When he compares the present to the past,
The past was better, infinitely so.'

LUCRETIUS, *ON THE NATURE OF THINGS*

Back in Athens, briefly, I met up in a café with Dimitris Ibrahim, who works for WWF Greece. He trained as a lawyer, before joining Greenpeace, and now he's with WWF and trying to alert people to the dangers of the oil and gas extraction that is planned for Greece and its portion of the Mediterranean Sea. He pulls up a brightly coloured map on his laptop and shows me the areas that are earmarked for exploitation: a great chunk of the north-west Peloponnese (about a fifth of the landmass), and then north over the Gulf of Patras and along the coast, past Astakos and Preveza, but far inland too, circling the Amvrakikos Gulf and wetlands, and north again over the wild mountains and woodlands of Epirus, to the very edge of the Albanian border (where the oil has been polluting the land and its people with minimal regulation for years).

The big blocks of colour on the map represent the areas that have been granted to corporations – Hellenic Petroleum,

Repsol Energean, Total, Exxon and more – the deals that have already been done. And he shows me the concessions along the coast and offshore: to the west of Epirus and Corfu, and then closer inland, past Kefalonia and Lefkada and other islands familiar to northern holidaymakers looking for two weeks of tranquility; and around the coast of the southern Peloponnese, digging into its fingers; and near to the Gulf of Kyparissia, where loggerhead turtles lay their eggs in the summer, and Pylos, where wise Nestor once lived and feasted his men on the beach (the most beautiful beach in Greece, some say).

At this place, but further offshore, is the Calypso Deep, where sperm whales surface, high above the shifting, tectonic Hellenic Trench, which curls down from here and then around the south coast of the island of Crete, once home to King Minos, whose palace was shaken apart by Poseidon, god of earthquakes, not long after Theseus had slain the Minotaur in its labyrinth. All of this has been offered up for exploitation. Apart from the effect on our climate, it is hard to imagine that anyone thinks it is a good idea to drill for oil or gas in these unstable and fragile seas. The plans stretch east, into politically volatile waters, where Turkey and Cyprus and Israel are all of a mind to lay their hands on what they can get.

Dimitris lays another map on top of the first, and this one shows in shaded orange the areas of Greece that are meant to be protected – the national parks, wetlands, forests and marine reserves that are part of the European Natura 2000 network, designated as off limits by earlier Greek governments – and it shows how much overlap there is, how much of the network has been opened up for exploitation, huge tracts offshore and along the coast and also smeared across the wondrous wooded mountains of the northern region of Epirus. We stare at the maps, and then Dimitris laughs. 'The Greek government has been unusually efficient,' he says.

The oil and gas corporations have been busy too, not only signing deals with central government, but making sure that local authorities and the people who live in the affected areas are either kept in the dark about the plans, or mollified with a new football pitch for their park, or dazzled with tales of the fabulous wealth that will flow. Most media are silent, or owned by the same people. It is a familiar story, wherever we live. And of course Greece has been under extraordinary pressure, ever since the financial crisis of late 2009 engulfed the country. The need for money for the bankrupt state lies at the root of much of this.

Dimitris tells me that concessions last for twenty-five years and 'the companies get the keys' to do what they want, with very little right of oversight. 'Local people think they are going to get rich,' says Dimitris, 'and there'll be development and jobs in areas that desperately need them. But what are the companies going to pay the Greek state? A median royalty of seven to eight per cent. It's what you'd tip the waiter in a restaurant. And what is the cost?' In lost tourism. In a blighted land.

We talk about the alternatives to fossil fuels, and Dimitris admits to feeling ambivalent about wind turbines and solar, especially when they are owned by the same companies that also control the gas and oil. Local ownership is best, but rare, and hard to achieve. There were horrific storms and mudslides on Kefalonia recently and local people blamed the wind farms, which are appearing on hilltops all over Greece. Our conversation drifts down a familiar spiral. The climate is convulsing. The forests are burning. Dimitris has a seven-year-old child and wonders what will be there for them. 'Have you heard of Medicanes?' he asks. 'They used to be rare, but we get them more often now. Mediterranean Hurricanes. There was one that tore through Thessaly recently. Epirus too. The strange thing is that most survivors of these events do not start worrying about climate chaos – or doing something about it. No, if anything they become optimistic: "if I can get through that," they say, "I can get through anything." And then these things become a normal part of our lives.'

'It is hard for us all to stay optimistic,' I say, worming towards my question . . . 'But do you still have hope for the future?'

'*Hope?*' Dimitris laughs. 'Hope is a curse.'

'I know I am in the business of hope,' he says, 'and there is what they call the optimism of action. At least I am doing something. We have to keep saying to ourselves that nothing is impossible. There are 43,000 households in Greece getting their power from renewable sources today, thanks to a tariff that was introduced in 2006 and activated in 2010. In 2008–9 we stopped four coal power plants from being opened.' He pauses. 'It has been a long time since we had a victory.'

And then: 'This is a mountain – and sometimes I wonder why I am climbing it.'

The next day I took the road south from Athens to Sounion, at the very tip of the peninsula, passing the international airport, tracing in reverse the route I'd made with Wild Bill a few days earlier. I hardly need to say it, but the sun is hanging hot in a cloudless blue sky. My little hired car seems happy, leaving the aggravations of Athens's traffic behind – I know I am – and we zip through wide valleys flanked by scorched, treeless hills (Plato would recognise them, if not the many pylons) along a dusty road lined with eucalyptus, olives and prickly pear. There are signs for a 'Dino Park', which I eye wistfully (no time for that), and off-roading, and something called 'Happy Dog', which may be a bar, or a taverna, or possibly a kennels. And then just about fifty metres later, there is a large yellow dog lying flat on the side of the road, entirely still, laid out in the sun, with a small pile of something crimson and grey by its side – guts, I think later, maybe brains? I don't know, I was past it fast. The dog was smiling, but it was also undeniably dead.

When the legendarily wealthy King Croesus asked the Athenian statesman Solon who was the happiest man in the world, expecting that the answer would be him, because how could it not be with all his money and power, Solon said that it was a man called Tellus, who had died in battle fighting for his city and been honoured by his countrymen, having lived a prosperous life, and was survived by every one of his healthy children and grandchildren. And then, said Solon (talking over Croesus), there were the brothers Cleobis and Biton. They had dragged their mother's cart to the temple of Hera, the queen of the gods, when her oxen had failed, so that she could pray. The mother asked Hera to grant her sons the greatest gift of all, at which point Cleobis and Biton lay down on the floor of the temple and fell into a deep sleep; and then, some time later, without waking, they were caressed into an easeful death. The point is, said Solon, that these people were dead. If a person lives for seventy years, that is 26,250 days (Solon's maths, not mine), and every one of those days will be different. So until you are dead, you cannot say that you are happy . . . you are lucky.

The road leads past Thorikos, where I stop to look at the ruins of a once busy ancient settlement on a hill, neolithic originally, which in the classical era had a temple dedicated to Dionysus, the twice-born god of ecstasy and madness, of wine and metamorphoses and dark prophecies. Someone (not just the passing of the years) has torn down his temple and scattered it across the slopes, leaving just a few hot flat splintered stones. There was also a theatre here, along with defensive walls and towers and an industrial quarter, although there isn't much of any of it left, just foundations and loose stones among clumps of dry brown grass. The theatre is 'worth a detour', though, as Pausanias might have said, if he'd ever got here. The fact that he didn't is mildly unsettling. There is no one here, not even an archaeologist, but that could be the intense noonday heat.

A rusted iron fence surrounds the archaeological site. Person-sized holes have been made in places by local teenagers or hunters, perhaps rogue treasure-seekers, maybe maenads. Close to the entrance there is the usual deserted beige Portakabin. There really is nothing to be seen at the temple of Dionysus. The god is long gone. A line of black ants is tiptoe-ing at speed over a layer of rough grit on the theatre's stone seating, ferrying loot into an underground nest. A solitary fly weaves through the air, trailing a high-frequency whine. A small brown bird skips between the ruined columns, looking for a late-summer snack. Gerald Durrell would be ineffably happy here, but I am feeling my ignorance, thinking of the path I have taken since the days when I read every one of his books, over and again, hungry for news about his trips to the forests of Madagascar and Borneo, and his unimaginable zoo on the island of Jersey, and the garden snails that I was inspired to keep and breed in an old aquarium at home, collecting them at night after it rained, out in the garden with a torch, despite my parents' palpable unease. (I should have been a zoolo-gist . . . but why be sad that I ended up trailing in the footsteps of Pausanias?)

Behind the theatre there is a pointed stone arch, about head high, its heavy stones scarred as though they have been clawed by a bear, but still standing after all these years. I walk through, passing from nowhere to nowhere, out of the sun for a second, and as I emerge, right in front of me the long grass starts to shake. A snake? It must be a snake! I step back in my sandals, skin cringing, wishing I'd worn boots (but it's so hot). Perhaps, I think, after I've taken three further anxious steps backwards, snakes choose to linger at old temples, where they were once fed and cosseted by priestesses. They could be sacred to the Greeks, as well as deadly. The city of Athens was interwoven with snakes. Athena, their patron goddess, wore them on her cloak, still writhing on the severed Gorgon's head. And one of the first kings of Athens, Erichthonius, the one who was born from Hephaestus' semen-soaked rag, was half-snake. Or perhaps he wasn't. It is possible that Athena put 'her' baby into a box to be guarded by snakes. Either way, when Cecrops (who was the king of Athens at the time and most definitely half-snake) asked his three daughters to guard the box, two of them could not resist looking inside, just like Pandora, and when they saw what was in there they threw themselves off the Acropolis.

The founders of the city of Thebes, resourceful Cadmus and beautiful Harmonia, were blessed by being turned into snakes after their long and fruitful reign had ended, so they could spend the rest of their lives together. Snakes were long-lived, shedding their skins, starting again. Tiresias was punished for striking two copulating snakes (if it is a punishment to be turned from man to woman and back again). Heracles strangled two of them when he was a baby. Hermes, the messenger of the gods, carried a staff with two intertwined snakes. The caduceus, it is called, symbol of trade, sleep, dreams and lies. Eurydice, the wife of Orpheus, was bitten by a snake and died and went down to Hades, where her husband followed her, but only he came back. And King Lycurgus of Nemea was warned in a prophecy not to let his son touch the ground before he could walk, although the nurse forgot (or never knew) and so the boy was killed by a snake.

The god Apollo, who shoots from afar, slew a huge snake when he wanted to become lord of Delphi, and it rotted away in the place where the holy priestess (the Pythia, named after the dead serpent) would deliver her clouded and enigmatic but inevitably truthful prophecies. Later, or earlier, we don't know, Apollo turned himself into a tortoise in order to nestle in the lap of a woman he was pursuing called Dryope, and then he transformed himself into a snake, and they had a son. The word is anguiform, I have learned – taking on the appearance of a snake. Later, Dryope became a priestess, and then a nymph, and that was when a black poplar tree sprung up in the temple where she had worshipped the god. At least, that's one story. Ovid has another.

In any case, it turns out it wasn't a snake that was sliding through the long dry grass, but a tortoise. Hermes, the dog-killer, also slaughtered a tortoise on his first, very busy day on this planet, turning it into the world's first lyre. This particular tortoise was bumbling about, very noisily eating some dried-out, fibrous leaves, and I sat on a rock about a metre away and watched him until he seemed to register my presence, and we considered each other for a stretch until he turned and took a couple of steps and then ground to a halt with his back to me in the desiccated grasses. Apparently there's no hurry. Apart from humans (and Hermes) there is nothing here that can harm him, now that the bears and the eagles are so vanishingly rare in southern Attica.

One of the reasons that the Greek myths have become stories for children – something they never were, of course, and in fact Plato wrote that children should be shielded from some of the more brutal or less obviously moral myths – but surely the main reason that we now consider tales about animals and trees and gods and spirits to be essentially childish is that we no longer see or feel the connection between us and them, between what happens within the realm of our own exclusively human concerns (as if there were such a thing) and away from it. We have been trained to think that we have risen above nature; and that when we grow up we should put away our childish tales about foxes and talking trees. In common with every other subject under the sun, it is easy to find an ancient Greek who also believed this. Aristotle arranged the world into a pyramidal hierarchy (with humans riding high above animals and plants). But the reason why there are so many nature spirits and actual animals and animal similes in these Greek tales is quite simply that the Greeks were more profoundly entwined with the world around them than we are. How could they not be? Most of them were farmers, living in a land that had changed very little since the last ice age.

They still managed to do plenty of damage. It has been many ages since there were forests on these hills. The lions and elephants (and giant shrews) are long gone. If they'd had our tools and technologies, I wonder if there was anything – any belief or code – that would have held them back from taking and using and killing anything they wanted. It is an urgent question. Perhaps the most important of all. This hill that I have now climbed is riddled with the disused entrances to mines, some of them thousands of years old. They'd have murdered for some dynamite.

The view to the east loops over a string of sparklingly blue bays. There is a container ship in one of them, at the end of a narrow jetty, moored close to a power station with tall red and white striped chimneys, and over the waters is a low, barren island, risen from the flat Aegean Sea. There are many wind turbines on the horizon. Everything in this direction is sun-blasted and worked to the bone. Or, as Sophocles once put it,

> Earth, too, the eldest of the gods –
> The immortal, the unwearied – he wears away to his own ends,
> Turning the soil with the offspring of horses
> As the plows weave to and fro
> Year after year.

To the south is modern-day Thorikos, with its marina and shops, split asunder by the main road from Athens, and here there are earthworks and houses and more cargo ships and the ploughings and scrapings of humanity and so many cars, including my own, parked far below, sending me an oily blue wink in the livid sun. Dimitris is on my mind, and not for the first time I am wondering how I can justify driving here, and all over Greece, even though I am looking for Hope and answers that may have been forgotten (although who cares?), and I flew here as well (which I never wanted to do but time was concertinaed this year), and I have been guzzling from plastic bottles and leaving them in the car because I couldn't find anywhere to recycle them (but this is Greece!), and tearing through the plastic gel and shampoo bottles in the hotels and eating too much chicken souvlaki and I am glued to my smartphone and the laptop glows all night and I may have left the boiler on and I forgot to offset the flight and . . . oh God. At least I'm not on a cruise ship. (Although what the hell good is any of this while the Amazon burns.)

This morning, I read these words from Professor Gus Speth, spoken in 2008 (tick tock).

> I used to think that the top global environmental problems were biodiversity loss, ecosystem collapse, and climate change. I thought that with thirty years of good science we could address these problems, but I was wrong. The top environmental problems are selfishness, greed, and apathy, and to deal with these we need a spiritual and cultural transformation. And we scientists don't know how to do that.*

I have heard back from the Oracle at Delphi.

I had asked about hope, as I am sure you remember. Specifically, where to find Pandora's Hope (Ποῦ ἐστιν ἡ τῆς

---

* Quoted in Hunt and Marlow, *Ecology and Theology*.

Πανδώρας ἐλπίς), and this is the reply I had now received, by email, from the intermediary who I had found (or been led to) in the byways of the internet. I do hope it is clear that it is a serious question. ('I am afraid that this sounds flippant, but I don't mean it to be so.') When I had first asked this man, who is 'a kind of Delphic Priest' ('although,' he wrote, 'the term "priest" carries a lot of baggage') about the possibility of consulting the Oracle, he had told me that 'while a certain amount of scepticism would be natural on your part – it would require you to be open minded that these things *may* be possible', and I was happy to go along with that. And he had also written: 'Keep in mind Oracles can often be pretty straightforward and simple in their nature – e.g. a simple confirmation of something one already knows or suspects. (Perhaps confirming an awkward truth or difficult decision that one already knows needs to be made.)' My question was asked in Delphi, on a Sunday morning, and I am assured that the appropriate prayers were offered and libations poured.

Anyway, here we are.

> *The Reasons for the sometimes tough and painful path,*
> *Are often hard to see,*
> *And Hope beyond many people's grasp lies.*
> *For without some understanding of who,*
> *Rules within the skies, and what,*
> *Purposes they have for us below;*
> *How can we expect to have true Hope,*
> *That these divine goals will be achieved;*

> *And reasonably suppose that Pandora's Hope,*
> *From our own hearts and souls will shine.*
> *. . . Know Yourself.*

So, something to think about.

Oh, OK, I admit that my initial reaction was disappointment. I am almost too ashamed to write this, but a small part of me had been harbouring the possibility that I might be told to go and look for Pandora's jar underneath the large brown rock that lies thirty-seven paces due east of the ancient olive tree of incalculable age that still stands just above the top left-hand corner of the theatre of Sicyon. Go and dig there, six feet down, and you'll find her, Hope, I mean, fluttering under the rim of the jar. ('Let me out.') Like Theseus lifting the stone and reaching in to grasp his father's sword, or Indiana Jones uncovering the Ark, a moment of global significance was trembling to be born. It cannot be a surprise that I read an awful lot of Mary Renault and Willard Price and Conan Doyle in my youth, and pored over the Greek myths. The Great White Saviour, ha ha.

But no. Although on closer examination, there really is something to think about.

Back in the car on the main route from Athens, I set off for Cape Sounion, where there is a temple to Poseidon, god of earthquakes and the sea, on which Lord Byron scrawled his name the first time he visited Greece. Or so they say. The texture of the road has changed, and I am passing gated driveways, and long tall fences and dense laurel hedges, spiked with dark cypress trees and ilex. The sky has shrunk. It reminds me of the richer roads around Los Angeles, where there is never any way of getting anywhere, except along the designated route, and certainly not down to the ocean. The sea has disappeared, although it is close. Who owns these villas, I wonder, that are only ever glimpsed in fragments at the end of their interminable drives? Rich Athenians, presumably. Russian oligarchs. It is a startling fact, a legacy of the Ottomans when everything ultimately belonged to the Sultan, that still no one knows who owns all of Greece. The Greeks can be very flexible about their 'public' land. Ownership is sometimes a matter of fact, not law. Like everywhere, inequalities are grotesque and widening.

I pass a tall man with wild black tangled hair, coming along the road in my direction (there is no pavement), past the opulent hedges and high fences. He is wearing about seven overcoats on this blistering day, mahogany fingers gripping and pushing an overloaded shopping trolley, his trousers thick and sheened, his boots open and flapping. Aquamarine eyes lock on mine – so fleetingly, but with such force – from above an explosive black and grey beard. He looks familiar. Many years ago a man of the road ('The Tramp' we called him, because there was no other) used to walk past our home in East Sussex, in every season, and my father would sometimes talk with him, while my brother and I stared on in awe. There is a shared look between people who live all their time, night and day, out of doors, or perhaps it is a look they already have, from before they set out.

Just about the greatest fear for an ancient Greek was to be cast out from their city. Wandering was a sign of madness or punishment, although the gods and goddesses would sometimes visit the earth to roam and mingle with humanity. Hermes especially (delivering messages, soothing or sometimes killing dogs), Athena too, helping her favourites, and even Zeus on rare occasions, not just for sex, but one time travelling around the world with Hermes so that he could confirm that people had become as cruel and depraved as he had heard, before bringing down his punishment. All of these gods and goddesses were almost always in disguise. You never knew when you might be speaking with an immortal. The man I have just passed makes me think entirely inappropriately of Poseidon (it's the hair and the beard) but presumably he is just a man who has found himself with almost nothing other than his coats and what is in his trolley, walking in a place where the people have so very much more than that, although I could not read what was in his burning eyes.

The societies of the ancient world were profoundly, disturbingly unequal. The golden city of Mycenae, rising behind its magnificent lion gate, with all its exquisite jewellery, sculptures and death masks, would have been nothing without the labour of slaves, and nor would any of the Greek cities that followed. Thera, with its life-changing Spring Room, high Corinth with its lovely pottery and eternal fountains, the heart-stirring Athenian democracy (no women need apply), Thebes of the seven gates, the city of great Cadmus, the dancers and the songs, Sparta (especially Sparta), Argos, the festivals of Olympia and Nemea, the flower parades, Cretan Knossos, Pylos, Elis, holy Delos, radiant Delphi, Eleusis with its unknowable mysteries, from beginning to end, it was the enforced, unpaid, labour of prisoners and the children of prisoners that kept the whole boiling afloat. They enslaved each other, in a cycle of brutality, prostitution, floggings, executions and early death. It is hard to comprehend.

And all those philosophers and playwrights, mathematicians, architects and engineers, who brought us so high and so far, all that wonder and beauty, their lives were made possible by slaves. They lived in dread of the same happening to them. Greek enslaved Greek, or they were marched off to a short vicious life by Persians, Romans, Lydians, Lycians and Macedonians. And vice versa. Or so it would seem to us – and surely to them. But Socrates was apparently more concerned about how to avoid being made a slave; he had nothing to say about the institution itself. None of this is news. Perhaps we could say that the ideas the Greeks fostered would eventually make the people who came after them question the morality of slavery – just not in their own time. Perhaps we could also say that the fear of slavery, and the violence, and the ever-present possibility of random death, and the life-long certainty that there is no afterlife (or nothing that had the vivid richness of this one life), perhaps all of this lent their existence an intensity that we have now lost. Perhaps. I guess in the end it was all they knew. Slaves were cheap, that was one thing, and the worst excesses were hidden from view. We should at least understand something about that.

The area from Thorikos to Sounion was once home to the silver mines of Laurion, source of ancient Athens's wealth. It was the riches that flowed from these mines that would fund the building of the modern navy that destroyed the Persians at Salamis (the most significant battle in European history, people have often claimed), not to mention the architectural wonders of the Athenian Acropolis and beyond. And all of the miners that dug up this vast treasure were slaves. For centuries, uncountable thousands of men, women and children were forced down into the dark, working for up to a week at a time, bringing out the ore from the cramped tunnels that ran for miles under this landscape. None of these slaves survived working in the mines for more than ten years, and it was usually so much less. They were squeezed underground, in extreme heat, malnourished, beaten, in collapsing tunnels with little oxygen, ingesting lead and mercury and other toxins. When the Spartan army invaded during the Peloponnesian War they sent word to the slaves working the mines that they would set them free. About twenty thousand are supposed to have fled to the Spartans – although it seems unlikely that the Spartans honoured their promise, given their enthusiasm for slave-ownership – but the number of slaves escaping from just these mines gives some idea of the scale of Athens's slave addiction. The population of the city was no more than two hundred thousand at the time, probably much less.

Of course, there wasn't only a human cost. Or rather, the human cost was mashed into the destruction of the natural world, because how can they ever be separated? Forests were felled for miles around – and then further into Greece and overseas – mostly clear-cut, the soil washed away, never to return. Mountains of toxic waste were thrown up. Rivers and streams were diverted and the water supply was loaded with lead, arsenic and mercury. If you are wondering what it must have been like, there is no shortage of places where something similar is going on today. I have never been to the gold mines of the Amazon nor the lithium mines of the Democratic Republic of Congo (nor the sweatshops of India, Indonesia and Leicester and elsewhere), but again, and as we all know, we have always been adept at not seeing what it takes to construct our perfectly convenient world.

But (deep breath!), the temple to Poseidon at Sounion is beautiful *and well worth a visit*. This is another small region of Greece that Pausanias never reached, although that didn't stop him from writing about it. He thought the temple was dedicated to Athena, but never dared get any closer because of the many pirates that haunted these shores and probably made their camp under the sturdy columns and collapsing roof of Poseidon's home. And there were still pirates here when Lord Byron visited, almost 1,700 years later. Even if they were not always so bold as to attack an armed English lord, they were still abducting local children and selling them into slavery in other parts of the Ottoman Empire.

There is a single olive tree here, at the foot of the temple, a reminder of the goddess Athena in a place that otherwise feels drenched by the presence of Poseidon. Athena and Poseidon would often fight over who would be honoured by a city. Most famously, they fought over Athens, and Athena won with the gift of the olive tree, which I could never understand when I was younger (who likes olives when they are ten?), although it has to be said that Poseidon's offer of a salt-water spring was also underwhelming. Later, I was told that these things were *symbols*, and that Poseidon was offering a sea-based empire, and Athena a bountiful supply of timber and food, so I suppose the Athenians' choice made sense, although in the end they got themselves an empire of the sea anyway. After hearing the decision, Poseidon fell into a sulk and unleashed a great flood over the plains and was then made to mop it up by his brother Zeus. It was sometimes impossible not to offend one of the gods. Bad things are going to happen, whichever way we turn.

I find it surprising that Poseidon was usually the loser in his battles for precedence and that there were so few cities with Poseidon as their patron. Were the Greeks really so blind to their reliance on the sea (and their exposure to earthquakes)? Not here – they have given the god his full honours, just as King Nestor did when he slaughtered eighty-one black bulls on the sandy beach at Pylos and cut out the thigh bones and the rich fat to offer to the lord of the seas.

What is left of the temple stands on a ridge of hard brown rock at the very end of the Attic peninsula, the views stretching from three sides, over islands and an easy sea, to a luminous blue horizon. There are still three weathered sides of columns, looming over a dozen masked and selfie-snapping tourists. This is the place where Phrontis the pilot, who had brought Menelaus almost home from the sack of the city of Troy, was swept overboard and drowned and where Menelaus later built him a memorial. And Lord Byron's name is here too, on the third stone up on a column on the west side, but I can't see it and anyway there is much doubt that it was in fact him who scratched his name into the rock. Give it enough time and it will become true.

I am gazing out to sea at the nearest island to the south-west, little Patroclus, whose surface seems to be entirely covered in wind turbines, and spiked like an angry sea urchin. By a quirk of light, it actually looks like it is floating above the sea, powered by the turbine blades, about to take off for other lands, like the island of Laputa in Swift's *Gulliver's Travels*, or indeed sacred Delos, which is not so very far from here. When the Titan Leto was pregnant with Zeus' children, she was pursued by the furious goddess Hera, who forbade the Earth to allow Leto to stop and give birth. But Delos was a floating island, and so Leto was able to make her way there, and have her children (even so, with great difficulty . . . but she eventually gave birth to Artemis and then her twin brother Apollo), at which point Delos became rooted to the sea-floor. All of which is to say that this is why we can visit Delos today, fixed just off the coast of Mykonos. It is empty now, but at its peak some twenty thousand people lived on the tiny, barren, holy island. And Artemis, who helped deliver her twin brother, became the goddess of childbirth (if not the only one), although she never had any children herself.

What, I wonder, would (or does) Poseidon make of the man who is buzzing about above his old sanctuary in a microlight aircraft, circling noisily to and fro, legs dangling from below an acid-green parachute? The engine is barking and clattering like a distressed lawnmower. With Icarus in mind, and the inexhaustible hubris of humanity, perhaps Poseidon might have struck him from the sky, like Apollo did when he shot Phrontis at the helm of his ship for no reason other than that he was the best pilot and helmsman that the Greeks had ever known. The gods can be jealous. Mind you, the view from up there must be stupefying. God-like. Terrifying. The wonder of it. What would Byron think? Or Menelaus? It is easy to forget how far we have travelled in just a few years. And now here is someone looking down on us, the dozen or so pilgrims at Poseidon's temple, and the scene cannot really be very different from how it must have looked two thousand years ago and more, except for our baseball caps and the missing temple roof.

Was life better for the earlier visitors than it is for us, when the building was freshly painted and loaded with statues, filled with incense and prayer and adorned with ivory and gold? If we could talk to everyone who has ever come here . . . priests, pirates, slaves, supplicants, soldiers, farmers, poets, doctors, traders, artists, builders, masons, wives, husbands, children, tourists . . . would we be able to tell if our lives are becoming better, easier, happier, richer and more fulfilling? It depends who you ask. And in fact there were plenty of Greeks who would have said that we cannot just talk to other people, we need also to ask the nymphs of the springs and the trees, and the river gods and the creatures of the sea, we should ask the deer and the vultures and the swifts and whatever is left hiding in the forests. Go talk to the lions. Let's ask the extinct giant shrew if we can. Perhaps ask Solon to check in with that dead dog – although surely we cannot just wait to the end of our lives to know if we have been happy or are taking the right path. Pray to the gods. There are some things we need to figure out before it is too late.

FIVE

Sweet Release

'And darkness delayed by the season.'
LOUISE GLÜCK, 'THE MUSE OF HAPPINESS'

If you were (un)lucky enough to be living in the classical world about 2,500 years ago – let's say in Athens, slap bang in the middle of its golden age – and assuming you were not weighed down with a blood crime for which you had not yet atoned (butchering a brother, murdering your father and then marrying your mother, or what have you), and also assuming that you spoke reasonable Greek, then whoever you were, male or female, even a slave, at some point in your life you would be encouraged to take part in the Eleusinian Mysteries. For many people it was the defining moment of their lives.

The Mysteries were an initiation ceremony, dedicated to the goddess Demeter and her daughter Persephone, the Queen of the Dead, that promised to reveal the meaning of life and death, and explain once and for all what we are doing here on this radiant planet. Everyone who took part agreed that it was life-changing – revelatory – but that is just about the only thing they would say. No one who celebrated the Great Mysteries was allowed to talk about what they had seen or felt at the climax of the nine-day festival, when they were ushered into the deepest recesses of Demeter's temple in Eleusis and shown . . . wonders. And although hundreds of thousands of people must have taken part (and these people were *Greeks*, for heaven's sake, the most loquacious people who have ever lived), no one said a thing. Well, almost no one. And even then not very much.

Some people think that the origins of the message at the heart of the Mysteries can be traced back to the kingdoms of Mycenae and Troezen. Others reckon Crete, and the bull courts of Knossos, once a home of the Great Mother (or so we are told). And if I could also wade in briefly (I've read a couple of books on the subject, smoked some weed, listened to a long podcast, and once disappeared down a rabbit hole on the internet for three days and nights), the Mysteries must be even older than that, prehistoric, I would guess, celebrated by the world's first farmers or even their predecessors, our hunter-gatherer ancestors. It is possible that the revelatory power of the message may reach further back again, beyond ice ages, to the time when we were just one animal species among many – nothing more, no less.

Still, we do like a mystery. And this one leaves much fertile ground for speculation. For example, you might believe that any place that has been on the receiving end of so much intensity of feeling, and for so long, would carry some signs scorched into the ground or pervading the air, a lingering spiritual afterburn. After all, this was the place where for centuries people would flock to be reborn and to find out why, in the words of Cicero, we can 'die with a better hope'. Every year in September the initiates of Athens would gather in the marketplace, men, women and their slaves, children too, before heading to the Athenian cemetery (death was at the heart of these Mysteries), from where they would set off to Eleusis, about thirteen miles in all, a half-marathon, dancing and singing along the route, telling filthy jokes at one point, waving the cut branches of trees and reeds, accompanied by priests and priestesses, strewing flowers, washing in the sacred waters of the bay, to be met at the borders by more priestesses who would tie the ankles and wrists of the pilgrims with yellow twine, before the procession crossed into the holy land. Tucked away somewhere near to the temples and the town, hundreds of animals would be waiting (chickens, oxen and suckling pigs), all unknowing, ready to be sacrificed on the altars of the goddesses and later consumed by the humans at the great feasts that followed the nights and days of fasting, prayer, torch-lit dancing and sacred song. We know something about what happened on the way to Eleusis, and also during the festival once the initiates had arrived, but what was revealed on the seventh and eighth days in the holy temple of Demeter remains a mystery.

I have been back briefly to Athens, after the trip to Sounion, visiting museums and ruins, before joining the setting-off point of the Sacred Way on a sunny morning at the end of October. I had wanted to walk the thirteen miles, but had ended up driving, and if you've seen what the Sacred Way looks like today you'll understand why. That morning my head was full of the sound of church bells, which had been cascading through the hotel room window earlier (very early) in the day, in an endlessly repeated but also infinitesimally varied tonal pattern. I had gone to sit on the tiny balcony, with its view (as promised) of the

Acropolis to the left, and listened to this surprisingly loud but thrilling call to prayer.

I have become troubled by how little I am dreaming in Greece, given my desire to record any possible messages. This morning, perhaps prompted by the bells, I had come awake to some fading images, burning up like a spool of film exposed to the light. I couldn't hold on to them, although there may have been something about headmasters and goats (#5). It is my fault, I have decided. If I could only go to bed earlier, perhaps without drinking any retsina, but certainly avoiding all Netflix, especially the trashier but undeniably addictive series that have nothing to do with my researches for this book, then perhaps my mind would be more open to the numinous. I should be tucked up in bed reading *The Homeric Hymns*, with a notepad on my bedside table, ready for the dreams that will surely come. But have you seen the German series *Barbarians*? It is compelling. The only way I could stop myself watching episode after episode ('starting in $5 - 4 - 3$ . . .') was by letting the battery run down on my laptop (which is an eco win at least). Maybe the bingeing classifies as research. According to the buff German tribal folk, sitting around a fire and tearing into their venison in the Teutoburg Forest, the Greeks believed that the planets are 'balls'. How the Germans laughed, although they did know that the Romans found the Greeks very clever.

Anyway, the drive from the centre of Athens to the ruins of Eleusis, which are now contained within the modern town of Elefsina (how pretty it sounds), tracking the route of the old Sacred Way, is no longer a flower-filled parade. This is the way that Theseus came, only in reverse, when he travelled from his home in Troezen to the great city of Athens to meet his father for the first time and claim his inheritance. He stopped at Eleusis to wrestle with and kill the hideously cruel King Cercyon (and, if you remember, to sleep with his many daughters). According to Mary Renault in her stupendous historical novel, *The King Must Die*, this was the moment when Theseus put an end to the supremacy of the 'old religion', the worship of the Great Mother, and with it the last major outpost of the matriarchal societies that had once existed all over Crete and Greece. Until Theseus arrived and refused to submit to the idea, the king of Eleusis had been wrestled to death every year and ritually ploughed into the earth to bring fortune to the kingdom and a bountiful harvest, his demise overseen by the queen who then took his killer as the new king. And so the years went by. At least, that's how Mary Renault saw it, high on the writings of Sir James Frazer and Robert Graves and others, who saw signs of the Great Mother and the dying god in every myth and legend, but the history books will tell you that Eleusis was absorbed into the Athenian Empire in the sixth century BCE with no mention of Theseus. Despite their subjugation, the people of the city and their descendants always retained control over the Mysteries.

To get back to it, the early stretches of the road from Athens to Eleusis, especially if your mind has been filled with visions of the Sacred Way and its procession of hopeful people, dancing under a clear blue sky, are a gut-punch of horror and despair. The pollution burns. There are convoys of trucks, bumper to bumper, endlessly replenished, crashing their gears, slapping and buffeting my little car, throwing out acrid plumes of diesel, huge tyres smacking into the potholes. Truck after truck, heading into the city or fleeing the other way. Has war been declared overnight? And how many petrol stations does any road need? Whatever the answer, Route 8 from Athens to Eleusis has more, BP, Aegean, Shell and all the rest. There's a Titan cement works and also one branded Heracles, the powerful old gods and heroes roped into the business of selling concrete.

Outskirts of cities are almost always bleak, but this road out of Athens is especially brutal, the coastline scorched and the hills to the north flayed and scoured clean of soil and trees. My mood lifts a little once I am past the city boundary and into the scrubby lowlands, but not much. There used to be a temple to Aphrodite along the route at this point, where initiates would sometimes stop and pray and make offerings to the goddess of smiles. But as the road curves north, and then further west, tracking the coast, past Salamis and along the Gulf of Elefsina, everything distils into a fly-by of trucks and oil refineries and cement works and aluminium factories and all the detritus and dirty scrapings of a decades-long hungry dash for profit and growth. The air is chemical.

A couple of days before this trip to Eleusis I had been drinking coffee with some friendly Athenians, who had politely asked about this book, and wondered if I minded talking about it (ha!), and after I had told them what it was called they more than once used the phrase 'beauty is in the eye of the beholder'. And I had been thinking about this later in the Benaki Museum in Athens, a stirring collection of classical vases and statues and Mycenaean artefacts, and paintings and armaments from the Greek wars of independence, and folk costumes, and so much more, a great deal of it, I would say, undeniably beautiful (including the views from the sunlit rooftop café, which is another place that is *well worth a visit*), and I thought well yes, it is all very well Keats insisting that 'Beauty is Truth' . . . but what exactly *is* beauty? Which I presume is what Jonathan Jones was pronouncing so emphatically on that poster outside the museum in Corinth.

Is beauty entirely relative? It is a well-worn question, but possibly a good one to ask in Greece, surrounded by radiant blue seas and the ruins of our inherited ideals about proportion and grace and form. No one seems to know, even while we cluster around certain agreed artefacts or views. We gawp at what is left of temples and frescoes, and are sometimes moved to tears. What we feel can depend on our mood, or the behaviour of those around us, or the weather, but any Greek could have told us that there is more to it than that. And now? Classical art and thought are overlaid with unease about Eurocentricity (even though the ancient world was a restless creative churn, embracing and spreading ideas and beliefs from Egypt and elsewhere in northern Africa and beyond, the Middle East, Greece and Italy, northern and western Europe, India and further east). It is a plain fact that humans interact and that borders shift and are often illusory. Ideas are born and spread. Some things emerge, who knows why, like the eruption (and assimilation) of science, philosophy and art in fifth-century Athens, which weirdly coincided with an equally transformative flowering of ideas (of *beauty*) in India and China, all at the same time. Only a fool would try and define what is beautiful, although if you ask me (here we go), nature is the template.

Pine trees on the seashore. Swifts in flight. Blue skies and a frost in winter. The budding of spring. The smell of cut grass. A garden of roses. A lover's laugh. And maybe it is worth stressing, at least as far as those last three go (because sometimes the idea can get lost), that our human presence can be welcome and fruitful and that our efforts do have the power to bring something meaningful into the world. Some thing of beauty.

I could tell you what is not beautiful, though, and that is this road into Eleusis. But even as I write those words, I realise that there are people who would disagree, devotees of edgelands or brutalism, who are impatient with aesthetics and who think it is cowardly escapism to ignore these marks of modernity – people who reject the very question itself. I once came across Jeremy Clarkson in an episode of *Top Gear* (this may be only peripherally connected), complaining about Swiss anti-pollution regulations, and then reversing his car up to a single flower in an Alpine meadow, possibly an edelweiss (he'd like that), his engine running hot, exhaust pipe dripping, drenching the helpless thing in toxic fumes. He should be pursued by the Furies to the ends of the earth for such reckless, knowing idiocy, even if his definition of 'beauty' is presumably different from a botanist's. Although I do remember that he lives in bucolic splendour, far from the poisonous outpourings of his beloved cars, so perhaps we can indeed agree – if only for what happened in Switzerland – that Clarkson should be pursued by Furies and his warm entrails torn from his living body.

I am sure I could find a way to define ugliness – or at the very least name some things that are undeniably ugly. A corpse-strewn battlefield, for example. No one would like to feast their eyes on such a sight, although I had recently been told by my new friends in Athens about the witches of Thessaly, who apparently did just that. One of them, Erichtho, was famous for trawling the aftermath of the Battle of Pharsalus, where Pompey the Great's vast army had been crushed and slaughtered by Julius Caesar's, looking for body parts to use in her spells, especially 'congealed eyeballs and . . . the pallid nails on a desiccated hand'. Or so said Lucan, who distrusted most things that happened any distance from his beloved Rome. It is also true that Mary Shelley's nightmarish monster longed to see his equally gruesome wife. So, yes, these things are relatively relative (let me know where to collect my philosophy prize); and beauty is an unhelpful but a necessary word; and that is more or less all I had managed, by the time I left the main road and rolled into the centre of modern-day Elefsina.

Pausanias made his way to Eleusis, of course, but he didn't like to talk about it. He wrote that 'the dream forbids me to write what lies inside the sanctuary wall, and what the uninitiated are not allowed to see they obviously ought not to know about'. So there you are. It is interesting that he describes his experience (or part of it) as a 'dream'. There is much theorising that psychedelic drugs were a key part of the ceremony, perhaps opium or ergot, a parasitic fungus that grows on grains such as barley or rye. Peter Levi, writing the footnotes to Pausanias' book in 1971, thought that 'to understand the spirit of the Eleusinian mysteries, one should not read the wild general books about it, still less the detailed archaeological arguments, but the Homeric *Hymn to Demeter* and Aristophanes' *Frogs*'. So, taking his lead, this, very briefly, is the story from which the Mysteries emerged. You already know it well, I am sure.

On a perfect spring day (and when was it ever not?), Persephone, daughter of the golden goddess Demeter, was playing in a meadow with her friends when she wandered off alone, distracted by the beauty of the flowers. Crocuses, violets, the most exquisite irises, daisies, hyacinths (*ai! ai!*), young roses and fragrant white lilies. Above all she was drawn by the sight and the perfume of a flower she had never known before, a narcissus, that was glowing on the fringes of the meadow, planted by Gaia, the Mother Goddess, the Earth herself, following the orders of Zeus. And as Persephone was stooping by the flower, to gather it up and take it home, the ground cracked open and Hades, king of the underworld, emerged from the darkness, standing tall at the back of a golden chariot, riding his wild black horses, and snatched her up, the skinny-legged girl, and bore her down underground, as she screamed for her mother and her friends. She had been ensnared by beauty.

No one saw what had happened, although Hekate, goddess of the night, of crossroads and the howling of dogs, had heard the girl's screams. Demeter was distraught. Inconsolable. She scoured the earth, with Hekate's help, a blazing torch in each hand, looking for any sign of her missing daughter. On the tenth day they went to ask Helios, the god of the sun, who sees everything, and they begged him for help. He told them that it was Hades who had abducted the girl – and he also suggested that it was an honour to be chosen to be the queen of the lord of the underworld.

Rage and grief tore into Demeter. She obliterated her own beauty, and walked in disguise through the world's towns and farmlands, until at last she came to Eleusis, where she sat down by a well and wept. And that is where the four daughters of King Celeus found her, when they came down to fetch water for their home. They were kind, and said they could easily find an old woman like her somewhere to live and to work, and the goddess thanked them and promised to tell them the truth about who she was, although this was a lie: she said she was from Crete (perhaps that bit is true), where she had been abducted by men, although she had escaped from them at Thorikos and made her way here, to Eleusis.

So far, you will notice, the only males in this tale are abductors, or the abetters or indulgers of abductors, although Celeus shows promise. But we carry on.

Demeter went to the girls' home and as she stood on the threshold her head touched the rafters 'and she filled the doorway with her light divine'. The girls' mother, Queen Metaneira, ran over and offered her a seat at the high table, but Demeter refused and would only sit on a low stool, where she drew her veil over her head and refused all food and drink and ached and wept for her daughter. And this would have gone on, perhaps to the world's end, except a female servant called Iambe whispered jokes in her ear – alas, no one knows what the jokes were any more, but they were *filthy* – and then Demeter cheered up enough to accept a drink from Metaneira, not wine, which she refused, but something called *kykeon*, of her own devising, a mix of mint and barley (and perhaps its ergot) and more, that would later be served to the initiates of the Mysteries.

Demeter now offered to look after Metaneira's baby boy. She nursed him herself, massaging him with ambrosia, and he grew fast and strong like a god, and at night she placed him in a fire because she was going to make him immortal, immune to old age and death, and that was a mystery, and it would have happened except Metaneira saw him one night, apparently burning in the fire, and she screamed for help. Demeter was furious ('witless are you mortals and dull to foresee your lot, whether of good or evil') and she snatched the baby from the fire and revealed herself as a goddess, wreathed in power and beauty. The boy had to be rescued by his sisters from the floor where Demeter had dropped him.

Demeter now made King Celeus build a temple for her, here in Eleusis, and she sat in it, weeping for Persephone, harrowed by grief, until the crops died, and famine spread, and every human began to starve and die. Now Zeus got involved (because what would existence be like if there were no humans to make sacrifices and offerings to the gods?), and he sent every one of the Olympian immortals to plead with Demeter to relent, but she would not. So Zeus sent his messenger Hermes down to the underworld to talk to Hades, who seemed happy to comply and allow Persephone to return to her mother, although, as he pointed out, it was by no means a small thing to be his wife, and queen of all the dead. Just think, he said, of the punishment and torments that await anyone who does not honour you and offer up the prayers that you deserve. I am after all the brother of Zeus, the king of the gods – and your uncle.

Even so, Persephone couldn't wait to get back to her mother. Clever Hades offered her a single sweet pomegranate seed for the journey and she ate it absent-mindedly and then she leaped into the golden chariot, driven by Hermes this time, and the black horses raced over the seas and rivers and mountains. Demeter was waiting for her in Eleusis, on the steps of the new temple, and ran towards her as soon as she saw her arrive and they fell into each other's arms. It was only later that Persephone told her mother about the pomegranate seed, and they learned that she would have to spend a third of each year with Hades, reigning in the underworld as his queen. Those months would be barren above ground, in memory of the time when they had been separated; but for the rest of the year the earth would blossom. An annual miracle, over and again, the arrival of beautiful Persephone trailing flowers, her mother running to meet her, and a world erupting into new life.

Hekate, the goddess of the night, joined them and hugged Persephone close, and swore to be her companion forever. And Rhea, the daughter of Heaven and Earth and the mother, in order, of Hestia (the home-loving goddess), Demeter, Hera, Hades, Poseidon and Zeus, was sent down by Zeus to the fields of Rarion, near to the city of Eleusis, to talk to Demeter, and they agreed that she should reverse the famine and heal the earth. Everything now bloomed. And Demeter taught three men – Triptolemus, Polyxeinos and Diocles – about the Holy Eleusinian Mysteries, and perhaps there were two more of them, Celeus and Eumolpus, but there is much that has been lost. What we do know is that Demeter went to live in high Olympia with Zeus and the other immortals and that no one must ever speak of what they see or feel or hear when they are ushered into the deepest recesses of Demeter's temple in Eleusis and shown . . . wonders.

May the golden goddess bless us all.

We have much to thank Persephone for. Her name means 'death bearer', an acknowledgement that she not only returns to the light, but also descends every year into the darkness, where she rules over the dead as queen. People avoided using her name. She was more often referred to as 'Kore', which means, simply, 'The Girl'. The *Hymn to Demeter* says that she spends four months of every year in the underworld, when the earth above dies, but others have said six. And we all assume that she returns in the spring, when the narcissus blooms, but some people think that it is the summer she spends underground, sheltering from the worst of the heat, when the earth in Greece cracks open and the rivers die, and that in fact Persephone returns in the autumn, bringing the healing rains; and this feels about right, what with the spreading intensity of the world's droughts and fires. Although the recent proliferation of Medicanes, which have started to rip through the land at the end of every summer, may show that she is not entirely happy about any of this.

There is no sign of a break in the weather on this late October day, as I sit myself down at the head of the well where Demeter once rested and wept. Although the sacred precincts of Eleusis were knocked down and rebuilt many times (until people lost the will to carry on), the well was left untouched after it was first constructed in the sixth century BCE. The area had been holy for very much longer than that. The 'maidens of Eleusis' used to dance by this well at a special festival, it says on a sign. The day is ragingly hot and I am being bothered by a fly and only just finding my equilibrium after the drive, and in fact I am recovering from Elefsina itself, which at first glance seemed clean and trim, and so much better than the hell-road I had just left, but also somehow washed out, despite the perky shops and scrubbed pavements. I don't know – was I expecting priestesses with flaming torches and a procession of sacrificial bulls with garlands on their horns? The place is no different from the neutered centre of almost any modern town, rubbed smooth by chain stores. Eleusis was once arguably the most sacred spot in the ancient classical world (there are other candidates), but it has been successively torn apart by invaders, eviscerated and left to die by Christians, picked up, pulverised and polluted by industry and now suffocated by the bland and nonsensical outpourings of late-stage capitalism. And that, I must quickly add, is still a vast improvement on the years of unemployment and decay, when Elefsina became a breeding ground for the far right Golden Dawn party. Apparently the place had an energetic mayor, who did much to drag it out of its slump, but he died before he could see the job through.

The museum is closed, possibly because of Covid. The site itself is being dug over by archaeologists and I am one of only ten people in the sanctuary, including nine workers sweating under the noonday sun. There is just one woman, which feels wrong for this place, although she appears to be in charge, which does at least have historical (or mythic) resonance. Over in the distance, a grey-bearded man in blue overalls and a white hard hat is casually bringing down a cascade of earth from the side of a trench next to a small stack of ancient stones. Does he imagine that if he digs down far enough he will find the meaning of the Mystery? Perhaps he will.* A workman wanders by with a long iron pole, lifting and lowering it above his head like Heracles with his club. Another man sits watching the others work, his mask on his chin, tugging hungrily on a cigarette. Metal scrapes on rock. A dog barks and the fly sizzles at my ear. The stones scattered by the well are becoming painful to touch.

The bottom chunk of a deep-grooved marble column is standing by my side, the rest lying in pieces on the ground, and I find myself caressing its tawny, buttery, crystalline flank (surprisingly soft and weathered to the touch), at the same time as I am staring down at the well and enjoying the feeling of being almost alone in this once holy place, with no one around other than people who are doing what they can to care for it. It must have been such a strange moment when the message arrived from the authorities in Rome that the golden goddess and her Mysteries were no longer to be worshipped. ('What, are we no longer praying to Demeter now?') The Emperor Julian the (so-called) Apostate tried to revive the ceremonies, fifty years after the Roman Empire had turned Christian, but by then there may not have been anyone left who remembered how to perform them; and anyway it is likely that the holy basket or chest that had contained the truth of the world had gone missing. Or maybe the container was still here, but in the end what is wondrous

---

* (Should have been an archaeologist.)

about a mouldering ear of wheat in a box, once you have stripped away the drama and the certainty of shared belief?

And also, perhaps, once you have forgotten how to mix a sufficiently psychotropic dose of *kykeon*. My friend Kenny, who follows these things intensely, had been urging me to eat magic mushrooms at Eleusis, because there are many people (serious academics among them) who are convinced that the secret of the Mysteries lay in the consumption of psychedelic drugs. Kenny suggested I take some 'microdose' mushrooms with me to Greece, in order to create and then carefully calibrate my response, and I would have done just that except I was sure that I would be arrested for drug smuggling at Eleftherios Venizelos airport and then my trip (to Greece) would have been over before it started. I am wary of the unpredictability of mushrooms, microdose or not, ever since the time I found myself in a Welsh wood, full of raw mushrooms, not to mention mushroom soup, stew and possibly tea, eating blackberries from the bush and all of a sudden convinced that I was chewing on a bee (I could feel its heavy hairy wriggle between my back teeth, and an angry, but furry, buzzing against the side of my anxiously probing tongue), and next thing I knew I was being told by a near-naked man I had only just met that we were no different from apes, separated by nothing more than our clothes and glasses, and then he was off, swinging round the hillside and hooting like a gibbon, and I was left alone in the Welsh rain with a mouthful of bumblebee or more likely berries and a feeling of gathering doom. That said, I am more than happy to put down here that the near-naked man's insight about us and the apes has stayed with me.

One reason that some scholars are sceptical about the use of psychedelics in the Mysteries is that they imagine that drug use is an individual or isolating experience, whereas the essence of Eleusis was that it was unifying and *collective*. It may well be the case that our most intense and revelatory experiences are shared, but that does not rule out drug taking. The priestesses of Demeter would have known exactly how to administer their *kykeon* so that the world cracked open in harmony for the hundreds of initiates who gathered every year in the torchlit chambers of the temple. All we can do now is lament that their knowledge seems to have been lost.

The other Olympian gods and goddesses feared and needed golden Demeter, goddess of the harvest. Her name 'De' means 'barley' or 'corn' (or even 'earth') and 'meter' – 'mother'. She is an old god, sometimes mixed up or mingled with, or somehow evolved from, the Great Mother. All the immortals had powers that the others respected and would defer to – and only Zeus stood above them all. But even he was reluctant to challenge Demeter and her daughter Persephone. 'The Two Goddesses' they were called, and they were often worshipped together, as one. Or so we are told. And some say that Demeter turned Persephone's companions, the ones who had not noticed when she wandered off to gather flowers, into the Sirens, who sang so irresistibly and lured men to their death. Demeter was the goddess who made the crops grow. But sometimes she also brought famine.

There is something serious about Demeter, not just in the way she punished the gods and humanity when Persephone was seized by Hades. She makes the others seem frivolous and often vile, even Zeus himself, with their stupid flirtations and arguments and cruel, violent abductions (their rapes of nymphs and humans), although Demeter must have also liked to laugh and dance.

When a king of Thessaly (or maybe he was the son of a still-living king) called Erysichthon brought twenty of his strongest men into the goddess's most sacred grove one day (they were men-giants, able to lift up a city), and they started to swing their axes, Demeter was enraged. And then Erysichthon began to chop into the most holy tree of all, a tall poplar that stood at the centre of the wood, and the nymph that lived in (or with) the tree screamed to the goddess for help. Demeter appeared, towering over Erysichthon, and gave him one chance to stop, but he wouldn't, although his men fled. He was mad with lust for wealth and he wanted to use the timber to build a vast banqueting hall, where he would feast and drink all day.

And so that night when Erysichthon was asleep Demeter sent Hunger to him, a hideous emaciated being that crept and latched onto the king's open mouth, and breathed an unas-suageable need for food into his stomach and guts and deep into his veins. Erysichthon woke up hungry, and started eating, and called out for food, and more food, but however much he ate it was never going to be enough. He consumed everything in the house, his horses too, his mother's heifer (which she had been saving to offer to the goddess Hestia), mules, wheat, bread, fruit, corn, even the house cat. Everything was eaten, and then they had to send out for more. And even that was not enough. The family's wealth was destroyed and still Erysichthon craved and moaned for food.

Ovid wrote that Erysichthon had a young daughter, Mestra, who was able to change shape, so he sold her as a slave, or sometimes as a cow or a rooster, getting money to feed his hunger, and each time she was able to escape and come back to be sold again. But that wasn't enough, and still Erysichthon ate, and eventually (or so writes Ovid) Erysichthon had no choice, with his stomach burning, lusting for food he didn't need, useless, empty, ceaseless consumption, when at last everything else was gone, Erysichthon had no choice but to eat himself. And that, I think we can all agree, is as perfect a description of out-of-control, grab what you can, self-pleasuring, screw everyone, world-ending capitalism as we could ever hope to find.

Or, to put it another way . . . it's us.

I have been wondering at what point the gods might intervene in order to put an end to our reckless consumption of the planet, but apparently it is not yet. Is Demeter going to stop the harvests? Will Poseidon rise from the seas, brandishing his trident, or send a tsunami or a sea monster? Will Dionysus drive us all mad? Apollo bring plagues? Perhaps it is already happening, only in slow motion (or slow to us). They cannot be happy with our destruction of everything they hold dear; and we know that in the past Zeus would have swatted us away and started again.

There is something violent about the ruins of Eleusis. If you climb as high as you can, you will see what a very small area they cover – just the shattered temples and Demeter's well and

Hades' caves – before your eye reaches the swell and spread of modern Elefsina and down to the empty blue bay. There is the smell of ships' fuel in the air. The ground is brown and parched, which makes me think that The Girl is no longer with us, although whether it is the end of her time in Hades or the beginning is anyone's guess. There is a sign at the top, just next to the inevitable, small whitewashed church, warning us that 'the ground is unsafe', advice they could have better saved for Persephone. The church has a couple of dead pot plants outside its front door (there are marks of Demeter's displeasure every-where) and anyway I am fairly certain that its builders have missed the point: any mystery to be found is not here, at the top of the hill, but in the cracks and caverns down below, where the archaeologists are currently rootling and smoking in their trenches. This is not a place where you should be looking up to the sky for your answers.

A clock strikes one from a tower. I decide that if I were unex-pectedly put in charge of this place, I would fill the rubble with trees and flowers: wild roses and crocuses, violets, irises, daisies, hyacinths (*ai! ai!*) and white lilies. Flowers everywhere, a riot of colour and perfume. I would plant many pomegranate trees, and their luscious red fruit would hang like burning lanterns floating in a sea of green. A tall poplar tree too, in the centre of everything, in memory of the nymph who was hacked to pieces by Erysichthon. There are a couple of olive trees here, I see, and a fig and a wild pear, but that is all, although it is good to see the pear tree coming into fruit (thank you great goddess). But how much colour there must have been in this place all those years ago, the temples and the statues painted and golden, the incense rising, and the noise from the drums and cymbals and pipes and the flaming torches and the chanting and the singing and the stamp of the dance. If we know anything, we must know that these precincts needed colour, noise and dancing – and not just the hot white silent stones, which is all that seems to remain of the secret Mysteries today.

Speaking of dance, ever since I arrived in Greece, I had been hoping to meet with a group of activists known as the Dancing Women of Vrisoules. It has not been easy to arrange, although it is true that I have been distracted by the wonders of Pausanias, Corinth and Athens (and the empty beaches of the Peloponnese). The Dancing Women came together in 2018, when the Greek government's ruinous plans for oil and gas extraction were becoming better known, even if the true details were hidden in dense text, or avoided altogether. They are mostly Athenian women, often with roots in Epirus, the wild north-western region of Greece, with its deep forests and gorges and famous stone bridges, which now stands in the frontline of the energy industry's onshore plans.

The world is full of voices raised against environmental despoliation, and so often these voices are quashed or side-stepped, or made to seem irrelevant, cranky or subversive, perhaps anti-patriotic, or economically illiterate or luddite, or privileged (or envious), or hypocritical, or young, or not local (or too selfishly local), and if you have any experience of protest you will know this, because the pockets of the corporations and their friends run deep – and anyway none of us likes to be told that the lives we are leading, and the beliefs we hold, are destroying everything around us. And so the women decided that the most arresting and inclusive way they could alert the public to what was happening was to dance, dressed in the traditional costumes of the women of Epirus. They dance in city squares and shopping malls, on the metro and outside the Ministry of the Environment and Energy, chanting songs of lament and loss. A fiesta and a demonstration, aimed at the Greek government's reckless energy policies.

'Why Turn Paradise into Hell?' it says on their Facebook page, over an aerial picture of a turquoise river weaving through a lush emerald forest. 'And for what?' asked Eleni Tzachrista, when I finally caught up with three of the group on a Zoom call from London (my plans disrupted in the dying weeks of the first year of Covid). 'Ask yourself. Why do we need more energy?'

'Vrisoules' are fountains, of which there are many in Epirus. And it is said that when the Ottoman Turks invaded the region, many women chose to dance off high cliffs, singing their songs, sometimes clutching their children, rather than fall into the hands of the Turkish soldiers. Although as Eleni said, we may be taught this at school, but no one actually knows if it is true. It was a desperate act, though, freighted with the power of myth – 'and that is what we need now, with the whole world, not just Epirus, threatened and dying,' said another of the women, Eleftheria Tsoyknaki. 'It is happening so fast, all over the world. Not just here. Everywhere.' Their dancing is a way of helping us to see the beauty of what is being taken from us.

The original dancing women of Epirus sang as they danced over a cliff, and the chorus of their song went something like this.

> May you fare well little fountains,
> forests, mountains, little ridges,
> May you fare well little fountains.
> Farewell to you, girls of Souli . . .

There is more to say about the Dancing Women of Vrisoules, but it will have to wait until I get to Epirus. The only thing I knew when I was picking my way through the wreckage of Eleusis is that they seemed like good people to ask about hope.

Just outside the entrance gates of the archaeological site is a café and guesthouse called Kykeon, so of course I headed straight inside, hoping to be served a cooling draught of Demeter's holy drink. No such luck, but I can tell you (channelling Pausanias) that the tree-shaded courtyard is wondrously peaceful and the mint tea is refreshing. You can ignore my earlier grizzling (or some of it) about Elefsina. This place has survived the ravages of Goths, Christians and capitalists and is slumbering in a magic of its own, although perhaps I was just happy to get out of the sun. Hippolytus of Rome, a third-century Christian who was eager to make the Mysteries sound absurd, wrote that the Big Reveal (the one that no one ever talked about) was 'an ear of grain in silence reaped', but I think all he has managed to do is add to its fascination.

What we do know is that the Mysteries gave people a way of seeing and understanding and even welcoming their own death. This is strange to us (as is so much of the ancient world) – the idea that there was no meaningful afterlife. But perhaps we are better placed to understand this part of it, if only because we live at the back-end of centuries of talk about heaven and hell and the paradise to come, and so even if we ourselves no longer have faith in a future life, we can at least more easily see that what the Mysteries of Eleusis were offering was hope. When Odysseus travelled to the underworld, he met Achilles, or the wraith of Achilles, who told him that he would rather live out his days above ground as an anonymous peasant than as a dead king below it. And this was Achilles, the greatest warrior who had ever lived, celebrated and sacrificed to by millions, who had known that he had the chance to return home early from Troy and live a long quiet life, but had instead chosen death and eternal fame. He regretted it now.

There is another thing we know about the last, most secret stages of the Mysteries, which is that initiates were shown something revelatory – something life-changing – in a casket or under the lid of a holy chest. And it occurs to me now, sipping my mint tea in this limpid courtyard, that maybe what people saw, or imagined they saw, hiding or fluttering under the rim of the sacred casket, perhaps struggling to get out – or maybe just floating there, a radiance in the darkness – what they saw when the lid was lifted was quite literally Pandora's Hope.

That's one possibility. The other is that the café owners have stirred about four tablespoons of liquid ergot into my surprisingly wheaty mug of mint tea.

SIX

Halcyon Days

'For she also haunts the Lake and passes over the dry
land that stands in the eddies of the surf.'

EURIPIDES, HIPPOLYTUS

One consequence that flowed from the dominant ancient
Greek belief that the afterlife was a dreary, meaningless void,
empty of all incident and passion, was that they lived out their
lives on earth with an intensity and urgency that most of us can
never hope to match. Or, as the poet Pindar puts it:

Do not crave immortal life, my soul, but use to the full
the resources of what is possible.

He was writing about Asclepius, a man who was so extraordinarily proficient at healing and medicine that he became a
god, although if you prefer you can say that he came to be
worshipped as a god. Either way, he was later transformed
into a constellation and you can see him in the night skies
even now, grasping a serpent, the symbol of his powers.
Asclepius had learned how to hold back death, and it was
even said that he could bring the dead back to life, and this

appalled King Hades (Persephone is not mentioned) who complained to his brother Zeus, and Zeus in turn became concerned that the number of living human souls would soon disturb the natural balance of the earth, and the world would become too populous (he should see it now), and so he struck Asclepius dead with his thunderbolt. The gods guarded their powers jealously – although it was also known that even they were not allowed to deprive Death of his bounty by prolonging a mortal's life. There were, as ever, exceptions to this rule.

Asclepius was the son of shining Apollo, the god of healing, plague and prophesy, of good order and fresh starts, who speaks obliquely and shoots from afar. His mother was human, the lovely Coronis, who dressed so beautifully. But even though she had been the god's lover, and knew she was pregnant with his child, Coronis chose to sleep with a stranger from Arcadia, because as Pindar writes 'she was in love with what was distant; and many others have felt that passion'. As she should have known, you cannot hide from the gods. Apollo went cold with rage when he saw Coronis making love with this man from far-off Arcadia, thinking they were safely hidden in the woods or under the covers of their secret bed.

Coronis lived in a town by the side of a lake, and so Apollo asked his twin sister Artemis, the goddess of wild places and lonely edgelands, to bring down his vengeance. And that is what she did, killing the people indiscriminately, until they put Coronis on a pyre of wood and threw on a flaming torch (burn the witch!). But then Apollo decided that he could not bear to see his child die, so he strode into the blaze and lifted the living baby Asclepius from the charred womb of his incinerated mother and took him to be raised by the centaur Cheiron in far-off Mount Pelion, like all good heroes once were. And that is where Asclepius mastered the arts of healing, and soon outstripped his teacher and even his father, and learned to perform medical miracles that have never since been equalled. It was the snakes that taught him. They renew their vitality by shedding their skin, and they know how to nurse and foster a longer life. At least, that's how Pindar tells it.

Pausanias had heard other stories. One was that Coronis had come with her father to Epidavros, a small town which lies on a raised thumb of land in the north-east corner of the Peloponnese. Coronis was already pregnant with Apollo's child, and she gave birth on a small local mountain called the Nipple, and there she abandoned the baby, which was found by a nanny goat and a sheepdog and raised by their owner to be the great doctor Asclepius. The shepherd knew that the baby Asclepius was special because when he first saw him he was crackling with divine fire, a sad premonition of his eventual doom, as well as his mother's. There is a lot of fire in this tale, and Hephaestus, the god of furnaces and metalwork, is in some way involved or important to Asclepius' healing powers. Pausanias had also heard that Asclepius' mother was not Coronis at all, but a woman called Arsinoe, but he thought that was the least likely version, because when the Oracle at Delphi was asked about it, Apollo himself, through the mouth of the Oracle, had stated that he had indeed 'mingled in love with beautiful Coronis in rocky Epidavros'.

I am drifting around what is left of Asclepius' sanctuary at Epidavros with Anna and Alex.* I can confirm that it is 'rocky', just like the Oracle said. Apollo never lied, but he did speak elliptically, producing his prophecies at an angle (*loxias*, meaning 'he who speaks obliquely', was his frequent epithet) and it is up to us to make sure the cogs mesh. As ever, in these late October days, the sun is hot and high in a cloudless sky and there is only a handful of people mooching in the ruins. (This is compared to the hundreds who would have been visiting this place in any other more recent year, or indeed 2,400 years ago. The sanctuary is impressive in itself, but it is also a short walk from the most awe-inspiring stone-stepped theatre you are ever likely to see.) The world feels distressingly off kilter. We all need Asclepius now, the man who became a god, and who could heal anything.

When it came to health (and to almost everything else), the Greeks believed that balance was the most important attribute of all. 'Nothing in excess' was the famous maxim carved into the stones at Delphi, but that did not mean that people were not expected to strive and fight and party hard. It was not an edict against passion, it just meant that for every action there is a reaction. If you dance and drink all night (and sometimes you should!) you will be tired and hungover the next day. If you carry on dancing and drinking all night, every night, you will lose control of your life – and that may be your fate, to follow Dionysus, the wildest god of them all, raving with the other dancers, mingling with the maenads, satyrs and leopards, hung

---

*   This journey has travelled back in time, to just after the moment when it was decided in Athens (by a democratic vote, appropriately) that what my book really needed was a closer exploration of the beaches south of Corinth.

about with ivy, your lips red with wine and blood, worshipping the god in ecstasy and madness, and never finding your way back home.

And the maxim was also a warning against carrying on like Erysichthon, whose unassuageable hunger was never satisfied, chewing up the world, craving more, burning and carving into the last forests and filling them with our farms, cramming in the animals we breed, shoulder-to-shoulder, caged, biting and bleeding, pumped with drugs, plagued by insects (which we fight with poison) and bitten by the last of the bats from the vanishing wilderness. There will always be a reckoning. Although it is worth remembering that those pronouncements at Delphi came from the mouth of Apollo, who may have been far-seeing, but he was also a famously distant god.

The worship of Asclepius as a god (or hero) was encouraged into Athens by the writer Sophocles, about ten years after the city was hollowed out by a four-year plague, said to have arrived from Egypt in the year 430 BCE. Its symptoms, and its effects on the people of Athens, are described in traumatising detail by the historian Thucydides, who contracted the disease himself but was one of the lucky ones who survived, when more than a quarter, perhaps a third, of his fellow-citizens did not. Well, we say 'lucky', but as he wrote of those who made it through the seven to nine days of excruciating pain, and who did not die afterwards, wasted away by weakness and despair, then,

> he that overcame the worst of it was yet marked with the loss of his extreme parts; for breaking out both at their privy members and at their fingers and toes,

many with the loss of these escaped; there were also
some that lost their eyes. And many that presently
upon their recovery were taken with such an oblivion
of all things whatsoever, as they neither knew themselves nor their acquaintance.

As Thucydides wrote, if anyone was sick when the plague
arrived, then their sickness became this one. And almost everyone else, however healthy, just went down with it. A brutal, tearing headache, inflamed eyes, a bloody tongue and throat, short-
ness of breath, sneezing, hoarseness – and then the pain spread
down the body, through the chest, producing a violent heaving
cough, and into the stomach, with vomiting and copious retch-
ing of bile. Most of the sufferers, says Thomas Hobbes in my
translated copy, had the 'hickyexe', convulsing with fever, which
could last hours or days. Their bodies turned a livid red, breaking out in rashes, and they burned so they couldn't bear the
touch of their bed linen or any clothing, but would seek out
fountains and cisterns and any source of cold water, where they
would lie consumed with a raging thirst, or dying, here and at
home and piled unburied in the temples, or sometimes rolling
themselves into the city's deep wells in a desperate desire to
drink. If they survived that, then the diarrhoea followed, an
unstoppable, wasting flow, and that is the moment when most
of the survivors ran out of strength. A quarter, perhaps a third,
of the city . . . made so much worse by the fact that Athens was
newly at war with Sparta, and thousands of people had left
their farms and surrounding villages to crowd in illusory safety
behind its high walls.

Of course, we should thank the gods for modern medicine. There was so much the doctors of ancient Athens did not know. When they went to help the early sufferers, they were among the first to get sick and die. People lost faith, too. What was the point in obeying or praying to the gods? It didn't seem to make any difference. And who in fact needed to care any longer about the city's laws or morals? Everyone was going to die. The poor died. The rich died. Someone inherited their wealth. And then they died too. Thucydides notes all of this, the descent from order into isolation and extreme hedonism, but it is also worth saying that their society did not collapse and its essential structures remained. Even when their leader, Pericles, died, life carried on, and so did their disastrous war with Sparta.

In the early days of the plague, Pericles had sent part of the Athenian army, about four thousand fighting men in one hundred ships, along with another fifty ships from Lesbos, horses too, away from Athens and into the Peloponnese, even though the Peloponnesian army, under Sparta, was burning the countryside around Athens and attacking the mines of Laurium (and urging its slaves to flee). The army was pleased to be far away from the plague-stricken city, and they sailed to Epidavros, just a short hop across the blue Saronic Gulf, with its many dolphins (at least in those days), and tried to raze it to the ground, but they were beaten back by the high walls and its determined citizens, so they drifted down the coast, looting settlements and ports, slaughtering and enslaving the people. Most of the ruins that you can see today in the sanctuary of Asclepius date from after the Peloponnesian War, but there was still a thriving shrine to the god of medicine in those days, and

I do wonder whether any of the soldiers stopped to think it might be better to seek help from the inhabitants and healing priests of Epidavros, what with the plague running out of control at home and killing their families and friends, or whether they just carried on with the carnage. I suppose it was war . . . and that was what they did.

Many years before these events (no one knows when) Theseus had stopped at Epidavros on his way to Athens to meet his father for the first time. He killed Periphetes here, a son of Hephaestus, who had been robbing travellers on the road and bludgeoning them to death with a big bronze club. Theseus took the club from him and beat him into the earth, close to the point where you could once find one of the entrances to the underworld. Theseus was one of those heroes who liked to tidy up – clearing roads of robbers, ridding the world of wild bulls, killing the Minotaur, traversing the labyrinth, uniting kingdoms, ending matriarchies, introducing democracy (or so they liked to say) – but he still spread chaos. It was as though he was followed all his life by a feral dog that tore into the people he loved. Inescapable tragedy. He was happy here, though, just sixteen years old, executing a violent and cruel man, on his way to meet his father, his life ahead of him, lovers, friends, wives, children, conquests, kingship. How do we know if we are happy? It is too early to tell.

Theseus had a beautiful son called Hippolytus, which means 'unleasher of horses', or even 'loosened or destroyed by horses'. Imagine being called that. You would have to wonder, growing up, what your parents had meant by giving you such a name. Hippolytus was the son of an Amazon queen called Antiope, or possibly his mother was Hippolyte, who had been carried off by Theseus from her home by the Black Sea, or maybe she had come willingly, having listened to a prophecy. Hippolytus was sent to spend his childhood in Troezen, south of Epidavros, just like Theseus had before him. Apparently Hippolytus had an instinctive feel for horses, and was supremely skilled at chariot- and bare-back riding. He was, as I say, beautiful. He worshipped Artemis, the goddess of the edgelands and the wild places, who loved to hunt with her followers, nymphs and female humans, all of them, Artemis especially (who had extracted a pledge from her father Zeus), sworn to be free of the company of men. There are the ruins of a temple, here in Epidavros, dedicated to 'Artemis Hekate', as she was known in this place, once deco- rated with the heads of boars and dogs. Hippolytus was also devoted to Asclepius, and Pausanias says there was a stone tablet in the sanctuary at Epidavros, 'separate from the others saying that Hippolytus dedicated twenty horses to the god'.

Theseus had married a young Cretan princess called Phaedra, the daughter of King Minos, and she had fallen in love with beautiful Hippolytus. Or lust, if you prefer – a burn- ing, limb-shaking, blinding, all-consuming lust to have this young man. They were close in age, and Theseus had already lived a long life. One story is that smiling Aphrodite had brought down this doom on Phaedra, to punish Hippolytus for his chaste devotion to Artemis. There was no limit to the jealousy of the gods. In the end Phaedra had no choice but to let Hippolytus know how she yearned and longed for him, or perhaps it was a nurse who acted as go-between, or let slip what was meant to be kept a secret (despite Phaedra's overwhelming desire) and Hippolytus was revolted, and raged against all women, or maybe he was tempted but terrified (he was so young), we don't know, but he didn't tell his father, because how could he?

Phaedra did, though. She may have told Theseus herself, or she may have left a note after she committed suicide. Either way, she accused Hippolytus of raping her – and Hippolytus would not deny it. So Theseus cursed him, and Hippolytus fled in his chariot, along the road from Troezen to Epidavros, and because Theseus was the son of Poseidon, a great bull rose from the sea (it was always bulls with Theseus) and Hippolytus' horses panicked, and he fell from the chariot, tangled in the reins and tackle, and the chariot overturned and Hippolytus was torn apart by the horses he loved. 'Ah, so that's why they called me Hippolytus' was presumably his last thought as the light faded. Some say that Theseus was weeping at his side. According to Pausanias, Hippolytus' mauled and trampled body was carried to Epidavros, where Asclepius brought him back from the dead and he went off to live in Italy, still worshipping Artemis and spurning Theseus' heartfelt and miserable apologies.

We all took turns lying on the stone bench in the Abaton in Epidavros, which is the long building with restored white pillars at the heart of the sanctuary. Well, the columns are white now, but in earlier days I imagine them decorated with gold and ivory or maybe painted with intricate, serpentine reds, yellows and greens. This was once the place where the sick and the weary would lie down to sleep. Abaton means 'impenetrable', in other words the building was open only to those who had prepared themselves with ritual purification to meet the god Asclepius, who would be waiting for them in their dreams. The Abaton was also known as the place of 'incubation', because the patients were dreaming and brewing a cure for their illness.

Running water was important (there was a sacred well here) but above all it was snakes that symbolised and at times enacted the healing. They would appear in the dreams of the supplicants, licking wounds, whispering in their ear, and they were also to be found in huge numbers in the Abaton itself, a pale yellow colour, slithering on the floors and quite tame with humans, or so says Pausanias. The Epidavrions were proud of their snakes and said that the ones that lived in India and Libya and grew to at least sixty feet in length were not real snakes at all, 'but some other kind of beast'. And also, Pausanias tells us, if you want a parrot you'll have to go to India for that.

Anyway, none of us fell asleep, or stayed overnight, or bathed in the sacred waters, so I cannot tell you about our dreams or any changes to our health. Indeed, it was around about now that I began to be nervous about how little I was dreaming in Greece. I had been hoping for a sign about hope, but all I had to go on so far (apart from the velociraptor and the mouse) was last night's dream (#3), which is an embarrassing one. We had been to the beach earlier in the day and in my dream I was standing waist-deep in the clear blue sea, pine trees and sand behind me, a soothing place, beauty and light, when all of a sudden, appearing from the right, an immense bronzed man came swimming on his front, face down, forging his way with unhurried ease through the water, the straps of his goggles showing through the damp curls at the back of his great head. A god-like figure. He was hugely muscled, with a back like a bull rising from the surface, oblivious to my presence, but closing in on Anna who was just the other side of him. And I thought: he is not going to take her away, is he? He is a god, or a hero at least, I am sure of it, and that is what they do. He moved in the water like an elephant seal or an orca. I was frozen. And Anna – what? She just stood there in the unruffled sea, impossible to read. Maybe she hadn't even seen him.

So, yes, not really the kind of dream I was hoping for, and I've only remembered or repeated it because I had so few to choose from. We left the Abaton (me flapping away a sudden, too-sharp memory of the dream) and went to visit the large open-air, stone-stepped amphitheatre, which as Pausanias quite rightly says is 'particularly worth a visit'. The acoustics here are beyond comprehension. There were just seven of us scattered around the seating, all as high as we could go, looking down over the ancient mottled grey steps to the stage far below, and then over a thick spread of green umbrella pines and beyond to the valley and up to the peaks of the bare-backed mountains and into the liquid blue sky, now brushed with a few early evening clouds. There was a smell of warm herbs and the softest of breezes. And then a French woman stood suddenly and left her seat at the top of the theatre. 'Écoute,' she said to her young daughter, who stayed where she was, 'Listen,' and she walked down to the exact centre of the stage and she lifted her arm high and she dropped a tiny stone, precisely there at her feet, and the sound of it, a delicate 'pip', leaped and rippled all the way up the dozens of steps right to where we were sitting and the child, who was about twenty metres to our left, gasped out, '*Oh!*' And then her mother started to sing, something choral and old, and it was beautiful, all of us sitting so high in this ancient theatre, the warm sky and the scent of the pines, listening to a human voice fill the air with the ache of her song. And the moment was over almost as soon as it had begun.

Hippolytus used to bring flowers to the goddess Artemis from a meadow that only he could visit, but he never even caught a glimpse of her. And in Euripides' play *Hippolytus*, Phaedra sings to the same goddess:

> Take me to the mountain: I mean to go to the wood,
> to the pine-wood, where hounds that kill wild beasts
> tread, running close after the dappled deer! By the
> gods, how I want to shout to the hounds and to let fly
> past my golden hair, a javelin of Thessaly, to hold in
> my hand the sharp-pointed weapon!

And the nurse (who would cause so much trouble later) tries to calm her. Why not get a drink from inside the walls of Troezen, she asks? Why go hunting in the mountains? Why do you want to kill deer? But the only thing that Phaedra knew was that she had to get away from the city and Hippolytus and run with the goddess in the wild places, far from the scenes of her pain. She was desperate to escape, but that wasn't going to happen, not once the wheels of this tragedy had started to grind and turn. It doesn't seem right or fair, but the only reason that Aphrodite had caught Phaedra up in her plans and pulled her so close and fed her obsession is that she wanted to punish Hippolytus for his neglect and for his worship of her rival, the goddess Artemis. She hated that such a beautiful young man should be so uninterested in love. Phaedra was being used. And anyone can get lost in a dark wood.

'Mistress of the Salt Lake,' Phaedra sings, 'Artemis, mistress of the coursing-ground for horses, oh that I might find myself on your ground taming Enetic horses!'

You may not be surprised to hear quite how much scholarly fossicking has been stirred up by the phrase 'Enetic horses'. It sounds like they are about to be sick, but the consensus seems to be that this breed of horse was especially vigorous. The 'Salt Lake', though, is easier, because there was once a temple to Artemis on a lake just north of Troezen on the road to Epidavros, and although the temple is long gone, the lake – shallow and salty and home to many wading birds – is still here, not far from a beach called 'Metamorfosi', or (in other words), the beach of changes, where forms are never fixed. The slippery beach. It could have been right here that the bull rose from the sea to drive Hippolytus' horses mad, although Euripides seems to think that he managed to ride a little further along the road. But then again, who really knows? The coastline has shifted many times since.

Still, if you are looking to catch a glimpse of the goddess Artemis, then these wave-licked shores would be a good place to start. I came here with Alex early one evening, at the cusp of the day, to see whether we could pick up her traces. I suggested it was a good idea to separate, to give us both a better chance, and Alex very sensibly opted to stay in the car with his phone, because you never know. I set off towards the east (the bay curls and faces north), away from the setting sun, with a brisk wind arriving from the sea on my left. It is cold in this direction. The beach is a sandy grey, with a restless clutter of pebbles and flat stones lying in a narrow strip between the waves and the reeds to my right, behind which is the salt lake where Artemis once had her temple and accepted her sacrifices. She haunts the edges of places, when the day turns, early and late: lakes, shore-lines, marshes, mountaintops and woods. She is unpredictable (she is a goddess). She likes to run and kill. She may be seen (or choose to be found) at boundaries and margins and the places where opposites meet, and at those moments when humans are more likely to feel the strangeness of things.*

The shoreline, to the Greeks, was a place of transition, between the danger and possibilities and hope of the sea (*'thalassa! thalassa!'*) and the more stable but blood-drenched land. Monsters (and bulls) could come from the sea; and humans could kid themselves they had more control over the land.

---

* Yes, I am choosing not to use the word 'liminal' at this moment. If I were a true NatureWriter™ I would be contractually obliged to roll it out, just as this 'place' would be a 'space'. But I do not like to write down words I can't use in conversation without wincing. The same goes for 'chthonic' – or even 'autoch-thonic' – which really does need to appear in this book, but it sounds like some-one is vomiting (perhaps the 'Enetic horses'). I will be breaking this general rule later. And I am certainly not suggesting that people should not be free to use any words they like. Liminal. Liminal. Liminal. There.

There is even something monstrous about Artemis, whose shrine at Patras, or so says Pausanias, was the site of a festival where every year the people would drive wild animals onto an altar covered in dry logs, all of it surrounded by a wooden stockade, and they:

> . . . throw alive upon the altar edible birds and every kind of victim as well; there are wild boars, deer and gazelles; some bring wolf-cubs or bear-cubs, others the full-grown beasts. They also place upon the altar fruit of cultivated trees. Next they set fire to the wood. At this point I have seen some of the beasts, including a bear, forcing their way outside at the first rush of the flames, some of them actually escaping by their strength. But those who threw them in drag them back again to the pyre. It is not remembered that anybody has ever been wounded by the beasts.

The people of Patras believed that Artemis wanted this annual incineration of wild beasts. None of the animals escaped. They were just thrown into the flames and burned alive. It wasn't even a proper sacrifice, as set out by Prometheus, when the best bits would be saved by the humans to be eaten later. Even while she was demanding this slaughter, Artemis was also the protector of wild places and animals. She was beautiful, beyond our understanding. We would say that she was cruel, but it is so very hard to understand how different these ancient people were from us. Of course, we kill millions of beasts every day. It is just done in a rather more orderly, and less public or celebratory, fashion.

Anyway, back to the beach, where the wind is getting stronger and the waves are chopping busily at the sands. At my back, the last of the sun is turning the surface of the sea a thin yellow, floating above cold grey depths, although in the distance, beyond the dark mountains, there is a last halo of pale gold, framing some slender wind turbines on the high barren peaks. Ahead of me the clouds are low and dark. I scramble on towards some scrubby hills, fixing my eye on a single pylon. There is a line of eucalyptus trees to my right and walls of tall reeds, masking the lake; and to the left, out to sea, there is a large rocky island, looking like it should be a home for Cyclopes. Not humans, anyway; there are no houses nor any lights. I don't really want to head this way, it looks so uninviting, but it seems to be what I am doing, stumbling over a ragged beach towards a dying sky.

My foot becomes caught in a plastic bag, so I stop to strip it off. This is the tideline, the edge of things, and night and day are slipping past each other, but I don't suppose Artemis has any desire to be here. There is more than one plastic bag. Cheap blue things, some of them shredded and faded from the sea. And there are also coffee cup lids and old ropes and bricks and torn fishing nets and a small decaying iron stove. There is a large crumpled and sliced brown plastic flowerpot. Dozens of bottles, most of them plastic, also glass, some with their lids still fixed and half-full of water. Odd shoes too, not just trainers but a strappy black one with a very high heel. And there are clumps of bright white polystyrene where the waves reach the shore, drifting in and out of the sea and being blown in flecks among the stones. Shells as well, but it is hard to tell the difference in the pale grey light. There is a bottle of salad dressing and chunky blocks of foam stuffing, the cheap kind that comes from old sofas and was discontinued because it burns too easily. And there's an empty five-litre tin can that once held engine oil, rusting among offcuts of sodden brown carpet.

One thing the ancient writers told us is that nymphs could appear to anyone who was open to the possibility. And Artemis was followed by an entourage of nymphs. But why would they want to spend any time on this desolate human shore? Even though this beach is really no different from almost any other, anywhere in the world. They are all scurfed with litter; and if they are not it is only because the locals are working hard to pick them clean, just as fast as more unwanted effluent arrives over the horizon. The discarded or lost detritus of our lives is drifting in the tides and the winds and fetching up on every coast in every continent, islands of plastic floating miles wide across the oceans. Much more has sunk to the bottom. And our babies are born with plastics in their blood.

So why would Artemis, the goddess of wild places, want to be here? More to the point, why would I want her to be? When Actaeon lost his way in the woods on the side of a tall mountain (it is easy to do) he followed a stream and found himself on the edge of a shady pool, where he thought he could cool off and wash away the blood and gore from his hands and arms. He had been hunting with his hounds, and had killed many animals: deer, boar, hares and birds of many kinds. He was a famous hunter. But Artemis was already there, bathing naked with her nymphs, and whether he saw her, or even tried to assault her, we don't know, but Artemis was shaken with rage, and she

transformed Actaeon into a stag, slowly so that he would understand what was happening, and when he tried to call out all he
could do was bellow his distress, and his hounds heard –
wondering, perhaps, where their master was – and they howled
the visceral lust of the hunt, one last run of the day, and Actaeon
wanted to say 'it's me, it's Actaeon', but of course he couldn't,
so he turned to run, his hooves tripping on the unfamiliar paths,
already amazed at his own strength, but even so they caught
him almost at once, burying their jaws in his back legs, dragging
him down, shrieking and pleading (not in any human voice),
and torn to bloody rags, Artemis not even bothering to watch.
The list of her murders is long.

I do realise I am writing about Actaeon because I don't want
to think about this heaped plastic beach. We have all lost our
way (it is easy to do) but I suppose the only question is whether
we can make our way out before we come to a place we would
rather not find ourselves. Or whether it is already too late.

I turn for the salt lake and am passed by a middle-aged man
in a bright red hoodie, making the same weary walk. We
exchange looks of caution. This is not an easy place. Plato
seems to have believed that every spot on earth has its own
essence, irrespective of human activity. And he thought some
places have a kind of 'heavenly breeze' and are under 'the care
of daemons, so that they receive those that come from time to
time to settle there either graciously or ungraciously'. I would
say that the jury is still out, here on Metamorfosi beach (and
beyond), about quite how gracious our welcome is going to be.

Looking out for daemons in the twilight, I find an opening
in the reeds and follow a raised path towards the lake. There are

empty 'Hell' energy drink cans to either side, as well as the familiar blue and silver sheen of Red Bull. I could go on: an orange plastic food tray, the large polystyrene lid of a cool box, a plastic cup with 'Everest' written on its side in pale pink lettering, a discarded empty fertiliser bag that makes me think for some reason of the Roc's nest in Ray Harryhausen's *Sinbad* film. But what is the point? And where is the hope in that? There are also crickets, leaping up with casual power and then floating across drifts of pale mauve flowers. And there are hides that have been made with love for the birdwatchers, in among the reeds and the dark juniper bushes. The ground is soft with a glittering sand. There are tamarisk trees, no longer in bloom, but feathered gold in the last of the sun, which has just appeared between the low purple clouds and the hilltops. And there are two large birds, cormorants I am sure, rising above the end of the lake, and when I look down I see that the whole distant shoreline is filled with wading birds, too far away to know what they are, and I have no binoculars (and I should have been an ornithologist), but there is a great black and white and grey mass of movement, over there, blurred on the horizon, a living backdrop to the silvery lake. Perhaps there are flamingos here. Kingfishers too. And on the foreshore, framed by tamarisk, with two rounded green hills behind him, fading blue sky above, there is a man at the side of the lake rhythmically striking the ground with a long stick. Slap. Bang. Slap, it goes. Is that Alex? It was probably not the best way to try and summon Artemis, but I was thrilled to the bone to see him.

There are many beautiful beaches running south from Epidavros Port to the tip of the peninsula beyond Troezen. We were staying in the Poseidon Hotel in the port, and very lovely it was too. The exceptionally friendly owner had seen his business badly battered by the first year of Covid, but he remained unfailingly cheerful. There were still plenty of French and German visitors in October, and the weather (did I mention?) was limpid, and when I unfurled my inevitable question he smiled and said that he expected next year would be better. 'What else can we do but hope?'

The best beach, we decided, was tiny Kalamaki, a short stroll along the coastal path from our hotel, but we did also find time to experiment with a few others between here and the island of Poros to the south. We crossed to Poros on a small car ferry, heading for Love Bay (because who could resist?), the journey taking about ten minutes. Pausanias warns us that this area is dangerous for swimming because of the numerous sea monsters, including sharks, that infest the local waters, and that was enough to put me off, even if he was writing almost two thousand years ago. The idea makes my skin crawl, but the Mediterranean needs its sharks back. The island of Poros was once sacred to Apollo, but he swapped it with Poseidon for Delphi, or so the locals liked to claim, and perhaps that is why there are so many monsters in the ocean, keeping their sovereign lord company.

We drove past Love Bay but decided there must be something better further around the island (there is always something better further around the island). And for once it worked, and did not end in recrimination and regret ('I told you we should have stopped at that bay'), and we found ourselves on an exquisite beach, with low flat rocks for our picnic, lapped by a lapis sea, fringed by pine trees, the hot sun in the blue sky, a ten-minute walk from the road, down a narrow goat track, past a burned-out car, and with just three middle-aged naked Germans for company. If you travel to the more remote beaches of Greece there are always three naked Germans for company, and it seems unnecessary to mention it, given that these shores (and gyms and athletics stadia) were once filled with oiled and naked men, not to mention erect phalluses at every single cross-roads and front door, and swinging lustily from the loins of the actors at the theatre, and there were beautiful sculpted naked bodies in the temples and public squares, both male and (later) female, but these days most of us have been schooled to find public nudity uncomfortable. In earlier times, it was the god Hermes who was most often proudly on display, or at least part of him, but there was always plenty to choose from.

One of the middle-aged German men had positioned himself on a nearby rock overlooking our picnic, and had spread his legs wide in what felt like a rather overenthusiastic interven-tion into our meal. At the very least it was hard to savour the view. Anna seemed to think so, because locking eyes on the man, she rummaged in the nearest bag, brought out one of the picnic cucumbers, held it firmly on the rock and then brought down a heavy knife on its narrow end with a swift *thwunk*, before tossing the severed tip to a passing gull, which spat it into the sea, where it rolled and bobbed and winked at the man. Artemis would have been so proud. It took the man another twenty seconds to pull on a towel, but we left soon afterwards, exchanging cheerful but contrite words with the bronzing trio, because after all they had arrived on the beach first and they must have been sad to see us arrive clad so modestly.

Epidavros Port faces east and the pink and orange sunrises bathing our hotel balcony were enough to get us up and busy in the reborn hope of each day. In the early evening, when the boats are tied fast and nuzzling the jetty, I found myself talking to a British woman who had moved to the area about four years earlier with her husband to run a diving business. Well, I say 'found myself' – she was briefly trying to persuade us to go diving. Her parents had owned a house here when she was growing up. 'It must have changed a lot,' I say, leadingly. 'Not at all,' she replies. 'Really?' I say, because this is not what we are used to hearing, wherever we live. It is true that this place has a heavenly breeze that Plato might recognise. Sun glittering low on the dark blue bay. A headland of green pine. The soft rise and fall of the boats. A few parked cars. A pulse of Greek music. The occasional long fart from a scooter. Laughter from across the water or behind the bar. A couple of late gulls in the sky. The murmur of Dutch or German and the slap of cards from the back of the boats and the tables. Pausanias says that people first settled here when the snake they had brought from home in their ship slid overboard and swam to shore. All I can say is that it must have been a snake of taste.

'No, not at all,' the woman says again. 'Not one bit. People just sort of discover this place. We hope it won't change – and it never does.' Of course, to bring the mood down, I could tell her that things have most definitely changed, even in the last four years. There are more houses, more hotels, more boats and cars. More people. All of it good for her business, let's hope. But change is incremental. A plot developed here. A car park there. Trees brought down. Litter spreading. Fewer fish in the sea. Temperatures rising. The baseline always shifting. Nothing major. We adapt fast. The frog famously does not notice when it is boiling slowly in the pot, or only when it is too late. And we don't see what is happening until one day we look up and the little fishing port has become something else. And anyone searching for a more peaceful life heads a bit further down the coast or deeper inland, until they meet the developers coming the other way. I am not saying this is simple. People need work. The Greek economy is in trauma. Much of what is happening is for the better. Life-enhancing as well as depressing. But look around – and then tell me that nothing has changed.

Change, as any Greek philosopher could have told us, is the only constant. I do not say any of this out loud of course. I have saved this wet blanket for you. The woman wishes me a very happy rest of my holiday and moves on to the next table and I gaze at a ginger cat lying flat out on the jetty, right by the edge, its eyes closed, breathing easy in the last of the sun. I will try and be more like that cat, I decide.

And so the very next day I am drifting on my back in a gentle sea, a couple of hundred metres out from the tiny but almost empty Kalamaki beach, which is occupied by just Alex and a Greek woman with her young son. Anna has swum round the headland. Pine trees crowd up and onto the rocky beach, with its sliver of hot sand, and someone's blue towel is drooping over a branch. The Greek woman says she saw the kingfisher that lives here a few moments ago, skimming fast and low across the bay, but it seems to have disappeared. I don't remember ever having seen a kingfisher before (surely I have, although maybe that was just on a screen or in the pages of a book), but after a few minutes of scanning the woods I close my eyes and float in the water, and watch outlines of snakes slide past my eyelids. I do not know if Asclepius is trying to say something, but I am too happy to care.

And anyway, it says in my books of Classical Mythology that kingfishers don't live on the seashore. I am not sure I should be getting my natural history knowledge from Greek myths, but what I can tell you is that a long time ago (no one knows when) there was a beautiful princess called Alcyone who loved a man called Ceyx. Perhaps they were too happy, and compared themselves to Hera and Zeus, or maybe they were just unlucky, but either way Ceyx was drowned at sea and Alcyone found his broken body washed up on the beach; or maybe she was told about his death in a dream, because he was already at the bottom, being eaten by the things that writhe in the deep. What we do know is that Alcyone threw herself into the sea after Ceyx, and the gods took pity and turned them both into kingfishers. And every year, in the days around the winter solstice, Alcyone's father, the god of the winds, makes sure that the oceans are kept entirely still and calm, so that kingfishers can lay their eggs in their nests on the shoreline, or even floating on the sea, free from any danger. And these are the times that we know as 'Halcyon Days', brief moments of peace, precariously balanced between the storms.

SEVEN

'It's Just a Simple Metaphor'

'We went inside and again returned to Mythology,
   searching
for some deeper correlation, some distant general
   allegory
to soothe the narrowness of the personal void.
   We found nothing.'

YANNIS RITSOS, 'NOT EVEN MYTHOLOGY'

If you had been born with the long-range perspective of an immortal (perhaps sprung fully formed, clothed and armed from your father's head), you might think that a single morning spent drifting on your back in the blue Mediterranean Sea would be an altogether meaningless crumb of time. And yet we never hear that the goddesses and gods thought that their days were pointless or that they ever felt listless or unengaged. Odysseus may have been, when he was trapped on the shores of beautiful Calypso's island, gazing out to sea, but the immortal goddess never wavered from her purpose. She might have been distraught and angry when Hermes arrived with a message from Zeus to tell her that she had to let Odysseus go, but it doesn't sound like she was ever *bored*. There was always so much to do, weaving and tending her garden and playing with her leopards by day and making love with her ageing mortal by night (still yearning for him after seven long years, even though he had lost almost all interest in her). Of course they understood better than us how fast time flies, or that sometimes it hardly moves at all.

The immortals occasionally tried to prolong the lives of the humans they loved, but that never seemed to work out. Age and death would always come calling. When the beautiful Calypso is lamenting the fact that she has been told to let Odysseus leave, she mentions Eos, the goddess of the dawn, and her human lover, the great hunter, Orion, who was killed by a giant scorpion and transformed into a constellation. At least, that's what some people say. Others reckon it was Artemis who killed him because she was jealous of his hunting skills, or perhaps she was even falling in love with him herself, and was tricked by Apollo into shooting him with an arrow when he was floating far out at sea. And Calypso talks about Iasion, who made love with Demeter in a 'thrice ploughed field' and that's how the god Wealth was born, and so Zeus killed Iasion with a thunderbolt. The unfathomable jealousy of the gods.

And then there was the time when Eos, the ravishing, rosy goddess of the dawn, persuaded Zeus to give eternal life to Tithonus, another of her lovers, but she forgot to ask for eternal youth, and so eventually (in the wink of an eye) he shrivelled into a tiny piping man, squeaking irritatingly in the corner of her palace, until he was transformed into a grasshopper. And there was Apollo and Hyacinthus (*ai! ai!*) and Apollo and Daphne (who fled from the god and was turned into a laurel tree) and Apollo and Coronis (who was burned alive) and Zeus and Semele (who tricked the father of the gods into revealing his true self and was fried to a cinder; Zeus had to stuff their still gestating child, Dionysus, into his thigh to be born later). And so on and on. It never ended well.

The thing is, mortal humans could be transformed into something else, and live on as a constellation or (for a while) as a tree, a flower or an animal. Or they would die and part of them would exist elsewhere, as a bloodless spirit in Hades, or (some said) as a full-blooded hero in a paradise beyond the seas. That is where Menelaus ended up, along with Helen and a favoured few. The Blessed Ones, these long-lived heroes were called. There were even a couple of exceptionally rare moments when a mortal would be raised to Mount Olympus as a god (well, they were rare until the Roman emperors got involved). But nothing, not even the gods, could hold back time. It is true (or it was said) that Zeus and Hera enjoyed a 300-year-long wedding night. But the earliest writers, Homer and Hesiod, never saw the gods as living outside time. They were immortal, and they were unfeasibly powerful, but they were still subject to the immutable laws of the universe. They were even waiting nervously for their own eventual overthrow . . . unlike some other gods we could mention.

There were five Ages of Man, most Greeks agreed, or that's how Hesiod told it. The first age was an Age of Gold, when people lived a life of ease and plenty. The fruit fell into their laps and the wheat and the corn grew by themselves, without any labour at all. Presumably this was before Persephone had been seized by Hades. Certainly it was before Prometheus had tricked Zeus out of the best bits of the sacrifice, and had stolen fire from heaven, and before Pandora had been sent to earth to bring disease, war, plague, famine and death (and also women, Hesiod grumbled). Hope too of course. There was always hope. Except that the golden age ended, and everyone died, and what came next was the Age of Silver, when all the men were so hopeless that they lived with their mothers for a hundred years, playing childish games, and then they would leave home to lead a life of crime. Zeus got rid of them, although Hesiod says that we still worship at their shrines.

Next up was the Age of Bronze, when the people were hugely strong, made out of ash trees, but they were violent beyond measure and slaughtered one another, leaving no trace of their deeds on their way down to Hades' dark halls. So we arrive at the fourth age, the Age of Heroes, and they were 'more righteous and noble' than the bronze psychopaths, but they also killed one another, in war and fighting. This was the time when immortals mingled with humanity, and they loved us, and fought for us, and tormented or ignored us. They hungered for our sacrifices. It was the age of Theseus, Ariadne, Heracles, Perseus, Medea, Medusa, the Minotaur and all the rest. Jason and his Argonauts. Nymphs, satyrs and Pan. Artemis and Actaeon. Oedipus, Helen and Cadmus. Achilles and Odysseus. The time of monsters and monstrous men. It didn't last long, this age, just a tiny handful of generations, before the heroes all died at Troy or were murdered when they got home or eked out a last few weary years roaming the seas. As Pausanias says, the gods once lived and walked with us, and now they don't, but that should not stop us from worshipping at their altars.

And here we are in the Age of Iron. At least, that's what Hesiod says, but of course he was writing over 2,700 years ago and maybe now we are already launched into some other era. The Age of Plastic, perhaps, or lithium. It is hard to know. Hesiod says he wished he had been born in some other Age – earlier or later – because the Age of Iron was a time of toil and misery and 'constant distress' (with the occasional good moment), and his desire to be born later seems to imply that he knew that there were some other Ages planned. This might be a hopeful thought. We can trust Hesiod because he was getting his information directly from the Muses, who danced and sang on the slopes of Mount Helicon, and although they are known to lie, they promised that they were not lying to him.

Hesiod also said that the Age of Iron would end when men are born with 'grey at the temples' and when 'there will be no thanks for the man who abides by his oath or for the righteous or worthy man, but instead they will honour the miscreant and the criminal' – and I don't want to jump to conclusions but I would say we are there already, except for the bit about the babies with the greying temples. Eternal vigilance, that is the key.

The gods are powerful, but as Pindar wrote, so are we. We share the same mother.

> There is one race of men, one race of gods;
> and from a single mother we both draw our breath.
> But all allotted power divides us:
> man is nothing, but for the gods the
> bronze sky endures as a secure home forever.

Nevertheless, we bear some resemblance to the
immortals,
either in greatness of mind or in nature,
although we do not know, by day or by night,
towards what goal fortune has written
that we should run.

The future is written. And time rolls on. That is the reason why prophecies and auguries were so important to the Greeks. All they had to do was to tap into what was already known and the future would be revealed. And so it was, time after time: people would consult oracles and seers, and they would be told what to expect. 'Does Perseus love me?' 'Which god have I angered?' 'Will there be a good harvest?' 'Should I get a new dog?' 'Do we go to war?' The more complicated questions might not get a straightforward answer (anything that needed a simple yes/no was best), and the truth that was revealed might emerge clouded or at an angle, especially from the Oracle at Delphi, where the priestess of far-shooting Apollo held sway, but in general people put their faith in prophecy, just so long as they remembered that it is only the immortals who can ever truly know 'towards what goal fortune has written that we should run'. And some things were hidden even to them.

I am back on the road, in the proper order of this journey (the future is no longer ahead of the past), and I have left the Isthmus of Corinth and am now heading for Olympia, threading my way through the mountain passes of Arcadia. Alex and Anna are back in London and October is nearly at an end. The sky is blue. With time on my hands (it is a short distance but the road thrashes dizzyingly back and forth), I am chewing over my prophecy from Delphi. You may remember (the full reply is in chapter 4) that we cannot reasonably expect to find 'true Hope' until we have some understanding of who 'rules within the skies' and what they have planned for us. This is not so very different from what one of Plato's characters once said:

> My child, you are still young, and time as it advances will cause you to reverse many of the opinions you now hold: so wait till then before pronouncing judgment on matters of most grave importance; and of these, the gravest of all – though at present you regard it as naught – is the question of holding a right view about the gods and so living well, or the opposite.

The gods exist. There are many people who think that they don't (even though their parents were devout and prayed and made all the proper sacrifices), but these people always learn in the end that the gods are real. No one reaches old age and remains an atheist. Or so said Plato. It is time for Richard Dawkins to put aside his childish views. And Plato also wrote that there are even some people who think that the gods do exist but that they have no interest in human affairs; or that the gods can be easily won over by our prayers and offerings. And these people are fools. If we want to know what we are meant to be doing on this earth, and above all if we want to live well (in balance with everything around us), we have to understand the gods.

Anyway, what is bothering me about 'my' oracle is that not only am I meant to be working out what the gods want or expect from us, and what their ultimate purpose might be, but I am also expected to 'know myself'. I mean, am I supposed to be looking up or out or in? Or everywhere at the same time? Or is there some kind of order in which to proceed? All I was looking for was a little hope.

The people who lived in Mycenae in its heyday, in all its golden glory, well over three thousand years ago, may not have thought that they were living at the beginning of something. They may have believed that their age of plenty was behind them, those languorous days of ease when the fruit just dropped into their laps. And yet 'Greece' was only just getting going, the classical world of incomparable statues, pottery, philosophy, poetry and maths, of light and drama and the rough stirrings of democracy. There was even a dark age to get through first, the three-hundred-year aftermath of the great cataclysm, when Mycenae, the city of gold, was destroyed and emptied, along with Tiryns, Troezen, Thebes and more. Pausanias, when he got to Tiryns, thought that its vast walls could only have been built by the Cyclopes, and it is true that the heft and scale of the walls is incomprehensible, their huge honeycombed slabs slotted together as if by magic or the unquenchable muscle-power of one-eyed monsters. I suppose what I am trying to say is that beauty and hope can arrive unexpectedly.

The Greeks believed that each new day started at nightfall. The darkness would come and the day would begin. And the night would be followed by the dawn.

As well as Tiryns, the Cyclopes were also involved in building the walls of Mycenae, the richest city of them all, home to the great King Agamemnon. Pausanias mentions the treasures that were hidden in the burial mounds, but it took thousands of years before Schliemann came along to dig them up. There were bones of lions mixed in with the excavated jewellery and pots, and the famous entrance gate to this royal city is crowned with lions, and indeed this whole place is majestic and dangerous and wild, high and remote and surrounded by bare rocks and torched trees. My first thought was why would anyone want to build their citadel and royal palaces here, so far from the sea, at the mercy of the unforgiving sun? What did they do for water? (It turns out there were springs.) It must have been easy to defend (although not in the end easy enough) but it is so remote and silent, especially in this first year of Covid, when the tourists are outnumbered by the guides. Henry Miller, who came here just before the outbreak of the Second World War, thought that 'the stillness of it today resembles the exhaustion of a cruel and intelligent monster which has been bled to death'. And Aeschylus put these words into the mouth of Cassandra, standing right here in high Mycenae, the city of gold:

> I scent the track of crimes done long ago . . . a choir
> chanting in unison . . . gorged on human blood . . .
> lodged within its halls. I know the deeds of sin, ancient
> in story, of this house.

Despite the sunshine and the smiles of the guides, there is something nightmarish about Mycenae. Henry Miller was too scared to explore the underground tombs and he was right. Bad things have been done here. The Greeks understood that actions have consequences . . . and that we are implicated in the deeds of our forebears, however unfair that may seem. This place has been sucked dry by daemons.

Or maybe that's just me. I had come here with Alex, a couple of days before he left for London, and he seemed very happy scrambling about the ruins under the huge blue sky, peering into the black tombs, bounding up the cement pathways towards the heart of the palace where the House of Atreus once ruled. When King Agamemnon arrived back here, laden with loot from his war with Troy, including Cassandra the grief-stricken Trojan princess, now just another piece of booty, Queen Clytemnestra laid blood-red carpets and tapestries along these paths (which were not, of course, cement in those far-off days) so that his feet would never have to touch the ground until he was home in his royal palace, the great lord, but also so that he would know (without knowing) that he was about to be butchered like a hog in his bath by his smiling queen, tangled and trapped in her net (weighed down by the luxuriant robes he had taken from Troy), unable to fend off the furious knife that sent him down to Hades and:

he gasped away his life, and as he breathed forth quick spurts of blood, he struck me with dark drops of gory dew; while I rejoiced no less than the sown earth is gladdened in heaven's refreshing rain at the birthtime of the flower buds.

At least, that's how Clytemnestra told it, revenged at last for Agamemnon's sacrificial murder of their daughter, Iphigenia, whom he had killed on Artemis' altar ten years earlier, in order to lift the curse that was holding back the winds from taking his great fleet to Troy. Some say that he had insulted the goddess and that was the payment she required. Others thought that Iphigenia was turned into a deer at the last moment, just before the knife fell, and the girl was spirited away. Either way, Artemis wanted blood.

And so it went on. Murder and retribution, over and again, Clytemnestra killed by her son, although we are told that the curse was finally lifted in Athens, and the Furies (high on human blood, thirsty for more) were at last appeased and transformed into 'the Kindly Ones'. I think it's more likely that they left Athens and came back to Mycenae and eviscerated the place. If they're still here, perhaps we can bring Jeremy Clarkson over. He will be able to contemplate the rocky hillsides with the dead black trees (the charred remains of yet another forest fire, one that reached up to the walls this time, turbo-charged by our reckless burning of fossil fuels), and the Furies can feast on his liver. Prometheus at the Wheel. Oh, I know there are many more deserving candidates, and the rest of us are not far behind, but we have to start somewhere. Or find a better way of living.

Despite all this, Mycenae has power, and a rough and wild beauty, and there is huge weight in its stones, and to stand on the great citadel under the enormous sky, gazing out over corners of mauve cyclamen shivering in the high wind and the twisted black olive trees, and then over the walls towards a rolling cascade of valleys and mountains topped by the distant clouds, is breath-taking and enough to make anyone giddy with history and hubris. You can see why they lost all sense of proportion, the people who lived here, and those who came later, from Pausanias to Schliemann to Henry Miller, it gets to us all. Cyclopes and murders and Furies indeed. It doesn't make any difference if you know nothing about Agamemnon or the blood that flowed. For once, this is a place that carries its own atmosphere. Plato would understand. The daemons do not welcome us, and they only grudgingly share their home.

A short distance down the hill from ancient Mycenae is the more modern village (these things are relative), with its cluster of tourist-friendly tavernas and shops. There is even a hotel, La Belle Hélène, which is where Schliemann stayed the entire time he was digging up and dynamiting the archaeological site, busy making his own ruins. Since then, any number of famous people have stayed here, including Agatha Christie, Claude Debussy, Hermann Goering (followed some time later, separately, by Goebbels and Himmler; boy did those Nazis love ancient Greece – or their idea of ancient Greece), and Virginia and Leonard Woolf and Allen Ginsberg and J. K. Rowling. Henry Miller stayed at the Belle Hélène, and was taken up to the citadel by his friend, the poet Katsimbalis. The owner in those days was a man called Agamemnon, and apparently his descendant (of the same name) is now in charge, so I insist to Alex that we have to stop here for lunch, even though there is no one else on the terrace, and the neighbouring tavernas are all busy and light-hearted with grilled calamari and carafes of chilled rosé. A tall man with a tragic black moustache unpeels himself from his computer at the front desk and shuffles us over to a dusty table with a smudged white cloth overlooking the sun-scorched road, where the dogs scratch and bite at their sores.

There are four things available from the menu, apart from a family of flies, so we ask the man for chicken souvlaki and a Greek salad. We are on a mission to find the best of both that Greece has to offer, although it seems unlikely that we are going to locate them here. We listen to the man's footsteps echoing off into the empty hotel, heading for what must be a moribund kitchen, and I have a spasm of unease about the chicken. 'These glasses are a bit funky,' says Alex, holding up a tumbler that is apparently laden with the grimy fingerprints of one of the Agamemnons (who knows, perhaps the king's). A dog comes to rest its drooling jaws on my bare knee. The flies hop and buzz and twitch and rub their forelegs, getting ready for our meal.

In fact, the chicken is good and the salad is one of the best (Pausanias eat your heart out). The man settles in with us. I ask him about tourism, and he looks desperate. Everything is falling away, the season is almost over, and no one is coming to Mycenae any more. Just the French and the Germans. But he is pleased to hear that we are British and is eager to congratulate us on leaving the EU. 'You have done the right thing with your Brexit, my friend.'

'Well,' I bleat, 'it's probably just as bad out as well as in.' (Which is as far as I go, or ever go, when I can feel a storm building.) Alex has buried his face in the souvlaki.

The man glares at me, moustache on the rise. 'We have to be strong,' he says. 'Do you think we can't look after ourselves? What do you imagine we did before? Why are we so weak? The German banks run everything. You think they don't?' (And what do I know, in my London home, of what the Greeks have been through ever since the great crises of 2009 and beyond?)

He looks around the empty terrace, I'm not sure why, but he is suddenly furtive and a little bit agitated. 'Not the German people,' he qualifies, leaning closer, 'it's not them. They have no power. None of us have any power. It is the banks.

'And democracy? What is that? It is nothing. People don't understand who runs things.'

I raise a greasy glassful of Coke to him in a toast. I think he's right. About the power, that is. We don't have enough of it. Or we haven't learned to use what we have. That's more like it, probably. There is so much happening to us of which we are unaware, or it arrives with no warning. We never seem to be given the right questions, and there is never enough time to react, before the thing that we didn't ask for has become the thing that is. Just ask the Dancing Women of Vrisoules. I would have hoisted a quote from David Graeber at this moment, if I'd known it. Still, here we are, some months too late:

> The ultimate, hidden truth of the world is that it is something that we make, and could just as easily make differently.

'It is all about power,' was all I actually said, heading for safer ground, waving up the hill towards the ancient citadel. 'It is always about power.'

This inane comment seems to puncture him and he rises fast but with diminishing energy from the table, like a balloon let loose in a room, and finally settles over his computer, where I imagine he must be spending too much time on the wilder shores of the web. Aren't we all? I wanted to ask him about hope, of course I did, but I am not sure I could have stood the answer.

The narrow road from Corinth to Olympia is kept in very good condition and is absolutely terrifying. I have been skirting Mount Kyllini, where Tiresias struck the copulating snakes and was transformed into a woman (and then, years later, back into a man). The god Pan loved these mountains, and he enjoyed tormenting or teasing humans, especially when they were alone in the wild places, although I am surprised he can be bothered with me and my small, mildly asthmatic car. Our word 'panic' comes from the half-goat god, of course, and I find I am gripping the steering wheel with unusual force as we stutter around the hairpins and scrape along the frayed edges of the gorge. I am certain that Byron was spooked by the leering statue of Pan in the grounds of Newstead Abbey, but according to Plutarch, who heard it from an impeccable source, Pan is dead (breathing his last some time in the reign of the Emperor Tiberius, perhaps around 30 CE). Whether he was one of those gods that died and rose again (like Dionysus) is not known. Some say that he was the son of Hermes, purveyor of dreams, and of beautiful Penelope, who was banished by Odysseus when he found out she had been sleeping with one of the suitors, although most people prefer to believe Homer, when he described Penelope as the most faithful of all wives (and forgiving, too).

Mount Kyllini was the birthplace of Hermes. Arcadia was a rough and savage place in the Greek imagination. Wildly beautiful, yes, but also threatening, and nothing like the honeyed paradise of vines and shepherds that the Romans and all those neo-classical artists liked to describe or paint. A king lived here who thought it would be amusing to feed human flesh to the gods and was turned into a wolf, perhaps along with his fifty sons. And people used to make offerings to Lycaean Zeus (the wolfish god). If they ate human flesh at the sacrifice they would be transformed into wolves, only reverting if they did not taste any more humans for nine years. A werewolf cult. And in historical times there were lions, leopards, lynx, hyenas, jackals and bears, as well as the wolves, living in these heavily forested hills. And some time before the Mycenaean Empire reached its peak, there were equally fantastical creatures such as dwarf elephants and hippos, giant shrews, hedgehogs and dormice. Or so we're told. One thing we do know (although we are reluctant to face it) is that as humanity spreads, other animals die, the larger ones first, but it never stops there. Not chickens or sheep, of course (or not immediately), but most of the others. Perhaps the wolves will make their rightful comeback to these stark and lonely mountains. They only need to find a way along the isthmus.

I am travelling to Olympia via the Stymphalian Lake, which was the scene of Heracles' Sixth Labour. This was the one where he had to get rid of a host of murderous birds with bronze beaks that had been terrorising the neighbourhood, killing farm animals and eating the farmers and their families. They had toxic feathers that they could shed at will (like a storm of arrows) and they farted their rancid and fatal dung at anyone who threatened them. Heracles hid in a wood on a hill that overlooked the foul swamp where the birds lived and clashed the bronze castanets together that Hephaestus had made for him, and when the birds took to the air, shrieking their ghastly cries, he shot them with his poisoned arrows. Most of the birds died, but some escaped to attack Jason and his Argonauts (including Heracles) later when they were on their way to steal the golden fleece.

The winding road is empty and Alpine, emerald pines under a sapphire sky. Cold and clear and with almost no other cars to be seen (thank the gods), just the occasional lorry that creeps around the impossible corners and belches up the hills. I follow one for miles, at a safe distance, up and down, ears popping in the altitude. It is easier not to have to think about what might be coming next. Ben E. King's 'Stand By Me' has become lodged in my brain and the radio has lost all reception so I'm stuck with its addictive refrain. 'Stand By Me' I hum, my eyes open for a glimpse of Pan, the lyrics and the snagged tune rolling around my head, until I realise that I am chanting alone in my car that 'the mountains are held up by the trees', which I am certain are not the words that Ben E. King sang, but that's what it looks like to me on this lonely road and in fact, as Plato once told us, it also happens to be true.

I say that the road is in good condition, but there are probably more untended rock falls here than you would find on, say, the hyperactively cleansed highways of Switzerland. I am driving cautiously, and it is just as well because at one point I emerge from a blind corner and almost plough into an Arcadian shepherd and her flock of sheep. She ignores my apologetic waves from inside the bubble of my car and whistles and flicks her sheep around us and onwards. I have come part-way down the mountains and the sky has swelled to an immense blue, illumined by one faint paw-brush of cloud. The ground outside is hard from this endless summer and the grasses are a desiccated brown, but the trees – pine, poplars and spruce, the occasional oak and beech – are still so green, with just a flutter of early yellow from the aspen. I can hear a river chuckling nearby. With the windows down I inhale the warm air and watch the sheep shuffle past, their occasional deep bleats mingling with the aggrieved trilling of a robin from the top of a fence post. The ringing stillness after a long drive. The lake is not far now, but I stop anyway, and get out of the car to feel and breathe the peace of this Arcadian idyll. It is a fact, brought on by falling birth rates and the lure of the towns, that there are no longer enough Arcadian shepherds in this world.

A dragonfly zips by, skimming the earth, a quick hard flash of yellow and blue. It looks like a southern hawker, sleek, beautiful and voracious. If Byron were a winged insect, I reckon that's what he'd be, gorgeous to look at and always on the hunt. The gangly Shelley, on the other hand, would be a cranefly, purposeful, but blown in the wind. Keats is easy (in this round-up of Romantic Poets as Winged Insects which I seem to have embarked on): he's a mayfly, lovely and gone. Coleridge is the great diving beetle. So lithe and untouchable when young, and then in later life bumbling hypnotically from lake to pond, usually at night. Southey (hated by Byron) is a woodlouse, and flightless, like his poetry. While Wordsworth (but this is harder) is almost certainly the peacock butterfly, so drab on his rotting log, when all of a sudden he's tumbling into the air, borne aloft in a long, ragged dance of revelation and untouchable beauty.

Our ideas about what is heroic are never settled. The Greek heroes killed monsters, and Heracles was the greatest monster-killer of them all. Zeus knew he was going to need him one day to help defeat the giants, when they finally launched their assault on Mount Olympus. I never much cared for him when I first heard about his Labours, and most Greeks also seem to have been ambivalent. He is one-dimensional. A man of force, with no humour or wit, although he did manage to trick the Titan Atlas into shouldering the burden of the sky. ('Can you show me how it's done? You're so much better at it than me.') He killed his own children in a moment of madness, sent down by jealous Hera, which is why he was forced to work for King Eurystheus and carry out his labours, but you don't see that in the Disney film.

Heracles' character was essentially blank, and people (poets, playwrights, storytellers) could add onto it whatever they pleased. He existed to rid the world of monsters, and to clear the wild and the wilderness, which is why he was sent to slaughter lions and boars and bulls, and carry off giant stags, and to drain the marshes of the world. He was necessary, for a pastoral people who needed to hack back the wilderness and get rid of the animals that might eat their harvests and flocks, but he wasn't much liked, I don't think. They must have known they were losing something, even as they praised him for eliminating the outsized lions and boars and fabulous creatures that once slithered and stomped through the forests and swamps and that have now disappeared so completely it is almost as though they never existed. Or maybe that's wishful thinking . . . about their sense of regret, I mean. Because the slaughter's still going on, in every corner of the globe, without any help from Heracles. And all we are doing is following in his bloody wake, mopping up what is left.

Henry Miller, roaming around Greece, held this now very unfashionable idea about Nature.

> Nature can cure only when man recognises his place
> in the world, which is not in Nature, as with the
> animal, but in the human kingdom, the link between
> the natural and the divine.

An ancient Greek – living among nymphs and satyrs – would recognise the sentiment, as would a Christian or any other monotheist (although I'm nervous of speaking with any authority; sometimes it can seem like there were as many opinions in archaic and classical Greece as there were people). What I do know is that nowadays there are many who prefer to stress that there is no real division between us and the rest of Nature. We are all part of the same Darwinian family – and it is the false idea that we are somehow separate from Nature, or above it, but certainly not part of it, that is the cause of our alienation and epic destructiveness. And of course this much is true: it is absurd to think that we can somehow carry on as we are (fracking and looting and reaching out for more) without burning down our own home. It is urgent now. But surely it is also a good idea to recognise our own special role in the mayhem (climate chaos, mass extinctions, the dying rivers and seas), because how else are we going to learn to say 'no' to more of the things that we think we want but really don't need? How else are we going to set limits on our behaviour, or divert our energies into better channels?

These were gloomy thoughts to carry to the Stymphalian Lake, but I should mention that I was at this moment driving past verges laden with heartbreaking quantities of toxic litter and plastic rubbish. It was everything I found on Metamorfosi beach – and then some. Do the Greeks not care? It's really not that. Just look around, wherever you live, and you will see that it is the same (unless you happen to be living in Switzerland or Singapore, in which case, congratulations). A few days ago I spoke over Zoom to a man called Elias Tziritis, who works at protecting the forests of Greece for the WWF, and he told me that 'in Greece we don't respect public goods. The Tragedy of the Commons is real here.' In other words, no one cares enough about what is shared. Individualism has triumphed. Like so many people I spoke to about these things, Elias then started laughing.

'Who is going to say that they hate the environment?' he asked me. 'No one! But here we are.'

Perhaps laughter is the right response (the initiates of Eleusis certainly thought so), but we also need mundane, everyday things like laws and regulations and governments that can help us change our behaviour. If we know what Arcadia can look like, why are we settling for less? Live well, said Plato, and cherish what is beautiful.

I was expecting the Stymphalian Lake to be a poisonous swamp, but it is nothing of the sort. It is Arcadia. There are very few birds, it has to be said, at least not at this time of day or year, in the shimmering, mid-afternoon heat of early autumn. There are some high-pitched bird calls from the high reeds (that stretch so far over the lake that I cannot see where it begins or ends). A low rocky hill follows the edge of the lake, starting from where I parked my car at the end of a twisting dirt track, and in the other direction there are a few knee-high walls, all that is left of the town of Stymphalus. There was a theatre here long ago, and a temple to Artemis that was described by Pausanias. He said that you could see images of the famous birds under the roof of the temple and statues in white stone of young girls with the legs of birds. These days the lake is famous for its many frogs, which are eaten in season by thousands of water snakes. I decide to keep to the high ground.

A man is circling a herd of goats on the flatlands towards the distant hills. There must be about five hundred of them, of every shade of brown and black, some white ones too, being harried by the man and his dogs. Mostly they just stand and stare at him, at other times they break into a jog, ears flapping, bells ringing hollow and loud, not always in the direction he'd planned, so he shrieks and calls and strides after them. He is as nimble as any of the goats and is carrying a long straight stick with a bright metal tip. Sometimes he whistles, high and looping, although I am not sure what the goats make of this. He is wearing a faded green baseball cap and carrying a machine which is playing some kind of Middle Eastern or perhaps Bengali music. He is so fast and lithe and he keeps popping up in unexpected places, behind lone olive trees or at the top of the low hills. At one point I look up and see him standing above me, about fifty metres away, silhouetted against the blue sky, hand on his hip and leaning on his crook, the fir-clad hills behind him (from where Heracles once shot at the birds). We smile at each other shyly from under our caps.

'Hello! Where are you from?' he shouts in English, starting athletically down the hill.

'London,' I half-shout (he's getting closer). 'Britain.'

'Oh, I assumed you were German,' he says, arriving at my side.

The goat-herd, it turns out, is originally from Persepolis in Iran (that explains the music), and he is a Christian who fled persecution. He's about thirty years old and has a close black beard and a beautiful smile. He was a computer engineer before he left, and knew nothing about goats, back in Persepolis, never even met one, he says, and now here he is, loping expertly in the fields. He's been here about two years 'but it won't be forever. I want to move on. I prefer computers to goats.' One less Arcadian shepherd.

I ask if people have welcomed him here and he gives me a huge smile. They have been so friendly, he says, finding him somewhere to stay, getting him this job. 'That's amazing,' I say, 'that they should welcome you in like this. Not everyone has such happy stories.' I am thinking wistfully of the ancient Greek belief in *xenia*, the 'guest-friendship' of the epic poems, when any stranger, however ragged or needful, would be led to a table or a chair by the fire, given food and wine, and no questions asked until they were comfortable. At least, that's how Homer tells it.

'Oh, not everyone was pleased to see me,' he says, the smile wavering just a little. 'About half of them were. Fifty per cent.'

'I'd say that figure would be the same just about anywhere in the world,' I reply. 'Or not nearly so high. In fact, in my country it would be forty-eight per cent.' Smiling, as my incomprehensible joke falls to the stony ground.

We talk about his family in Persepolis and how he longs to see them (and how they would like to get out and worship freely). How he can't go back. We talk about Athens and London and the world's need for computer engineers. We talk about goats.

'And how about you,' I say, 'are you happy when you think about the future? Has this been a good thing for you?' (His incredible journey. His improbable life in this remote and random part of Greece.) 'Do you have hope?' Because his smile is so warm and his eyes are so kind and wise and he has come such a long way with such inexhaustible energy, I am certain that he will have something that is worth hearing.

'Hope?' he says. 'I see. Hope. Yes . . . of course. Hope.' He seems stuck on the word.

And then: 'I'm sorry, I have to go look after the goats, they are moving again.'

And he was off, up and away and over the nearest hill.

With Iran and Persia on my mind, I set off again for Olympia. Thinking about it, I am not sure I heard the herdsman right when he said he was from 'Persepolis'. For some reason it strikes me as unlikely that he grew up living among the ruins of the capital of the old Persian Empire, although there is absolutely no reason why he shouldn't. Someone has to, after all. It's just that the name is so redolent, and in my mind what is left there is no more than a jumble of fallen walls and toppled statues and (bear with me) the shattered head of Ozymandias. Alexander the Great reached the city in 330 BCE, having defeated Darius, the last Persian emperor, and not long afterwards the whole place was burned to the ground, perhaps by accident, maybe on his orders, and it never recovered, although the last few remaining standing columns and walkways look sumptuous on Google Earth.

War was a constant in the ancient world. It is possible that the Greeks were especially fractious (that was certainly their reputation), but I am not sure the facts bear this out. They seem to have resented Ares, their god of war, or worshipped him grudgingly or fearfully and only when necessary; it was the Romans who changed his name to Mars and set him high above almost all the others. Even so, we have all been steeped in Greek battles, the warriors and their gleaming armour. Troy.

Agamemnon. Achilles and Ajax. The invasions of the Persian Empire, the three hundred at the pass at Thermopylae, Marathon, Salamis and Plataea. Macedonia and Alexander. The Greek cities and their incessant wars against each other: Thebans versus Athenians, Athenians versus Spartans, Spartans versus Thebans. Corinthians, Spartans, Macedonians, Cretans, Argives, Euboeans and Arcadians, all at war.

Every city had its part-time army and its famous battles. They may have entered alliances, but they never united as a whole, at least not in ancient times, not even when the Persians invaded. Very much later, after the world had been remade many times, large numbers of Greeks came together (with mutual suspicion) to declare independence from the Ottoman Empire on 25 March 1821, and after a nine-year bloodbath, the country was recognised as an independent state in 1830. The history of unity since those times has also been a little, shall we say, patchy; although this fact is usually over-emphasised by outsiders who manage to forget the incessant divisions in their own riven countries.

Driving through these narrow valleys, through high passes and deep gorges, with the mountains looming above, it is easy to see why a larger unity of the Greek-speaking peoples proved elusive. The fragmented terrain is said to be why the ancient Greek style of fighting evolved, and why they spent so much time at sea, and why their main foodstuffs were olives and fish, and why when the population grew they left to form colonies in other, less aggravating landscapes. It is why so many of their cities kept their autonomy, even though they were built so close to one another (it is just a day's walk from Thebes to Athens).

And it is why it is taking me most of the day to travel from Corinth to Olympia, a journey of under two hundred kilometres across the Peloponnese, although I do realise I have taken the scenic route.

The Greek style of fighting was swift, brutal and bloody. It horrified foreigners who witnessed the slaughter, and who were more used to battles that left lighter casualties, even for the losers. In the age of Mycenae and Troy, the Greeks fought as individuals, one hero against another, riding up in their chariots to do battle, wheeling away. But the Greeks of the classical age fought as heavily armoured infantry, the hoplites, packed into a tight phalanx of men. Shields on their left arms and to the front; shins and torsos covered in metal; their heads encased by their heavy bronze helmets, so that all they could see was a narrow band ahead of them, chins to their chests, sweat in their eyes. The men at the front held out long iron-tipped spears, and the men in the rows behind pushed theirs through, a nightmarish vision of slicing metal, like you might see in an industrialised abattoir, if you could bring yourself to look. They were vulnerable from the side, especially on the right where they had no shields. But they lined up in their tight valley passes or on the narrow plains, and they pressed forward together, pushing and hacking and gouging, hundreds or sometimes thousands of men, more stepping up when the ones at the front fell, until one or the other lines gave way and the heavier, more relentless side, with its armour and blades, broke and rolled over its victims, or got at them from the side or even behind, trampling, stabbing and spearing, into the vulnerable inner thighs or throats or eyes, blood and entrails everywhere. When the great Persian army met the Athenians at the Battle of Marathon, they did not understand that their vastly superior numbers and thousands of archers would count for nothing once the Athenian juggernaut started to roll . . . and then *run* towards them, that vast weight of men and metal, smashing through the Persian wicker shields, through their padded jerkins, on and on, the lightly armed infantry on the Persian wings, the so-called Immortals in the centre, all of them pulverised by this monstrous lumbering armoured killing machine.

Alexander the Great and his father Philip adapted the phalanx, adding more cavalry to their armies to protect the flanks. And Alexander trained his men to attack at an angle, rolling up their opponents, tipping them off balance. He was never defeated and the essential formula never changed: a tight-knit band of citizens, called to war – farmers, merchants, potters and shopkeepers – knowing that if one of them fell, they would be replaced by another. If one of them broke, or left the line, they would put the lives of the rest in danger. It was brutal – terrifying – but it was a pure expression of community. And it was ancient knowledge, this absolute reliance on each other. The understanding that they had to work together, or fall together.

It is a simple idea, and an irresistible analogy for the importance of collectivism over individualism. We stand firm. We hold the line. Nothing is impossible if we only stick together. We can turn the tide of destructive consumerism . . . and reverse every one of the threats to our planet and its species. But only by working as one. Join us. And lock shields! Sadly, just 150 years after Alexander had ridden in triumph into Persepolis at the head of his unconquerable army, his successor in Macedonia, King Perseus, watched and then fled as his impregnable phalanxes were turned and obliterated by the altogether more nimble and single-minded Romans. So. The analogy doesn't work every time . . . but David Graeber was still right. We need to remember how much power we can wield.

EIGHT

Fun and Games

'Who knows, but that God, who made the world,
may cause that Giant Despair may die.'

JOHN BUNYAN, *THE PILGRIM'S PROGRESS*

I arrived in Olympia late one night, and ended up staying a few days. It was easy to do. David Stuttard in his Pausanian-esque book *Greek Mythology: A Traveller's Guide* calls it the 'most magical of places'; and Pausanias himself confirms it:

> Many are the sights to be seen in Greece, and many are the wonders to be heard; but on nothing does Heaven bestow more care than on the Eleusinian rites [yep!] and the Olympic games.

On the first night in my out-of-town hotel I dreamed (#6) that I was standing in a sunlit field, up to my knees in poppies, corn-flowers, ox-eye daisies and lush meadow grasses, playing musi-cal chairs or something slightly more complicated involving buckets and coloured sponges with a group of white-robed men and women, one of whom was Lord Byron. I didn't get a good look at him, but I knew he was there. Everyone drifted away into the hedgerows and I was left with a feeling of missed opportunities. I am not sure these dreams are helping anyone, certainly not me, but I can't seem to hold onto them. On the other hand, I am through Netflix's *Barbarians* and am embarked on the violent, conspiracy-laden, deadly pandemic series *Utopia*. Are we really going to amuse ourselves to death? It seems as though we are.

In the morning the skies were a thick grey and it was raining a soft rain. (Welcome back, Persephone, you have been missed.) It was early, but I was surprised, even affronted, to find that there were already at least seven other tourists ahead of me at the site of the ancient Games. They soon evaporated in the ruins, though, leaving me standing alone in front of all that is left of the temple of Hera: three decaying grey columns, the slabbed floor, a low wall or two and a line of lichen-smeared stone stumps. The Queen of the Gods was worshipped here long before Zeus and the other immortals arrived.

Perhaps it was something about the site, or the alignment of the remnants of the building, or my meagre breakfast, but all of a sudden I decided that I could feel the faintest breath of the goddess's presence. I am sorry to spring this out of the blue (I know it sounds intense), but at that moment it became at least a possibility that Hera was present, and that she is the one, ahead of all the rest, to whom I should be paying the most attention. And if I had been living 2,500 years ago, I might also have hoped that she would follow my interests more closely than the others, although that would have been presumptuous.

I have been nursing the idea that every one of us has a god or goddess to whom we are most linked. With Byron I thought it might be Hephaestus, although Apollo and Dionysus are other, more obvious choices. And now Hera has appeared. I don't know . . . I realise she is best known for her watchful jealousies and vendettas. That the gorgeous peacock is her bird. That her efforts to restrain Zeus were often presented as comic and her marriage was a source of misery and pain. But still, I feel drawn to her. Maybe it is because she hated Heracles. And she watched over Jason when he gathered his Argonauts and went to steal the golden fleece.

In the 1963 film *Jason and the Argonauts*, the one with the terrifying skeleton soldiers brought jerkily to life by the peerless Ray Harryhausen, she haunts the boat on a beam of oak from the sacred shrine at Dodona, and she whispers with Jason about his worries and plans, both of them somehow imagining that the rest of the crew cannot see them talking. She is majestic and powerful, and (in the film) colourful, too, an idea which was surely ahead of its time. We all now know that the surviving white temples, columns and statues of classical Greece once glittered and blazed with rich paint and gemstones, ivory, silver and gold (and, for that matter, that worshippers shouted and sang and danced to a wild beat), but this has been a relatively recent revelation for most of us. Anyway. It is probably best to walk away from the unsettling idea (and the temple where it started) that the gods may still be watching us. At least, that is what I did. I have been alone on this trip for too long – untethered – and am starting to babble.

Zeus arrived at Olympia some time after his wife, and tiresomely outdid her with the size and splendour of his temple. One of the wonders of the ancient world was kept here, the statue of Zeus that was made by the fifth-century sculptor Pheidias in a custom-built workshop next door to the temple and whose ruins you can stand in today, washed by the autumn rain. The statue was chryselephantine, a word I am relishing, meaning it was made from gold and oiled ivory, not to mention every kind of precious metal, gems, ebony and colourful ribbons. The Romans tried to cart it off not too long after they arrived, but the statue groaned in protest, so they left it alone a while longer, before taking it to Constantinople, where it disappeared in a palace fire. Pausanias describes this wondrous creation in awestruck detail, narrating the legends that were illustrated on its vast bulk, although he must be right to say that a mere list of its dimensions cannot give any true sense of the 'impression this statue has created in those who see it'. Not unlike Lord Byron's beauty.

It is said that Cronus was still king in heaven when the first Games were held, and the people of the golden age (who never had to work to feed themselves) were the earliest contestants. And then when Zeus overthrew Cronus, the gods held a Games in celebration, shining Apollo outrunning swift-footed Hermes to win the races and then overwhelming the brute Ares in the boxing. Zeus was everywhere. There were altars to Zeus the God of War and Zeus of the Thunderbolt, Purifying Zeus, Courtyard Zeus and Underworld Zeus, even Zeus of the Flies – a Zeus for every occasion. I wonder if at some point people got tired of having so many gods and decided it would be less confusing to have only one. Or did the gods get bored of us? There is something exhilarating about this teeming multitude of immortals. A god for all seasons. Even a different version or aspect of every god, to be worshipped or placated or entreated for favours. Did it mean that the ancients had more flexible or nimble minds than we do, or stretchier notions of what might be possible or allowed? Or were they lost in a fog of anxiety and superstition, worrying that they had neglected to honour Artemis or Pan or Ares? Did most of them, in the end, welcome the certainty of the written word and a single deity?

Heracles, the man-who-became-a-god, was everywhere in ancient Olympia. He is said to have re-started the Games and went on to win all the events himself. The other omnipresent beings on this trip around Greece are the three Germans I met on the beach at Poros. Here they are, sheathed in long raincoats, shielded by baseball caps from the drizzle, almost unrecognisable with their clothes on. A damp wind is blowing through the drifts of cyclamen and the late leaves on the many oak trees (Zeus' tree) that are rooted among the ruins. I am keen to get to the Oracle at Dodona, across the Gulf of Patras in the northwest of the country, because Zeus used to reveal his truths through the whisperings of the leaves of a great oak there, and although that first sacred tree is long gone, there may be someone who can help me find another so that I can ask about hope. It might not be possible. There is a rising tide of news from home of threatened lockdowns and closures, also here in less grievously affected Greece, and our horizons are shrinking. Even in this holy sanctuary, and after our friendly words on the beach at Poros, the Germans and I are circling each other warily, still smiling (I think), but at a distance, and from behind our masks. One of them steps too close to Hera's altar and a guide emits a shrieking double whistle-blast, like an enraged gym teacher scolding a daydreaming child, and the Germans scuttle away.

There were many laws associated with the ancient Olympics, some of which we might want to think about adopting. For instance, there's the one that stipulated that all trainers had to enter the stadium naked. This had been the law ever since the time a mother had trained one of the athletes. He won his race and in her joy she hurtled down the stands and onto the track and revealed – shock – that she was a woman. The male athletes all competed naked anyway (apart from the charioteers), but women had their own running race and ceremonies and perhaps other competitive events in honour of Hera, at least as old as those of the men, and were forbidden from attending the male Games. I am not sure if men could watch the women compete, although I doubt it. They ran, says Pausanias, eager to fill in the details, with 'their tunics rather above their knees, and the right breast and shoulder bared'.

The first athlete to cheat at the Games was a man called Eupolos and that didn't happen until the ninety-eighth Olympics. He bribed the other boxers to throw their matches, and every one of them was fined. Until that time, the Games had been cheat-free. The next scandal was in the 112th Olympics, a full fifty-six years later (life comes at us faster these days), when an Athenian pentathlete called Kallippos bought off his opponents. The Athenians refused to pay his fine, but stumped up when they heard that the Oracle of Delphi was not going to answer any more of their questions until they did.

The punishment (and this is something we should most certainly consider) was that the cheats had to pay for a statue of Zeus to be displayed at the entrance to the athletics stadium, with their names and their crimes written indelibly underneath. It is how we know who they were. Their infamy lives on, like the all-in fighter called Sarapion at the 201st Olympics who ran away the day before his event and was 'the only Egyptian and in fact the only man ever to be fined for cowardice'. Hey ho. But the wrestling must have been terrifying, an oiled and naked fight to the end with almost no rules, kicking and punching, squeezing, crushing and clawing, but remember, no biting, eye-gouging or finger-breaking.

The sun came out as I walked down the tunnel and into the stadium. It is a good place to fantasise about sporting glory, even now (I mean both its age and mine). The Emperor Nero lived the dream by taking part in the Olympics in the year 67 CE and he had an absolute blast, winning all his races by day and strumming his victory lyre at night. Strolling down the narrow, walled walkway, with its one surviving (or reconstructed) stone arch, that leads into the wide stadium, is incredibly moving, especially when you think back to how many have come this way, tense and ready for the race or the fight. This morning, there are three young men lined up at the start, about to launch their own 100-metre sprint (dressed in hoodies, long shorts and hiking boots), but otherwise the stadium is empty and even, perhaps, as it once was, a low oval bowl of sloping banks and soft grass, adorned with white autumn crocuses and yellow buttercups, spread out under a grey sky now making way for the blue. Seven tall cypress trees fill one corner on the far side, and beyond them there are hills of scrub and olives and oak. It is quiet here, behind the victory whoops of the men. An absence of clatter. Remote from the world. And somehow the grass has turned thick and lush and dark green overnight.

Endymion is buried here, in the corner of the stadium by the entrance. He was a beautiful and powerful king. The goddess of the moon, Selene, fell in love with him and they had fifty daughters together. Zeus had told him he could choose his own fate, so he asked to be allowed to sleep forever, keeping his beauty and his youth, and that is what happened; he dreamed away the years in a cave on Mount Latmus, which is not far from here (unless it's the one in Texas), and Selene visited him at night, especially when she was full, and gazed at him in wonder, or sometimes she woke him up so they could make more daughters (he must have been put to sleep when he was still young and before they had all been conceived). That's one story, although it doesn't explain why he is buried here, unless he'd had enough of being woken to make babies by the lovely but insatiable silvery moon and he begged Zeus to put an end to the business. Others don't mention Selene at all and say that Endymion was invited by Zeus to visit Mount Olympus and that's where he saw Hera, who was drifting around in the shape of a cloud, and he made a clumsy pass at the radiant mother of the gods, and was sent straight down to

Hades (perhaps leaving his body in this corner of the Olympic stadium). Either way, this is what Keats had to say about the matter:

> A thing of beauty is a joy for ever:
> Its loveliness increases; it will never
> Pass into nothingness; but still will keep
> A bower quiet for us, and a sleep
> Full of sweet dreams

Although you cannot always count on the dreams.

One of the many differences between us and the ancient Greeks (and I am talking about a core difference here, a fundamental, tectonic, non-alignment of our ways of thinking) is that they could expect stability. I know, this sounds wrong, because after all they were taught that the Ages were on the turn and that time was moving ever onwards. They knew that they might wake up one morning a slave, or that their city could be all but wiped out by a plague. That empires would rise and fleets would be lost at sea. So many of them died young (although if they survived childhood and wars and childbirth they could expect to live as long as us), and it must have seemed that there were things over the horizon which they could never know or would not ever be able to explain. They knew in theory that everything changes. But I am still guessing that they believed that the essentials of their lives (and the lives of the people around them)

would be no different from the day they were born to the day they died, and that they would hand the reins to their children, and their grandchildren, and on to the end of the Age of Iron and the arrival of the grey-templed babies (which they had probably not heard about anyway). Life would carry on, much as it always had. Harvests and worship. Wars, gossip and love. The same old plough and village tree and sometimes a new rug on the bed.

And here we are. With the sun out, I went to sit in the large empty courtyard of a shop and its café near the Olympia Museum. There was no one else, just me relishing the quiet, and the three people who worked there, no doubt wishing for more custom. Two of them (a woman and her mother, I guessed) sat at a table nearby and made dream catchers and friendship bracelets, which they hung on the already heavy displays at the door and inside the dark but spacious shop, which was itself also overflowing with perfectly aligned rows of miniature Greek vases, statues and fridge magnets, jewellery, honey, scarves, puzzles and plastic toys. A shop of wonder and plenty. It was so beautifully done, with such care and love, and the people were so kind and friendly, the Greek music playing in the empty aisles, so of course I bought something. (Some silver and turquoise earrings, made by 'a Greek lady', I was told. 'But don't buy those,' the husband added, pointing to the horizon-less rows of ancient-Greek-themed objects, lined up to perfection, some of them identical to the earrings I had just bought, 'they're from China. They copy everything.')

So I returned to my table with its waiting Greek salad and put aside my Pausanias and opened my phone and checked into the news from home and abroad (which I had been trying not to do), and I read about how our world is going to end. And on the day I am writing this (but it could have been any day), another report arrived in the media, from yet another group of agitated scientists.* Or Cassandras, as they are sometimes now called, after the Trojan priestess who was given the power of prophecy by Apollo, except that when she refused to become his lover he changed his gift, so that she would always tell the truth but would never be believed. She was the one who screamed at the people of Troy not to drag the giant wooden horse into their city and was pushed to one side as everyone celebrated the end of the traumatising ten-year war. No one likes a killjoy. She ended up in Mycenae, her family dead, the slave of Agamemnon, murdered by his wife.

The cold truth, the report says, is that we are on the brink of 'a ghastly future of mass extinction, declining health and climate-disruption upheavals' that threaten human survival. So. All of us – even the scientists who are working in these fields – are struggling to understand this core fact, that *we* are the cause of a collapse of biodiversity, and that the earth's ability to support complex life may not survive. We don't have the political systems to cope with this knowledge, and we don't have the time or maybe the attention span, and in fact as things get worse it is going to become even harder to pull together to find a solution. There are many who are working hard to stop us from seeing this.

---

* Bradshaw, *et al.*, 'Underestimating the challenges'.

The headings alone are chilling: 'Biodiversity Loss'; 'Sixth Mass Extinction'; 'Ecological Overshoot: Population Size and Overconsumption'; 'Failed International Goals and Prospects for the Future'; 'Climate Disruption'; 'Political Impotence' . . .

And the report winds to its weary conclusion:

> Given the existence of a human 'optimism bias' that triggers some to underestimate the severity of a crisis and ignore expert warnings, a good communication strategy must ideally undercut this bias without inducing disproportionate feelings of fear and despair.

In other words, as Nietzsche once wrote, it is HOPE that is going to kill us. Zeus' punishment, the last and cruellest of them all. Of course, this may be what all humans have always thought, that they are living on the edge of the apocalypse, but I don't believe it. I think this deep knowledge of imminent ecological collapse is something new, and we cannot bring ourselves to look it in the face . . . but it seems that I (like you) also suffer from 'optimism bias'. Because why else would we carry on doing the things that we do?

Perhaps it is time to stop looking for hope.

This is not a thought I can sustain for long (which kind of confirms the point). Anna was very happy to receive the earrings. The morning after I had spent a day dreaming of victory in the Olympic stadium, and marvelling at the statues in

the museum, and prostrated by despair in a local café, I set off
for a day's hiking in the Forest of Foloi. I was heading first for
some kind of environmental or learning centre on the edge of
the forest, which a blog I had found recommended as the best
place from which to start a long hike through the gorges and
wooded hills (I would find maps and guides and useful leaflets
about the local flora and fauna), but on the way I took a wrong
turning and followed a sign to the village of Foloi and found
myself in a small square with the inevitable dead or sleeping
dog and bushels of bougainvillea and a couple of old men who
stared at me from the dusty terrace of a bar with an early glass
of retsina in their hands.

I asked them the way to the 'environmental centre', heaven
help me, but they didn't speak any English (or not that kind of
English), and pointed me towards a young, plump, lushly
bearded priest standing by the small church, who was super-
vising the erection of some wooden scaffolding. The priest
was very friendly, but regretfully let it be known through signs
and smiles that he didn't know what I was talking about. I
gave up on my 'environmental centre' and tried the words
'learning' and 'teach' and even 'museum', which led to a
flurry of arm-waving and a few simple words for slow foreigners ('*sosta*', 'yes!', '*aristera*'), and so I headed back to my car
parked in the dusty square, with the priest following (looking,
in retrospect, rather surprised), and I set off, the old men staring, and after only about a hundred metres I arrived at the
front of the village school, which I now realised was where he
had been trying to send me. It was closed, though, and when
I looked in my rear-view mirror, there was the priest, huffing

towards me along the street, smiling and waving at the boarded-up school and flourishing an enthusiastic thumbs-up. I gave the horn a short, apologetic 'toot' (into which I think I also managed to inject a symphony of gratitude, sorrow and regret) and I drove away.

Some time later, I found my 'environmental centre', a small wooden shack set back from the road in a straggle of oak trees. It was also closed, but that didn't matter because I had my phone with its GPS and I just wanted to get walking, I didn't care where, so long as it involved a cool river and a shaded bank. The day was already very hot.

The Forest of Foloi is one of the largest old-growth beech and oak forests in Greece, and once upon a time it was home to the centaur Pholus (hence its name), who was a great friend of Heracles. Centaurs were men with the hindquarters of a horse (or horses with the heads and torsos of men), and the Greeks regarded them with suspicion and fear. They were primitive and prone to violence and you would regret letting them anywhere near your wine stores. Mary Renault rather surprisingly portrays them in her second Theseus book as a lost tribe of horse-riding Neanderthals. One of them, Cheiron, was unusually civilised and intelligent, and he was the centaur who educated Achilles and Asclepius and many of the other heroes, and brought them up on the wild slopes of Mount Pelion, nourishing their understanding of nature, before they headed off to slay monsters or heal the world. Pholus was the only other centaur you could trust, and one time when Heracles was on his way to capture the terrifying Erymanthian Boar, he stopped for a meal with Pholus in his cave, and the other centaurs got wind of the wine they were drinking and a fight broke out, and Heracles killed most of them with his poisoned arrows (dripping with the blood of the Hydra) and the survivors fled south to Cape Malea, but Pholus (who was kind but also maybe a little bit dim) picked up one of the arrows and dropped it on his foot and died in agony. One more magical creature extinguished.

So obviously I am not expecting to meet a centaur (if they're anywhere, they're in Malea), but I thought I might see some signs of a boar. Erymanthia is just north of here, connected by the sprawling forest. And there are also eagles (sacred to Zeus), owls (Athena), vipers and rat snakes (Hermes), doves and sparrows (Aphrodite), crows (Apollo), goats of course (Pan and Dionysus) and howling dogs (Hekate), but no peacocks for Hera. There are also pine martens, hares, weasels, foxes, skylarks, squirrels and badgers, and the acorns from the ancient oaks draw in a teeming mass of birds and mammals, and the foliage and the fungi seethe with insect life.

It is the very end of October. Inside the woods, what human noise there was has vanished, the cars silenced on the faraway road, and I am alone with the shrill chirping of the robins, a slight wind stirring the oak leaves, and the distant complaint of goats and the hollow dongle of their bells, somewhere out there in the hidden forest. There are times when, heading down the hill, I leave the tree cover and join a wide, red earth path, baked dry and powdery in the sun. Fat bees drift by, nosing at the thyme. The smell of herbs and yesterday's rain in the sunshine is intoxicating and my mighty hike has already dissolved into a languid, summer's day stroll. I find a few shreds of snakeskin and stop altogether and stare at them. I have only been walking about twenty minutes. I am in a clearing at the top of a high gorge, the river far below, way down over the green of the trees, mostly oaks – Hungarian and holm – snared with ivy and the tangled cotton heads of old man's beard, but there are groves of olive trees too, kept clear for the harvest.

Anyway, what with the bees in the thyme, and the butterflies on the sage, and the lizards crouched on their red rocks, progress is desperately slow. And then there's the sound of falling water . . . and the views, honestly the views, there is nothing to see except for the tops of trees, radiating a livid green, streaked darker by the holm oaks, and the valley moulded into a deep 'V', from the high hills on either side down to the invisible river, which weaves a shadow through the distant canopy, and sometimes there's a cleft of red or light-brown rock, where the soil has slipped, and then straight ahead, up to the pale, far-off mountains, there is still more forest, and more trees, and only the very tips of the mountains are bare, tickling a couple of clouds in the blue ecstatic sky.

I sit down on a smooth rock next to a small bush of sweet marjoram and give up on the very idea of a walk. It is too hot and everything is too beautiful and the warm embrace of the herb is drugging. Marjoram was created by the smiling goddess Aphrodite as a symbol of good luck. Just behind the marjoram there is a myrtle bush, with its dark-green, spear-shaped leaves and pale purple berries, some of them already turning a pure midnight black. People say that this was also Aphrodite's favourite bush, a symbol of love and innocence.

According to Pausanias, the first king of Pisa in the Peloponnese (Pelops was his name) brought myrtle here from Asia Minor. That would have been before he was said to have founded the Olympic Games, although it can't have been him as well as Zeus, Cronus *and* Heracles. He'll have to get in line. What we do know is that he murdered his father-in-law in order to marry his wife. No, that's Oedipus . . . almost. What we can say is that he murdered his father-in-law in order to marry his father-in-law's daughter, who then became his wife. It is very hot here on this rock, and so very peaceful, and I am sure that's a skylark riding high in the blue. But he did this by bribing a servant to put wax lynch-pins on the wheels of his father-in-law's chariot and then he threw golden apples to the monster with one hundred eyes who . . .

My reverie (drifting on the margins of a mid-morning snooze) is torn into by the loud revving of an engine somewhere up the track and coming from the deep forest. I snap awake, on instant alert. I have been reading a great deal recently about the bandits of Greece, who were widespread and deadly in the time of Lord Byron, and even more so one hundred years earlier, when the first French and British travellers were sometimes held to ransom or murdered in the pursuit of antiquities. I never know whether I am welcome when I am walking outside Britain. It is true that Greece has a great deal of public land (no one knows how much), but I feel safer following a Public Footpath sign. Of course, far too much of Britain's land is private and concentrated in too few hands, but that is another story.

Walking in the US is even edgier. Never leave the path, is my advice, or even get out of the car. Their land is privatised and they harbour a visceral sense of ownership, sometimes with guns. A friend once strayed a few metres from a public beach to scramble on some rocks (the tragedy of the notion that beaches can be private), and he was followed by a coast-guard boat, rocking just offshore in a slight swell. 'Sir,' an officer crackled through his megaphone, 'step away from the rocks.' And I once had a shotgun pulled on me by a man in a pickup by the side of a small lake somewhere in rural Kansas. The memory has come back, hard and sharp, now that I can hear that the engine in the woods just up the hill from where I am standing belongs to a jeep or a van and that it is crunching down the track towards me. A vanful of Greek brigands. Who else can it be?

The Kansas Incident happened a lifetime ago. I was with a couple of friends and we were looking for somewhere to sleep in the back of our car, so it seemed ideal when we saw a small lake, fringed with reeds and aspen, a hundred metres off the main road. We were very young and had no idea that the citizens of the US are prepared to kill to protect their property from marauding Europeans. In fact, we had only been there about ten minutes when the pickup arrived, and a man in a brown baseball cap wound down his window and asked us what the hell we were doing. 'Oh, I'm sorry,' I brayed, thinking this would soothe the situation, but sounding horrifically like Bertie Wooster, 'oh, I'm sorry, but we're from London, you see, London, England, and we thought it would be OK.' The man produced his gun and pointed it in my face. I could have counted the hairs of the stubble on his chin, he was that close. 'Just walk on out, boy,' he said, and spat on the ground at my feet. And now, over thirty years later, this memory is speeding me down the hill, with the pickup revving closer, still hidden from view behind the trees, and I'm sure I can hear the good ol' boys whooping in the back, high on moonshine, cocking their guns, closing in on their soft city prey, the plot of *Deliverance* unfolding in the remote Arcadian forest.

The track went into a hairpin and I hurried from it in a spray of dust and grit onto a narrow path and watched from behind a tree as a red tractor trundled past me down the hill, a couple of young men sitting in a trailer at the back, rolling around in a heap of olives from the harvest. I half-emerged from my tree and they smiled and waved, happy to be working in such faultless weather in this perfectly beautiful place.

And so I carried on down the hill, through olive groves and myrtle, no longer on any path, and at last I was at the bottom of the gorge, in a meadow by the side of the river, and it was like it was spring all over again, there were so many flowers, just daisies and yellow dandelions, but butterflies too, rising and settling in the sunlight. They had no right to be here so late in the year. I had walked into Narnia after the snows melted. It is here, the Elysian fields. And the sun was so hot in the fragile blue sky, but that was fine, I was walking through long grasses, shaded by olive trees and tall poplars, breathing deep of the cool, fast, glittering river. A frog leaped from under my feet and soared ten feet into a small pool.

I yearned to be in that river. The current was fast, and most of the time the banks were steep and slippery with a light-brown mud, but there was one stretch where the river swung round and widened, with olive trees growing close to the sides, and there was an easy path down to the water's edge. There were large flat stones to sit on, and small black birds dipping in the river, which slowed here to an easy flow. Sunlight freckled the surface. There would never be a more perfect place to sit and drift my feet in the cooling waters and watch all the detritus of the world pass by.

So of course I carried on. I don't know why, but perhaps I thought there would be other places, just as good, maybe better, and I had remembered that I was on a long hike, and although it wasn't late, I had come a long way down into this gorge. There was a village downriver, I had read about it in the blog I had found, and seen it on the map (even though my phone no longer had any reception) and I wanted to get there. It had a bridge that was 'well worth seeing'. I left the most perfect place I would ever find in the dream-like Elysian fields, and followed the racing river, but for some reason, I don't know how, the path (which was sometimes not even a path) edged me away from where I wanted to be, and the woods grew thicker, and the hills steeper, and although I tried to turn down to the river, or even thought about turning around (but I had now come too far, and who ever wants to go back?), the clefts in the hills and the thick woods took me further away and there came a moment, in a clearing in the trees, when I looked down the hill and saw that the river was already far below, and although I told myself I would get back to it, and there would still come a time when I would drift my feet in its cooling waters, I just could not seem to find the way.

I arrived at a wide earth track, baked red in the sun, no doubt used by the olive harvesters, and I turned right up the hill because the other direction seemed worse. And anyway I was now starting to feel very thirsty (I'd finished my water bottle a long time earlier) and my thoughts were turning to the village and maybe a taverna in the shade. I passed strawberry trees, and I trudged uncaring through their scarlet fruit, and yet more olive trees, and a black squirrel bounded through the branches. None of this was as exciting as it had been. It was hot, and the path was rocky, and every time it turned left (in the direction of the river and the village) I felt a little pulse of hope but in truth it was taking me up and away, I had no idea where because I had no map and my phone no longer worked. The sun was so hot and my mouth was so dry. There have been other moments, just like this, when I have had the chance to dangle my legs in the waters of a river and forget about the relentless passing of the hours and yet for some reason it almost never happens. There is always something or someone stopping me, and now it has happened again. And it is unsettling to realise – stumbling, lost and alone on this roasting path – that the aggravating person who always gets in the way, or taps on his watch, is me.

I blame the teacher at my school who read us John Bunyan's *Pilgrim's Progress* in bite-sized chunks every morning for a year when I was aged about ten. 'Onward Christian Soldiers!' There was a lot about hope in that book, I remember, and never leaving the path, but 'Hopeful' was also a rather naive and feckless character, and easily led into the arms of the Giant Despair. At least I think that's how it unfolded. I do know that the Pilgrim was fleeing his city before it was consumed in the fires of God's holy wrath, but it never seemed right that he left his wife and children and all his friends behind. I know they wouldn't listen to him, but perhaps he could have stayed and tried a bit harder before setting off on his exciting journey. And what happened to his city and everyone who remained? Did the hellfire descend? I am not sure we ever found out.

These thoughts kept me busy in the heat, trudging up the hill. Who knew that gorges could be so very deep? I am the world's worst wild hiker, always lost and under-provisioned. Never accept an invitation from me. There are clouds gathering. Is it actually going to rain? Will night fall? I am so thirsty. At the top of the hill (although it is another false summit), my phone claws a momentary thread of reception out of the sky and I see that there is a village only about three kilometres away and I take some screenshots. It is not the village I was aiming for, but apparently it has a shop. I could drink an aisle of bottled water . . . but of course, when I get to it, the place is closed. At least I am out of the woods and I know the way back to my car, a two-hour hike along the road.

On the outskirts of the village, an old woman gestures at me from her front garden. Where do they all come from, I wonder again, these Greek women with their headscarves and aprons and snaggle-toothed smiles? How come they all still look like this? Should they not be dying out, replaced by old women in leisurewear? There seems to be an endless supply, replenished from some central repository, ever since I first visited Greece in the 1970s. 'Yargy,' says the woman, with an emphatic, head-scarved nod in my direction, drawing her ancient husband into

the scene. He too is stooped and familiar. 'Yargy,' she repeats.
The pain and isolation of being without language. What does
she mean? 'Look at the crazy dehydrated German'? She doesn't
seem eager to talk, so I confirm her analysis with an unhinged
smile, and walk on.

The great thing about living in Roman times was the roads.
Lucky Pausanias. Lucky us. I am out of the wilderness (which I
have decided is overrated) and am marching towards my car.
Sure, I am being barked at by dogs, laughed at by old women
and sucked dry by the sun. I want fruit. I want water. I want
beer. I want a Greek salad. But I have come across a bush laden
with late blackberries and the afternoon sun has loosened its
glare and the trees behind the hedgerows loom green and heavy
with olives and chestnuts and I arrive back at my car, parked by
the shuttered environmental centre, weary and ragingly thirsty
but grateful for everything we can still find in this wondrous
land. Although I probably speak for more people than ever care
to admit it when I say how happy I was to find myself once
again among the tourist shops of Olympia, drinking iced water,
roaming the aisles and marvelling at a set of lovingly illustrated
and bracingly acrobatic playing cards labelled 'Sex in Ancient
Greece'.

I mean . . . who knew?

Another day, another river.

I have come to gaze at the Alpheius, which is 'the greatest of
rivers in its volume of water, and the most pleasure-giving to

the sight', or so says Pausanias. It curls just south of the ancient site of Olympia, and it is thanks to the Alpheius that there is anything at all left of the temples of Zeus and Hera and the great athletics stadium and the training grounds. After the site was looted by barbarians (Romans among them) and abandoned by the locals, the river silted over the ruins, and hid them under a layer of earth, grass and trees, and there they lay, as the centuries rolled by, until nineteenth-century archaeologists located their remains. Which is just as well, because in 1730 a French explorer called Michel Fourmont was at Sparta, having destroyed everything he could get his hands on, working night and day with a team of thirty men, wondering where to go next, with Olympia on his mind, but he decided not to make the journey.

'If I could do at Tegea, Antigonia, Nemea and one or two other cities what I have done at Hermione, Troezen and Sparta, it would not be necessary to send anyone here [to Greece]. There would be nothing left,' he wrote.

He was meant to be looking for inscriptions, and he tore down anything that might be concealing them. Perhaps he was hoping for immortality by being the last man of his generation to see the ancient wonders. He may have been driven by religious hatred. I don't know. He may even have made up the things he claimed to be transcribing. The impossible fragility of it all. What has somehow made its way down to us, through the flames and the greed of the looters and philistines, is just the tiniest fraction of what was once created.

But Alpheius saved Olympia for us. He was one of the greatest of the river gods, riding down from Arcadia into the sea near Pyrgos. He fell in love with a water nymph called Arethusa when she bathed on his shores, but she wasn't at all pleased with his attentions and fled to the bay of Syracuse in Sicily. He followed her there, under the sea, and mingled with her waters, and that is why (as everyone once knew) the river Alpheius flows all the way from Arcadia to Sicily, and why, wrote Pausanias, it 'became fabulous for love'.

It is a fast-flowing, powerful river, even at the end of a summer when there has been so little rain. It is 31 October, my mother's birthday. She would have been ninety-eight, if she had lived that long. Born on Hallowe'en. 'I'm a witch,' she always told us. It makes her a follower of Hekate, the haunter of crossroads, goddess of the night and the howling of dogs. Hesiod worshipped Hekate above all the rest. She could bring great fortune to farmers and fishermen, if she chose.

It is not easy to get down to the banks of the river Alpheius, at least not from ancient Olympia, but I have found a tenuous track through the tall reeds. After my travails in the Forest of Foloi, I have been gripped by a strong urge to visit another river, and I have found a place with wide, stony banks, where the river flows slow (although not in the middle, where it pulls with insistent force), and there are grey and white pebbles and teasels on the banks and a fallen willow growing defiantly in the shallows. Sunlight is rippling up and down the stems of the reeds on the river's edge.

A large bird has walked these slippery banks, probably a heron. There are prints in the slime just under the shallows. I am gazing at the water skaters, floating at their ease on the thick of the river, and wondering if I should have been a potamologist. The surface is grey on this sunny day, with a deeper green rising from below. Just to the right of me, the river divides at a small island and then shakes itself to the side with a burst of bubbles and foam and rolls around into a deep, moving pool. Minding its own business. It feels like a private place (but not in the American sense). This is Alpheius' domain. He is patient. When we have finished whatever it is we are doing, he will still be here.

There is a eucalyptus tree behind me in the reeds, a sometimes unpopular non-native tree, and maybe a fire hazard, but I am happy to see it. My mother once planted one in her garden and when it died, after about twenty years, we put in an amelanchier, two of my young children scampering about, getting under the spade. I hope it is still there, with its delicate blossoms in the springtime and golden red berries at the turning of the year.

The philosopher Heraclitus said that you can't step in the same river twice. Presumably (no one really knows) he didn't just mean that the river and time are always flowing ... he meant that it is also us who are never the same. Some things – perhaps all things – are defined by change, and there is nothing that is not always in flux. Rivers and fires and the winds are movement and loss and rebirth. So is all of life. Mountains too. If things don't change, they are no longer what they were. And a thing of beauty is not a joy for ever. Endymion will wake in his cave. Nothing can be fixed for all time. The ruins up the hill in Olympia, and the remnants of the faultless statues in the museum, are shifting and silting and ripe with decay. The world and its rivers and forests, and what is left of its creatures . . . all of it . . . it is all so unbearably fragile. People say otherwise, that the world is resilient, but the changes we have set in motion, and are feeding, have knocked us and everything else off balance.

But what are we supposed to do? We can't just stop.

NINE

We Live in Hope

'The god is no longer far away.'

CALLIMACHUS, 'HYMN TO APOLLO'

November was underway and I was up early in the fresh and sparkling morning, full of hope, leaving Olympia and heading to Delphi where I was going for a further consultation of the Oracle of shining Apollo. Well, not the priestess herself, she is no longer there, her halls have fallen into decay and her waters have run dry, or at least that was the final message she sent, to the last pagan Roman Emperor Julian in the year 362 CE. He had asked her how to bring back the old ways of worship, but the roots of Christianity were already sunk deep and people no longer had much faith in her prophecies and were turning away from the gods. Her advice was to embrace the new reality and leave her be. Or so said the early Christian fathers. I am not too worried about this, because if I can't find her hiding in a shed, I might still be able to talk with one of her priests. And then I am going to breathe the holy air.

I had only been driving for about ten minutes when I picked up a couple of hitchhikers on the outskirts of Pyrgos. I probably shouldn't have done, given the worsening news about the global pandemic, but it was such a warm, optimistic morning, and they were into the car before I remembered, and then it was too late. We strapped on our masks and they told me they were heading for the airport at Thessaloniki and would be delighted if I could drop them just over the bridge at Patras.

The young woman who sat at the back was French and was studying for a Masters in Paris. She had wanted to study in Britain, 'but, you know . . . Brexit'. The young man sitting next to me in the front was Austrian, his vast frame filling the small car, burly knees bumping against the dashboard, and he was on a break from military service so he could meet up with his French friend and travel around Greece. They had heard that their countries might be closing their borders soon and they were heading for the airport. They were very grateful for the lift. People were still stopping for them, they said, but it was mostly Albanians, and they never travelled more than a few kilometres, dropping off food at markets and shops.

I told them that I often wanted to stop for hitchhikers, ever since the England cricketer, Phil Edmonds, had pulled over in his beaten-up estate car on the A274 in Kent in 1982, and although I had been too shy to ask him any questions until the very last moment, he was extraordinarily friendly and so very kind, sweeping empty cans and cigarette packets into the front well with his famous left hand, making room for a scruffy young hitchhiker. I don't think my new friends grasped quite how exciting it had been – this was Phil *Edmonds*, for heaven's sake, the *England cricketer* – but my story kept the mood buoyant as the car wheezed towards the bridge at Patras.

The Austrian man had plenty of questions, his great thigh pounding up and down next to me in rhythm to the music coming from the car radio. 'What do you do?' 'How long have you done that?' 'Do you make any money?' 'When is your deadline?' 'Isn't that rather soon?' 'How much have you written?'

Is it possible that he has been sent here by my editor, Sam Carter, to check on progress? I start talking, fast, 'well, yes, it is soon, but I couldn't get here in March, and then in June, and I have been taking loads of notes, and you could say that some of the chapters are practically written already, and yes OK I haven't had so long because of the pandemic, but in a way maybe that's a good thing, because I've read more, and . . .' The man laughs. 'Really it is OK,' he says, apparently on the brink of folding his great hand over my knee, 'really, I am just the same any time I have a deadline.' At what age, I wonder, am I going to start feeling older than people? We talk about Salzburg and universities and Brittany, where the French woman grew up, and so did my father, at least some of the time, but that was almost one hundred years ago.

We arrived on the bridge at Patras, talking about oysters. 'Now that is beautiful,' said the Austrian, leaning his great head and shoulders into the windscreen to get a better look, loosing off a volley of photos and selfies. And then we were over this engineering miracle, its white sails flying high above the turquoise bay, the toll was paid and the hitchhikers were out of the car, now waving from the side of the road as they dwindled and then vanished. Be kind to strangers. You never know when they might be gods.

My way turned east towards Delphi, following the coast. I drove through deserted villages at the foot of tall hills, and along almost empty roads, wondering at the number of olive trees and dogs. Sometimes the dogs were ranged along the streets in packs and one of them would rush after the back wheels of my car, but most of the time they just lay there, waiting for something more exciting to happen. At around about lunchtime I started paying more attention to the villages and their tavernas, and there was one grimly familiar moment when I dithered just a fraction and drove past the small, half-hidden turning to a perfect curve of a bay, with a taverna right there on the beach, the tables spread out under their snowy parasols, and then almost at once I found that there was no other way down, perhaps not for dozens of kilometres, and I couldn't turn, and all I could do was stare at the violet sea in the shining bay as it disappeared forever in my rear-view mirror.

I came up to Delphi through the Crissaean plain, which was once the territory of the city of Crisa. Apparently you can still see what's left of its amphitheatre in the hills. The city had sent ships to the war at Troy (or so said Homer), but had provoked the rage of the Oracle by waylaying and extorting money from her pilgrims, and she had ordered her people to:

> fight against the Crisans day and night, and utterly ravage their country, enslave their inhabitants, and dedicate the land to Pythian Apollo, Artemis, Leto, and Athena Pronaia, and for the future it must lie entirely uncultivated – they must not till this land themselves nor permit any other.

So the inhabitants of Delphi and their allies from Athens and Sicyon and maybe Thessaly went to war, and it lasted ten bloody years (just like Troy), until the Oracle suggested they poison the people of Crisa by putting hellebore in their water supply, and then at last the city succumbed and its people were killed or taken away as slaves and its walls were torn down and strewn across the plain and no one ever lived there again. The Oracle was implacable. This all happened over 2,500 years ago. For many centuries no one dared cultivate the fertile plain (the Athenians asked once and were told to back off), but these days it is busy with olive groves and farmland and whitewashed villages with terracotta roofs.

You had to choose what you asked the Oracle very carefully. The questions were often public. Whole cities would wait for the answer, on whether they should go to war, or start a colony, or poison the aqueducts of their neighbours. The questions could be private – and personal – but you had to be rich to indulge your curiosity. Croesus, for example, who was indeed legendarily wealthy. First, he had tested all the greatest oracles of the world, by asking them what he would be doing exactly one hundred days after he had written the letters that his messengers were carrying. And only Delphi had known that he would be (or was) cooking lamb and tortoise in a bronze pot, which I think we can agree is a specific enough reply to make even the greatest illusionist tremble, although I do wonder what Croesus was doing, making his own food, given that he had enough money to employ ten thousand chefs. And also – tortoise and lamb? – what kind of meal is that?

The messenger god Hermes had a taste for tortoise flesh – or at least he made one into a stew on the day he was born, so that he could turn its shell into the world's first lyre. He traded it with Apollo in exchange for the older god's cattle, as well as a golden staff, which meant that Apollo became the god of music as well as prophecy, with his home in Delphi. He lived here for nine months of the year, spending the three winter months among the Hyperboreans. No one knows who these people were, but their miserable country was somewhere in the north, tormented by damp and icy winds, so I suppose it is possible that the Greeks were describing the island of Britain. I wonder if Apollo's absence coincided with Persephone's. She was in Hades, he was in Hyperborea, and all through the winter the god Dionysus held court in Delphi, dancing and drinking wine and urging his followers, the satyrs and maenads, into an orgy of drunken lust.

He makes me nervous, Dionysus. You should never offend any of the gods (Artemis destroyed cities), but Dionysus was vicious and he planned exquisite punishments for those who offended him, like the time he sent King Pentheus up to the lonely slopes of Mount Cithaeron to be clawed into bloody chunks by his own mother and aunts. He is not a jolly, red-faced drinker. He was born from Zeus' thigh, and torn apart by Titans, and he rose again to lead his followers in ecstasy and madness. You have felt his pull, I am sure, when the third drink turns to the fifth. The Greeks understood that you have to let the horses run, just so long as you can find a way to bring them back home.

People like to set up Dionysus and Apollo as opposites, encouraged by the idea that they shared the shrines of Delphi but never lived in the city at the same time. The ecstatic frenzy of Dionysus; the cold purity of Apollo. But the two gods had more in common than this implies. They both loved music. The first time Apollo came to Delphi, he transformed himself into a dolphin, and led the Cretan sailors here who would become his first priests; and Dionysus turned pirates into dolphins when they tried to take him as a slave. Apollo burned with the heat of the sun. Some say that there was no shrine to Dionysus in Delphi, only his tomb – he was born again every year, harbinger of new life. Apollo claimed that he was the only god who knew Zeus' mind, but people also went to Dionysus to ask about the future. They said that his prophecies were darker than anything Apollo might produce, although that ignores the bleak humour of some of the older god's oracles. They were both cruel and proud. The immortals had their own essence, but change was in their nature. Moments of metamorphosis were something else that these two gods shared. In truth, I am worried that I may be too late in the year for Apollo, now that November is here, and it may be Dionysus who is waiting for me in the dark of his tomb.

You have to guard against rushing to judgement when interpreting the oracles of the gods. Croesus pressed treasures beyond comprehension on Delphi (once they had proved that they had the greatest oracle in the world), and was told that a great empire would be destroyed if he attacked the Persians. So he did, and of course it was his own empire that fell. The prophecy was baited to ensnare an overconfident man. It is funny, though (at least from this distance). Croesus was taken to be burned alive by Cyrus, the victorious Persian emperor, but some people think that he was saved at the last minute by Apollo and sent to live among the Hyperboreans, although perhaps that was just a different, more lingering punishment for his greed and hubris. He would spend his last fog-laden days pondering Solon's words, that we can only truly say we are happy on the day we die. Maybe (to get back to it) we all feel an affinity for one particular god or goddess, but their identity changes through our lifetimes, or even depending on the time of day. I mean, they change, and so do we.

Anyway, there's plenty to think about as I grind up the steep and narrow road to Delphi, swinging around the hairpins, the resplendent views swelling in the car's grubby windows. I had treated myself to a well-reviewed hotel (TripAdvisor, not Pausanias) and when I arrived the lobby was empty, until a middle-aged Yorkshireman came clumping down the stairs and told me on no account to accept Room 207. 'We're moving,' he said, 'it absolutely stinks of smoke.' The receptionist arrived soon afterwards, a little flustered, and handed me a swipe card. 'It's our last room,' she said, 'but a good one. Room 207. Second floor, at the end of the corridor.' 'Thanks,' I replied.

The room was narrow and backed onto an ivy-covered outside wall and smelled strongly of pine air-freshener, laced with a cross-current of sour tobacco. For some reason the smoke was being replenished with a new supply every thirty minutes or so, and I eventually tracked this mysterious happening down to the air-conditioning in the small shower room, or maybe it was even coming from the taps in the basin. It was hard to tell, but I know what I smelled. Soft voices were whispering in the ducts and pipes, and I wondered whether my room was in some umbilical way attached to the staff's smoking room. I am a precarious ex-smoker, and my main worry was that the regular infusions of fresh smoke would coil into my dreams and trigger an irresistible night-time craving for deep, joyous lungfuls of nicotine, but I needn't have fretted because the hotel had thought-fully laid on a neighbour on the other side of the wafer-thin walls who was in the last desperate throes of tuberculosis, and his heartbreaking coughs kept me awake and thanking my negligible willpower that I had managed to give up smoking thirty years earlier.* At one point in the long night, an arm groped around the edge of the door and a synthetic voice from the corridor announced that my room had not yet been adequately secured, although that may have been fever Dream #7.

At breakfast the next day, with the masked Yorkshireman stand-ing too close behind me, I mumbled 'room number 207' to a member of staff at the buffet and watched him flinch. I then carried my tray to a table and lost myself in Michael Scott's book *Delphi*, while I chewed dryly on a Greek croissant. I read that there were only nine days in the year when the Oracle could be consulted. Just nine days – the seventh day of each month (except those months when Apollo was living among the Hyperboreans) – and I was here on the first of November. Nine days in the year. The Greek months were erratic, though, and every city seems to

---

* More or less, just so long as I avoid the warm terraces of tavernas overlook-ing a moonlit bay . . . and above all Birmingham.

have followed a different calendar, so I don't suppose we now know when their dates might be aligned with our own.

It had always been hard to get a consultation with the Pythia, Apollo's priestess and mouthpiece. There were rules about the order in which cities and citizens could approach her (Delphi first, then other Greek cities – their order changing depending on shifting alliances – and finally non-Greeks, more commonly known as 'barbarians' after the repetitive gurgling of their incomprehensible languages). The Pythia sat on a tripod somewhere in the inner sanctuary of the god's temple, wreathed in smoke (possibly emanating from a fissure in the mountain that is no longer there), and conveyed her indicative but elusive glimpses into the future. She had a laurel tree in the room with her, sacred to Apollo, or laurel branches, and maybe it was them that were smouldering. She may have chewed the leaves. Priests were gathered in an outer room, waiting to interpret or sometimes write down her pronouncements. The *omphalos* was most certainly there, the stone that had fallen in the place where two eagles met, soon after they were released by Zeus at the furthest edges of the earth, beyond the outer ocean, and ordered to fly towards one another so that he would know the exact centre of the world. And here it is – here it still is! – or a convincing copy – right here in Delphi. The heart of everything. Or so said the Greeks. Other peoples had other stories, but it's like Xenophanes once said:

> If oxen, horses or lions had hands, with which they could draw and work as men do, horses would draw gods like horses, and oxen like oxen, and each would make their bodies like their own.

The Pythia expected the sacrifice of a goat before she was ready to answer any questions. I don't have a goat, but that's fine, because as you know I have already consulted the Oracle and received my answer by email. I am here to soak up the atmosphere. Anyway, who in their right mind would not want to come to Delphi? It was a centre of worship for 1,500 years, perhaps much longer, and of course it has been damaged by earthquakes and looters/archaeologists and religious zealots, but it is still a wonder of the world. The site was once sacred to Gaia, the Earth Mother who was here before Apollo. Whether she was also here before the eagles no one knows, but Apollo followed soon after Leto had given birth to him on the floating island of Delos, travelling across Greece, stopping many times, looking for the perfect place for a holy sanctuary, until at last he arrived at Delphi and killed the great python that was already living here and it rotted into the ground, and this is where he ordered his followers to build his temple. There is always a snake. It's a chthonic thing.*

---

* See? Incidentally, the meaning of the name Erysichthon (the man who chopped down the sacred tree and was punished with unassuageable hunger) is Erysis = 'wound', and 'chthon' = earth. So Erysichthon wounded the earth, which makes his punishment even more apt. 'Chthonic' means to belong to, and emerge from, to be rooted in the earth. The Athenians liked to claim that they were 'autochthonic' – i.e. they and their ancestors had always lived on the land in and around Athens, sprung from the earth, which is why snakes featured so prominently in their story. This was unlike other Greek cities, they said, which were usually thought to be inhabited by the descendants of (relatively) recent arrivals. The Athenians also considered themselves unusually welcoming to those who had been cast out by other cities (Oedipus, Orestes). I have read that they welcomed refugees from wars and famine, but that it was hard to become a full citizen. Academics debate this and everything else, some of them lost forever in a labyrinth of etymological uncertainty, where minotaurs lurk.

I am also expecting that the answer I received to my question about Pandora's Hope will carry more weight in the place where it was given. I have arranged to meet with the person who acted as an intermediary with the Oracle for me, and I am seeing him tonight. But meanwhile the whole day is ahead, and up here in the high mountains the sun is ablaze in the roofless blue sky, and it is quite clear that shining Apollo has not yet left for the freezing north, and I am suddenly in a heart-pounding hurry to get away from the miasmic clutches of Room 207 and up to the archaeological site, ahead of the crowds, to be alone in sacred Delphi, to see if anything remains of the holy aura that captivated and shook untold generations of supplicants. It was once a place of pilgrimage, as great as any other.

I was almost the first through the gates of the archaeological site, gleeful to be up so early. I followed the sacred way through flurries of white, yellow and red butterflies, and watched lizards whisk from the tops of fallen stones. We are close to the sun – this place belongs to it – and the rose brick walls and the honey-coloured stone and the grey paving of the path and the cliffs high above are radiant with its power. It is nothing like the thin, arid home of Helios in Acrocorinth. Delphi is green and alive. The sky is mountain blue, threaded with wisps of white. There are dark cypress trees growing among the ruins, olives too, and fennel and thyme. I am past what is left of the golden treasuries, that were once laden with gifts for the Oracle. I am driven by the need to get higher. I am at the *omphalos*, the navel of the world, it is half a huge and perfectly smooth snake's egg buried in the earth, right here in the place where the giant python was killed and rotted away, with my back to the temples and the cliffs, the valley a blur and far below, the distant hazy mountains, umbrella pines to my right, and cypress in the long dry grasses, and birdsong and mauve cyclamen and crocus and even narcissus and more butterflies and the sky so achingly blue. Just me and three other stunned tourists. We could be flying. Except that the air is so intoxicatingly fresh.

The way passes the rock of the Sybil, where the first prophetess stood and gave her answers, and then the wall with the tight-fitting polygonal stones that the early British travellers wanted to remove (if only they'd had the mules), and round to the ruins of the temple of Apollo, where a woman in a wide-brimmed hat is sketching in the shadow of one of the only remaining columns, looking like she has emerged from the pages of Virginia Woolf. Everything is perfectly still.

And then I am standing near the stage of the ancient stone theatre, looking up at the tiered seating, cracked and clumped with grass but still recognisably able to put on a show, sweet music for shining Apollo, and there at the very top, sitting high above the theatre, legs dangling over a low wall, is a man carrying on a long and absorbing phone conversation in English. He has a huge and bountiful laugh that flows down the aisles, the theatre's perfect acoustics working in reverse, and he is enormously at his ease, all alone in the Delphic sun, dappled by a cypress tree, talking ('I was going to come and see you . . . wonderful . . . yes . . .') and laughing loud and merry. Soon he is joined by a German woman, also on her phone, and I look back and see the first stirrings of a coach party advancing up the hill behind me, so I press on around the corner and as soon as I reach the man on the phone he stops his call ('sorry, must go') and rises to meet me.

'Peter Fiennes?' he says. And here (who else?) is James, the man I had asked to consult the Oracle on my behalf, who I will not describe in any detail, because he guards his privacy . . . but of course it is him. 'How did you know it was me?' I ask, not expecting wonders, but still. 'Well, I had an advantage,' he says, 'your picture is in your books.' And it is unsettling, not just him knowing me, but the very idea of meeting the person who has been communicating with the Oracle and asking my foolish but heartfelt question, but what was I expecting? White robes and gold sandals? Religion permeated every aspect of the ancient Greeks' lives, even though we are told they had no word for 'religion'. Just because we have been taught that the gods and their exploits are stories for children, it does not mean that for thousands of years people did not worship them with sincerity and passion. The spirits lived in the rivers and the trees; the gods graced their temples; and their priests and priestesses could also be farmers and soldiers and shopkeepers. In later years, the Pythia herself was a mother chosen from among the citizens of Delphi. My grandfather was a vicar, for heaven's sake, so I should be used to mingling with the priesthood.

Even so. We agreed where we would meet later, and I walked on . . . somewhat ruffled. Further up is the stadium where they used to hold the Pythian Games, to rival the ones at Olympia. I believe Nero had a great success here. I was looking for a bay tree, to honour Apollo, but it was surprisingly hard to find. So I wandered back down to the place where I had met James the Oracle Man and sat where he was sitting and soaked up the sunshine and the incomparable views of ancient Delphi, still feeling off balance. Propped against the wall there was a dry and hollow fennel stalk, just like the one Prometheus used to store the fire he had stolen from heaven, so I picked at it and stared at the many large black birds soaring above the distant cliffs (definitely not Apollo's bird, the crow, but I'm not quite sure what they are . . .)* and shielded my eyes from the glare and wondered if it is true that the spirits of Greece appear in broad daylight, unlike the shadows of the North. My parents were here, some time in the 1970s, and I would like to see them now, my father shuffling up the path under his floppy white sun hat, my mother wondering aloud about the different varieties of cypress tree.

Of course I am still looking for hope. Or Hope. And wonder too, although that has been easier to find. There is beauty all around, in this numinous land. Perhaps they are all the same thing, though. Beauty and wonder and hope. Coming back down the path, steadying myself on the smooth lined trunk of a cypress, my open palm resting on the warm bark, I am sure I can feel a soft pulse from under the surface. Nothing intrusive, but there is a current I recognise. 'Here I am.' A shy tug on the sleeve. The trunk belongs to one of three cypress trees in a row, the shaggy kind, not wrapped tight in tall tapered cones, but tumbling outwards and laden with seeds. They're standing on the edge of a narrow path, running between low walls, and there is a channel of cool water splashing alongside. The nymphs and the muses and their lovely dances.

---

* Should have been an ornithologist.

Someone has placed a crystal in a cleft in a branch of one of these trees, in an act of worship or prayer. An offering to Apollo, perhaps. It comes to me then, looking at this fragile and hopeful crystal, that I am tired of cynicism. It is no way to live or survive. I know that entire schools of philosophy say otherwise, but now is not the time.

And in fact Lord Byron has been in my thoughts again. Maybe it was my night in Room 207 that brought him back. He liked to boast that he slept 'like a top' whenever he was travelling. It didn't matter if he was lying in a cowshed or beset by 'hard beds and sharp insects', he always dreamed the night through. But that was the younger Byron, aged just twenty-two, dawdling around Greece with his friend Hobhouse, and not the later, more troubled man. He came to Delphi on his first journey to Greece and carved his name onto a column in the gymnasium, but he didn't have much else to say about the place. In 1815, aged twenty-seven, married just nine months, floundering in a chasm of depression, he wrote this in a letter to his friend Tom Moore:

> but what is Hope? Nothing but the paint on the face
> of Existence; the least touch of truth rubs it off, and
> then we see what a hollow-cheeked harlot we have got
> hold of.

So he and Nietzsche would have had plenty to discuss. Interestingly, as he got older Nietzsche seems to have unbent just a little, but Byron was always heading in the other direction, despite his frantic involvement with the Greek cause of independence. I am surprised to discover that I have spent less time with Byron in Greece than I expected, certainly compared to what I imagined might happen when I was standing by his dead tree in the grounds of Newstead Abbey, but perhaps after all he was not the right spirit guide to accompany me on my journey. Because if I have learned anything at all over the past few weeks, it is this: we need to leave room for hope.

A couple of days before I arrived in Delphi, I had set off to spend a day on 'perhaps the most idyllic beach in all of Greece' – which is the kind of reckless statement I find impossible to ignore.* Pausanias never had to worry about killing the thing he loved (there were very few tourists in his day, and the population was falling, and anyway I don't think he actually sold very many copies of his gargantuan *Guide to Greece*), but these days every guidebook- and travel-writer has to consider whether they actually want to expose their favourite local bar or hidden cove to the millions of people who are searching the web looking for a place that is undiscovered and unspoiled, whatever that may mean. Henry Miller, who travelled around Greece in the days before mass tourism, sort of predicted the problem (and more).

> Whatever we cling to, even if it be hope or faith, can be the disease which carries us off.

---

* Stuttard, *Greek Mythology*.

The idyllic beach is called Voidokilia, and it is just north of the town of Pylos. Many years ago (no one knows when) King Nestor, whose voice was sweeter than honey, ruled over the city with wisdom and strength. He had gone to Troy to help bring Helen back to her husband, and unlike most of his fellow-fighters, he had returned home safely. Some time later, Telemachus, the son of Odysseus, had gone to ask Nestor if he had any news of his father (who was still lost in the arms of Calypso), and had found Nestor on this beach with his sons and his men, sacrificing eighty-one black bulls to Poseidon, the god of the sea.

So, something to look forward to. But before I reached Voidokilia, I stopped off at a place called Agiannakis, which is one of a string of beaches in the miles-long Gulf of Kyparissia, with its pale golden sands and voluptuous dunes. Even though it wasn't the season, I wanted to see where the loggerhead turtles come ashore and lay their eggs. My cousin Sicily once volunteered for a charity called Archelon (the Sea Turtle Protection Society of Greece) and it sounded so hopeful, what they were trying to do, keeping the eggs and new generations of loggerhead turtles safe and nurturing them into the sea so they could return one day to the place where they were born.

I parked almost on the beach, next to a French family in a campervan, and walked through the dunes and the reeds, where blue dragonflies hang, and down to a restless sea. I had planned to walk north, perhaps up to where the river Neda joins the coast – Neda was the eldest of the three nymphs who hid and nursed Zeus after he was born – but there was a naked middle-aged couple in this direction, Germans I presume, and although

I'm short-sighted he appeared to be about to lower himself into her arms. They were both looking in my direction and even if they didn't seem bothered by my arrival, I still turned around, back into the sun, and went to search for signs of turtles in the sand.

There was a tree trunk washed up on the shore, looking like a wet black seal, so I sat down on it and listened to the waves, which were making an especially satisfying, rhythmic smack and swish as they rolled and tumbled up the beach. What an illusion of purpose it gives, staring into the endless waves, rather like settling in for the determined pull of a train journey. The foam had the swirl of royal icing, and the water was murky brown as it slapped and withdrew with a bounty of sand. Further out, the sea was misty blue. It was almost November and there was something northern about the beach, even British – I'd like to say Hyperborean, or maybe Northumbrian – particularly because it was so empty, on this warm sunny day in late October, just me and the naked Germans and the French campervan hidden somewhere behind the dunes.

Menelaus, the husband of Helen and the brother of Agamemnon, once lay down with his three strongest men in the middle of a spectacularly smelly herd (or harem) of seals. He wanted to catch the god Proteus, who could change shape at will, and this was the only way he could get close enough to him without being seen. Once they had him, they all held on tight, while Proteus turned from lion to snake, from boar to tree, and even flowing water, until in the end he settled on his own, essential form, and gave Menelaus what he wanted, which was to know which one of the gods he had offended. The message, if you ever want to know why you are marooned with no wind on an island far off the coast of Egypt, is to rub yourself down with wet fish and find a seal colony.

Sadly, there are no real seals on Agiannakis beach today, and of course there aren't any turtles either because it is the wrong time of year, even if the number of their nests has grown every season. The work that Archelon is doing is starting to pay off. When I returned to London, I spoke with Yiannis Chalkias over Zoom. Yiannis is working on his Marine Biology Masters at Falmouth in Cornwall;* but he grew up near Agiannakis and he was one of the first and only locals to work for Archelon. Yiannis has a smile that lights up my screen.

'It is an act of hope,' he said, 'it is everything that you could ever wish for as an environmentalist. Just think, you see these baby turtles setting out into the sea, and twenty, maybe twenty-five years later, they are back as adults, at the same beach, to lay their own eggs. The fledglings that left the beach in the year I was born, they are now returning as huge adults.' Yiannis, who is not yet thirty, tells me that it's a generational thing, that the 'older locals didn't understand what the first volunteers of Archelon were trying to do. They didn't trust them. They thought they were a bunch of hippies, or that they were working for Brussels or the government in Athens.'

'The turning point,' said Yiannis, 'was in 2013, when a development company from Athens came to the area to build fifty luxury villas. Not a hotel or a resort. Fifty private villas to be used all year round by different rich people.'

---

* A life free from regret.

'Well, that must have finally got the locals on your side,' I say.

Yiannis laughed. 'Not at all,' he said, 'they wanted the jobs. They believed what they were told, that there would be money and work for them. It was only stopped by the government, because the whole development was illegal. Archelon was part of the protest, and was blamed by the locals when it didn't go ahead. They thought they were all a bunch of foreigners . . . It has been a big conflict,' said Yiannis, looking briefly gloomy. 'The locals came up to the dunes. Tyres were slashed . . .

'But still,' he laughed, 'the development was stopped.'

'I presume it helped that you were there, a local?' I asked, leadingly.

'Yes, maybe,' said Yiannis. 'At least they opened their doors to me. But it didn't change much. They're farmers . . . they just want to make a bit more money. And you know, I hate to say it, but the people who really understand what Archelon are trying to do are the big developers. They're the ones who can see what it means to keep the beaches clean. To have the turtles there. They see the value of it. The small businesses? The locals and farmers and small tavernas – they don't understand why you are telling them to turn out the lights.'

We talked for a while about this – about how vital it is to involve local people. The laws that were passed to protect the area were rushed through by the government in Athens, bad laws, done in a panic, and no one thought to ask local people what they thought, which only led to yet more conflict.

'Let's talk about hope,' I said, because I really needed to.

Yiannis didn't hesitate. 'Hope is what gets us through. We are adrift without hope. It is the fuel in our engine. Being involved helps, being part of it. But hope means working on something that is not going to happen for twenty years. Maybe not even being alive to see it . . .

'I know everything can seem so bad,' said Yiannis, 'and that sometimes we think that humans must be the very worst of species. But really there is nothing wrong with us. There is just something wrong with our choices.'

He paused.

'Because, you see, hope is the moment when the turtle comes back.'

I didn't linger on Agiannakis beach. It is beautiful, and slightly wild, but I had 'perhaps the most idyllic beach in all of Greece' to get to. And anyway, although I was happy on my olive tree that looked like a basking seal, gazing out over the foaming waves, dreaming of Proteus, my reveries had recently been punctured by sharp cries coming from somewhere up the beach or among the dunes, borne to me on the north-westerly breeze, ululations of anguish or joy and even, once, a man's hoarse voice and a wheezing 'mein Gott!' They can't be, can they? I wondered. Indeed they could.

So, I set my phone to take me to Voidokilia beach, and hung on her jaunty voice as she steered me through groves of olive trees, many of them twisted and scored with age, and the dusty road wove past low fading houses and sleeping dogs and rivers flanked by tall banks of reeds. In the small car park for the beach, still hidden from me by rocks and dunes, there were four campervans and a couple of cars and more blue dragonflies skimming the surface of a muddy stream. Shoals of small fish swirled in perfect synchronicity in the shallows. I walked bare-foot along a hot sandy path, not there yet, pine trees covering the slopes to my right, dunes to the left, the sea ahead of me. I can smell it, but I haven't seen it. This is the beach where Nestor sacrificed the black bulls, and feasted Telemachus, his royal guest, and the goddess Athena, perhaps the most idyllic beach in all of Greece. I am following the stream, the dunes to the left, a low hill ahead and to the right, deep green with pine trees, the blue sky behind and all around, the sounds of gulls and the lapping caress of gentle waves. I am determined to tread care-fully in this precious place. I turn the corner and stop . . . and at that moment the phone pipes up from my pocket.

'You have arrived,' she says, in a voice of absolute certainty.

I followed olive trucks all the way home. It was harvest time, and they were loaded with fruit, the workers in the back staring at me as I rattled through the potholes in my car, sometimes someone waved, or smiled, more often they just looked, with no particular expression at all, or they lolled and slept on the sacks piled high on the flatbeds. It was a huge harvest, trucks heading both ways, orchards on either side, olive trees stretching into the distance, the sun low and a great yellow moon rising over the reeds. Selene the long-winged, radiant goddess, harnessing her strong-necked horses, not waiting, but riding her shining, long-maned team up into the roofless sky.

Hail, white-armed goddess, bright Selene, mild, bright-
tressed queen!

It is the end of the day, and a new one has already begun.

I met James the Oracle Man in a Delphi restaurant and I ate a
beautifully tender chicken souvlaki with a side dish of stewed
'mountain greens', small squid-like vegetables that I had to
drench in lemon juice to render them less bitter, washed down
with bottles of cold Mythos beer. The view over his shoulder
was stupefying, the sun god disappearing for the night in an
orange and acid-yellow atomic blaze over the Crissaean plain.
We talked about Plato (or he did) and writing, and of course, at
some point in the meal (when I wasn't wrestling with the faux-
squid), I asked him about the Oracle, specifically mine, and
how it is done and also what it might mean.* Because I was still
not entirely clear whether we need to be trying to understand
what purpose whoever (or whatever) 'rules within the skies'
might have in store for us, or whether we should first be looking
inwards, and searching our hearts and souls so that we can,
more than anything, know ourselves.

What I mean, I say to him, is that 'the Oracle's answer seems
circular. Know the gods, understand what their purposes are,
and then Pandora's Hope will shine from within *us*. So we have
to know ourselves. I get that. But, then . . . *where do we start?*' I

---

* See chapter 4.

yelp, with perhaps too much emphasis, already on my third Mythos. 'Are we looking outwards to the gods, and then in? Or in, then out?'

My instinct, I tell him, is to look 'inwards', and he seems to nod, but . . . also . . . What about Pandora's HOPE? Specifically, the hope that we are not a plague on the face of the earth, poisoning everything that makes life worth living. And (although I did not bring this last bit up, but only because I didn't think of it until later) what if I get to 'know myself' and find that what I want, more than anything, is to live my life inflicting no lasting damage on the earth? But perhaps there are others, who also get to 'know themselves', who have very different ideas about what they want. What happens when Jair Bolsonaro (let us say) really gets to know himself and finds that what he wants more than anything is to squeeze out the last drops of oil and gas from underneath the charred remains of the Amazon rainforest, and then race around the wreckage in a diesel-powered SUV? There is a conflict here. Or maybe (help!), what happens if I look deep into my own heart and find that this is also what I want? The unassuageable hunger burning in every one of us.

Or perhaps none of this matters. Because who are we to interrogate the gods? I've never liked that idea – and nor did most of the Greek philosophers, who wanted us to ask questions about everything. But the gods know best, don't they? At least, they are stronger than us. Although even that may no longer be true. Look at Apollo, or his Oracle, hiding in a shed. What if the gods have gone?

I am thinking about Henry Miller and the whole long history of human thought (at least the dominant part of it, and for as long as we can remember) that puts us outside or separate from the rest of nature. Is that actually a good thing, if it means we recognise our unique capacity for destruction and waste? (But also, let us hope, our feeling for beauty. Our readiness for love.) Or should we stress our similarities with the rest of nature, the negligible differences between every living thing's DNA, the apparent truth that we are just another thread in the infinitely varied web of life? In short, is humanity woven into the web, connected at a deep level with everything else on this planet and beyond? Or are we on our own?

James was happy to talk more about my oracle and his part in it . . . but I didn't actually bring up most of this babble at the time, because it only came to me later when I was back in Room 207, brooding and scribbling over a few more Mythos beers. I find the maxim 'Know Yourself' daunting, especially when I am alone in a hotel room that smells of rancid tobacco smoke, facing another night without dreams.

But one more thought. If we really are now living in the Anthropocene, an era whose name acknowledges that there is nothing in the world and its life-enabling atmosphere that has not been influenced or affected by us, most often for the worse (climate, other species, every one of the earth's systems), then it is time we shouldered some responsibility. Or got the fuck out of the way.

The next day, I came down from the clarity of the mountains at Delphi and into the heat of the plain below. There were at least eight pillars of oily black smoke rising from different places, whether from forest fires or industrial or agricultural effluence it was impossible to know. I was heading for Missolonghi, the town where Lord Byron died. There were more dogs than ever before, all of them apparently waiting for something, like Penelope in her palace, longing for Odysseus' return. At one point I swerved past a perfectly scruffy white terrier, looking like Harry the Dirty Dog from the children's books, lying dead across the lines in the centre of the road. The idea that he is happy now no longer makes any sense. I bet he had more fun as a pup.

Lord Byron arrived in Missolonghi on 5 January 1824, suffered severe convulsions on 15 February and died there on 19 April, aged just thirty-six (although he felt and looked much older). In other words, he lived in the mosquito-ridden town for only three months, even if he had arrived in British-ruled Kefalonia in August the previous year, looking for the best place to join the campaign to overturn Ottoman rule in Greece. Byron was prepared to sink his fortune into the cause of Greek independence (for the first time in his life he was rich, having at last managed to sell Newstead Abbey), but his name was even more valuable. He was the most famous writer in Europe, and not just for his Byronic poses and scandalous affairs. The fact that he was a British Lord also resonated in those far-off days. As well as a stack of cash (and access to funds in British banks), Byron brought his own ship, and a band of soldiers (five hundred Souliot tribesmen from Albania), a rather overblown uniform and helmet that he probably never wore, the usual hangers-on (as well as Pietro Gamba, the brother of his Italian mistress) and a genuine readiness to fight and die. It is easy to imagine that Byron had a death wish by this stage. He had buried his friend Shelley on the beach at Viareggio in 1822, his daughter Allegra was dead aged just five, he talked and wrote often about his wasted and wearisome life – but even so there is no reason to suppose that he *wanted* to die. This Greek adventure was not necessarily a last reckless throw of the dice: it was very plausibly the beginning of something new, even if it didn't turn out that way.

In 1824 Missolonghi was a fever town, fought over by the Turks and the Greeks. In 1826, in a pivotal moment of the war of independence, it was captured by the Turks and its inhabitants massacred or enslaved. Today it is a sleepy place, with a life-affirming café in the park next to the Garden of Heroes where Byron is buried. I arrived in the middle of a Monday morning and joined a crowd of men and women who were easing themselves into the week with a leisurely coffee.

I say that Byron is buried here, but there seems to be some confusion whether it is his lungs or his heart that lie under his statue at the centre of the Garden, in among the tombs of the many Greeks, as well as the Germans and other young foreigners who gave their lives fighting for the new nation. The rest of Byron's body was embalmed and shipped back to Britain, to be buried at Hucknall Torkard near Newstead Abbey. Different books tell different stories. We do know that Westminster Abbey would not take him, or even take notice of him, at least not for another 150 years.

Byron understood the power of a symbol. His rather dainty white statue stands among pine trees under the proud blank gaze of the bust of a man with a threatening moustache on a tall plinth, and next to a naked young girl, whose toes have been rubbed pink through the grey marble by supplicants and pilgrims. Someone has laid some dyed blue roses by her right hand, and Byron is looking the other way.

I am surprised how moving it is to stand here by Byron's statue, thinking about his final, lonely days. He cared so much more than he liked to pretend ('I am afraid that this sounds flippant, but I don't mean it to be so'), and he understood himself better than we ever will. His last coherent words, as the inadequate and panicked doctors bled the life out of him, were an affirmation, perhaps a statement about his poetry, but more likely an understanding that his death would mean something to the cause that he had taken up as his own. 'I leave behind something precious in the world,' he said in Italian, and the words were conveyed to Gamba. Or so they say. Others think he just muttered 'good night' and turned his face to the wall. He wasn't the only one to understand the power of a symbol. But even so, perhaps Byron has been a better spirit guide than I have realised. He had hope, after all, right up to the end. He was even prepared to die for it.

TEN

Half Full

'Did he not restore the world to health when almost at the last gasp?'

FUNERAL ORATION FOR THE
EMPEROR JULIAN THE APOSTATE

Epirus is beckoning, but time is running out. Lord Byron visited the region on his first trip to Greece, aged just twenty-one, and met Ali Pasha, ruler of the land from Albania down to the Gulf of Corinth (although he nominally reported to the Ottoman sultan in Istanbul). It was joyous, the young Byron wrote to his mother, riding into 'Yanina [Ioannina] the capital after a journey of three days over the mountains through a country of the most picturesque beauty'. Ali Pasha, who was aged about seventy at the time, but still restlessly ambitious, was delighted to see the young lord and said he was certain, wrote Byron, that 'I was a man of birth because I had small ears, curling hair, & little white hands' – and in fact his enthusiasm for the dainty and undeniably beautiful English lord was so great that Byron had to get out of town before the old goat led him to his palatial bed. Or so said Byron, who later described him in *Don Juan* as:

> The mildest mannered man
> That ever scuttled ship or cut a throat.

In 1803, only six years before Byron met him, Ali Pasha had waged the last in a series of vicious wars against the Souliotes, an Eastern Orthodox people who lived in the villages and mountains in the western part of modern-day Epirus. It was Ali Pasha's troops that are said to have cornered the sixty Souliot women on the rocky cliffs of Zalongo, and these were the women who had sung and danced and thrown themselves over the edge, some of them holding their children, rather than be captured and taken as slaves. Slavery was a fact of life in the Ottoman Empire at that time – as it was in the British.

And these were the women who were the inspiration for the Dancing Women of Vrisoules, who dress in traditional costumes and sing their own versions of the old songs, while they dance in protest at the reckless exploitation of oil and gas in the beautiful forests and gorges of Epirus.

> The fish does not live in dirt,
> nor the flowers flourish in toxic waste
> and girls from Epirus cannot live in gas fumes.
> May you fare well little fountains,
> forests, mountains, little ridges.

'It was a desperate act,' said Eleni Tzachrista over Zoom, 'when the Souliot women threw themselves over the cliffs. At least, that is what we were taught at school', and she waggled her eyebrows at me over the flickering screen, a smile of doubt riding the airwaves from Athens to London. 'But these are also desperate times. No one knows how bad, or what the government and the companies have planned. They don't mention fracking once in their proposals, but we know that is another thing they are after. That, and so much more. Just look at Pennsylvania, it is almost totally fucked up.' It is true. Just look at the fracking zones of Pennsylvania. The scorched earth, the wreckage of human health. The irretrievable cost to the world's climate.

'And now,' said Angeliki Kanelli, another Woman of Vrisoules on my screen, 'the government has taken all responsibility from local authorities. They couldn't always get them to give the companies what they wanted, so they took away their power. They sneaked it through in the pandemic. Everything is done in secret, between the same people. That is why we dance, to bring attention to what they are doing. Everyone loves the traditional dances. It is not at all threatening. In the Herodion theatre in Athens and in the Cultural Centre of Ioannina, they thought we were part of the presentation. That was, until they saw our banners and heard our song.'

'But the companies and the government lie all the time,' said Eleni, 'they tell us we are going to be rich, like the Saudi Arabians! And that's how they get local people to sign away their rights.'

'Oh sure, we have hope,' said Eleftheria Tsoyknaki, beating back my inevitable question. 'You have to have hope. But hope is a twin-faced god, like Janus. We cannot live without hope, but . . . also . . . . "Abandon Hope, all who . . ."' she laughed and left it hanging.

'Hope is two-edged,' agreed Eleni. 'People can feel defeated. But many people have started to realise that this affects them. Not just in Epirus, but all over Greece. We have been forced to talk about our energy problems. They have woken us up! Everything is connected, across the world. Energy, democracy, war, peace, poverty, inequality . . . and biodiversity is at the centre of it all.

'We have to start somewhere, and awareness is the first step. People want to live better lives. Not just the one per cent. All of us. That is why we got involved.

'The world always moves forward,' said Eleni, 'but ask your-self . . . why do we need more energy?'

There is never enough time to consider these questions, before someone else (who never asked) has already given their answer. As Dimitris Ibrahim told me in Athens, the deals are signed and the seismic testing is underway. But I am on my way to Epirus at last, with a stop-off at Mitikas, just north of Preveza, a town on the coastal edge of the Ambracian Gulf.

Almost as soon as I leave Missolonghi, I pass a sign for an 'undersea tunnel', and then there are more, every kilometre or so, 'undersea tunnel' it says, in a large liquid script. How excit-ing, I think, it's going to be like something out of Jacques Cousteau, or *The Life Aquatic with Steve Zissou*, an underwater drive-through perhaps, with flatfish and dolphins knocking at the perspex, or a scene from Disney's *Bedknobs and Broomsticks*, with cartoon sea lions and coral reefs (there was a lot of time for the excitement to build), but in the end it was just another blank concrete hole, taking me up to Preveza and round to the Iraklis Hotel in Mitikas.

I was meeting the author Julian Hoffman at the hotel. We had arranged to spend a couple of days together, exploring the classical sites and the nearby Ambracian Gulf, and Julian was also eager to see more of Epirus. He lives in Prespa in north-western Greece and writes nature books, including *Irreplaceable: The Fight to Save Our Wild Places*, a detailed, poetic and devastating exploration of the world's dwindling wilderness, although somehow (like Theseus) he manages to hold onto a thread of optimism. I was very pleased to see him, especially when he pulled binoculars and a powerful telescope from the back of his car, and I saw that he would be able to tell me something about the birds I had been staring at for the past few weeks.

'There was a great flock of large black birds at Delphi,' I told him, as we settled behind an unsteady formica table at the low-key but genuinely unmissable 'Doctor of Hunger' steak house in Mitikas (I mean, who could resist?). 'They were wheeling high above the cliffs. But they weren't crows.'

'I think I might need a bit more information than that,' said Julian, with admirable restraint, chewing on his 'scopped pork'. The Doctor of Hunger was already working its magic. There may be other restaurants in Mitikas, we will never know – but in truth, I thought, as we watched the owner lurch towards us with a chocolate crepe the size of a tractor tyre, it is unlikely that we will ever need to find out, or indeed eat again. The logo on the menu is a racing ambulance, and Erysichthon would have had them on speed dial.

The Ambracian Gulf is a large inland stretch of low-lying water, narrowly open to the Ionian Sea where Preveza meets the town of Aktio, or ancient Actium if you want to revel in the fact that this is the place where Augustus defeated Antony and Cleopatra in the great naval battle, just offshore from the route of the 'undersea tunnel', and Antony and Cleopatra committed suicide (with sword and snake), having retreated from their camp on the headland at the southern entrance to the Gulf, after watching their men die and:

> The breaking of so great a thing should make
> A greater crack: the round world
> Should have shook lions into civil streets,
> And citizens to their dens.

There are still dolphins in the Gulf, they say, and some improbable flamingos, but no lions, of course, although they too were here once. The world became smaller that day.

The first birds we saw, as we stopped the car on the northern edge of the Gulf, and before Julian had time to drag his telescope from the back, were two kingfishers, flying low and fast over the grey water just a few metres from the path. 'Good lord,' said Julian, not for the last time that day. A blue and gold blur, moving fast, speeding into the reeds, slipstreams of yellow and white, then back out again, skimming the surface, a high 'neep-neep', one of them stopping now in the low-slung branch of a dead alder, maybe thinking about a nest, its halcyon days ahead. They are the first kingfishers I have ever seen, I would know it if they weren't.

And there are little rock nuthatches in the scrub around the olive trees, grey and beige, their tawny shanks and long black beaks, darting and bobbing earnestly among the dried twigs and leaves; and great white egrets standing still and snowy, up to their knees in the water; little egrets too, closer to shore; and Dalmatian pelicans further out, riding the swell, flat orange beaks resting on their grey-white chests; and then ('good lord') in the hazy distance, towards the far shore, there are the flamingos, and Julian leads me to the telescope and I find myself staring at dozens of them, a fantastical creature on a European shore, still here, and in such numbers, strolling together, stalking the waters on their spindly legs, the knees buckling backwards, and the curve of their long necks, some-times bowing to the water to feed, or held high like a swan, but pink and absurd (Lewis Carroll inescapable), but also so grace-ful, and even strangely menacing, like lifting the lid on a box of snakes.

'But look,' says Julian. And there are pygmy cormorants, so close we could throw them a lifeline, and the regular-sized cormorants I know from the river Thames, standing on logs or barely submerged stones, holding their wings wide, turning with the wind, these prehistoric birds. There is a tall grey heron behind the nearest stand of reeds, so absolutely still I hadn't even seen it (and anyway I have been turned giddy by the distant flamingos). And hurrying through the water there is a little grebe, its bright eyes busy. There are sandpipers wading even closer, dabbing at the shore, crowding out a solitary ringed plover. And then ('look!'), incredibly, there are two marsh harri-ers, far off beyond the flamingos, but drifting closer, circling above the lake. The sky is the colour of oysters, the harriers standing out sharp and black against the low, pearly clouds. There are black redstarts dancing in the tamarisk and (don't worry, I have this one) robins calling in the trees above the rocks at our backs. The rock nuthatch has a beautiful song, a soft liquid trill, drenching us in music. Do you know why the nightingale sings? That is an old story, a sad one too, best kept for another day.

We drive on and find another place to stop, next to a perfectly preserved church, with a bell tower and a cluster of empty outhouses. There is a well with a zinc bucket wound tight on a new rope, and tiles sliding from its broken roof. 'Monastery of Rodia' is written in yellow on a brown sign. An old man is here before us, gathering purple cyclamen from the stony banks. He has a mustard-coloured shirt, burned-toffee-coloured dyed hair and a nose like a flamingo's, and he squats down on the dusty track that leads to the monastery to speak with Julian, relaxing into the moment, unleashing a squall of Greek. He holds a small bouquet of cyclamen in front of him, like an offering. 'He insists on us having these flowers,' says Julian, 'apparently he gave some flowers to some beautiful models last week, but they had "no minds" and threw them away.' We promise to cherish the flowers. But how?

The man's name is Costas and he is an ex-teacher. He wonders what we do, and Julian tells him I am writing a book about the area and Costas wants to make sure I have heard about Maria Callas and Aristotle Onassis. 'They used to meet in a boat, off the coast, here!' he says, over and over. 'They were lovers,' he says, 'not just friends. A couple. They were lovers.'

And it is true, or so we are told. Maria Callas, 'the Divine one', and the shipping magnate Aristotle Onassis, who married Jackie Kennedy, and was as rich as Croesus.

We stroll around the monastery, but not inside because it is locked. We find a plain tiger butterfly, which Costas says was first depicted in art 3,500 years ago. And then we have to go. Costas hands us each the cyclamen, and there are tears in his eyes, but we are all three of us unaccountably moved. 'Remember,' he says to Julian, 'what men are here for. It is to share stories about the things that matter.'

We follow the five-kilometre causeway to the tiny island of Koronisia, skimming the water-line, the faintest waves rippling the reeds, prickly pear and clumps of sedum growing along the line of large, white, road-side rocks, placed there to keep the drunk (or twitching) drivers of Greece out of the Ambracian Gulf. I am staring at flamingos landing in the water in a whirling blaze of pink, or flying across the lagoon, their necks so long and straight, the blurred grey mountains behind. Shoals of fish swirl in the shallows, stalked by herons and egrets. We are so blasé by the time we near the end of the causeway that we have started looking for coypu among the reeds. They are said to live here too, released or escaped from farms.

We stop for lunch on the island, and find a deserted café with tables facing the Gulf. Perhaps in a normal year this place would be busy with yachts and holiday-makers, even now, in

early November, but this is not a normal year. We sit and listen
to the silence, the occasional splash of fish from the lagoon, the
water so still, a sheen of mother-of-pearl, the misty hills over the
water. There are olive trees at the shoreline, a small rowing boat
tethered and sinking in the shallows, a faint vapour rising from
the Gulf, and then, into this reverie, one, two, three dolphins
break the surface and softly submerge, and then up again, so
gently, with the grace of Apollo, the dolphins lift and dive along
the bay, swimming with untouchable power to the far shore,
where they disappear forever into the past. 'Good lord,' says
Julian.

We sit in the empty café.

'And that may be a merlin,' he says, punch-drunk with
wonder.

We have not been on these shores for more than half a day
and I do not know why it should be so hard to remember that
'Hope', as we are so often reminded, 'is the thing with
feathers'.

To Epirus, then. We stopped at Nekromanteion on the way,
because I wanted to see the place where Odysseus called up the
dead and spoke with Tiresias and Achilles. And here it is, on a
hillside on the edge of a small village, just above the car park
fringed with cypress trees. There is no doubt: simply follow a
path littered with the droppings of beech martens (thank you,
Julian) and trace your way down steep, worn steps into a cold
narrow room, your fingers brushing the heavy dead stone, the

warmth leaching from your bones on this sunny November day, and you will feel a sliding creep of anxiety or dread, because Hades and Persephone were once worshipped here with the blood of generations . . . and they are nearer than you would like. Some people say that this is not the true Nekromanteion, which was written about by Homer and Virgil, but is a later shrine, over which a more modern (but still ancient) fortified farmhouse perches, but perhaps those people would like to spend the night here alone, in the cold dank room under the farmhouse, with all the lights extinguished, the next time Hekate's moon is on the turn.

One thing we do know is that the river Acheron, the river of woe, over which Charon ferried the dead to Hades, is very close, even though its course has changed many times over the centuries. I asked a young guide whether we could walk there and she looked at me as if I had just asked where I could slit the throat of my sacrificial goat, but I have learned that the Greeks are generally unenthusiastic about hiking. Anyway, she and her friend were preoccupied with the sight of a small Dahl's whip snake sunning itself on the crazy paving. They told us that a bust of Persephone had been found here, and that we could see it in the museum at Ioannina. The strange thing is that it feels like spring, on this mid-autumn day in Nekromanteion, the snakes and lizards basking on the hot stones, clouded yellow butterflies and dragonflies rising in the sunlit air and the leaves green on the trees. Persephone is not in the museum. She is close.

Odysseus, standing here, had to slit the throats of a black ewe and a ram and let their blood flow into the pit he had dug with his sword (one cubit wide and long – follow this recipe carefully) and sprinkled with barley, milk, honey and sweet wine. And then the spirits of the dead came. He wanted to speak with the prophet Tiresias, who could see into the future, but first he had to push back the ghosts that had gathered around the pooling blood. His mother was there, and after he had spoken with Tiresias he let her drink, and she told him that Penelope was waiting for him, and his father was alive, his son too, and Odysseus tried to embrace her but it was like trying to hold onto a dream. And he spoke with Agamemnon, who told him he had been murdered by Aegisthus, along with all his men, butchered at the feast held to celebrate his return (and not in his bath as others say). Odysseus spoke with Achilles (who just wanted to get back home and lead a long, anonymous life in the hills), and Elpenor, one of his men, who had died on the island of Circe, breaking his spine when falling out of a loft, and who begged Odysseus for a proper burial. And Persephone sent the ghosts of famous women to talk with him – Tyro, Antiope, Alcmene, Chloris, Leda, Iphimedeia, Phaedra, Procris and lovely Ariadne – all of them lovers or victims of the gods. And there were so many more, the ghosts crowding round, craving blood, the agony of the dead separated from the warmth and the light. You can see why a religion that offered the hope of escape from this nothingness would prove irresistible.

If you want to know what Pandora's jar looked like, there are some beautiful examples at Nekromanteion, fashioned from warm terracotta, almost intact after more than two thousand years, with wide openings and lips and curved sides, most of them large enough to hold a body. A writer called Theognis, who lived not too long after Hesiod, believed that Pandora's jar contained all the good in the world. After all, that is the meaning of her name, Pandora. All good gifts. We don't know if Theognis thought that the jar also held everything evil, because not all of his poem survives, but he does write that the gods of Truth and Restraint and the lovely Graces all flew off to Mount Olympus, leaving only Hope behind. In the end it doesn't seem to matter who you ask. They all agree that Hope was the only one left.

When we got there we discovered that the river Acheron is beautiful, and nothing like the dreary river of the dead that marked the boundaries of Hades. Perhaps it was one last twist of the knife, to drink in everything that you were about to lose. Pausanias never visited (not until he breathed his last, that is, and clambered aboard Charon's ferry), but he does quote these verses from a lost epic called the *Minyad*.

> The dead men's ferryboat, which the old man
> Charon rows, was not moored at the bank.

And those are just about the only lines we have from the *Minyad*. So much has been lost, perhaps ninety per cent of everything that was ever written by the Greeks. Some may count that as a blessing.

Anyway, there is still no sign of a ferryboat down by the shores of the Acheron, just bands of yellow chiffchaffs whirling between the banks, barging into the willows, hoovering up late autumn stores of insects. The river is the colour of iced vodka and there's an old man fishing on the far side, but not for trout, he says, even though the waters are running fast and cold and clear. His son arrived to help him carry away his catch and Julian and I stood in the river of death and listened to the chiff-chaffs and the splash and chatter of the water and I thought of the gorge in the Forest of Foloi and made a silent promise to myself (while sending up a prayer to the god) not to miss these moments again. Although as Bacchylides once wrote, in words that have somehow survived the last 2,500 years,

> It is hard for men on earth to sway
> the minds of the gods.

I have received an email from Dimitris of the WWF, his happiness bursting through in a fanfare of exclamation marks. It is so good to hear from him after what must have been an uncharacteristically gloomy conversation in that café in Athens. What a rollercoaster it is.

> Repsol is on the verge of exiting its upstream portfolio in Greece!!!! This portfolio consists of two onshore blocks (Ioannina, Aitoloakarnania) and one offshore (Ionion). Repsol has deprioritised Greece as part of its decarbonisation target and new business plan (2021–2026) . . . and the company will reduce its oil production and upstream activities over the next five years.

We cannot take sole credit for this thrilling development, but we can surely say that our campaign has contributed decisively to it. It also acts to reinforce our campaign's strategies to increase investment uncertainty (through raising local opposition and mobilising legal action) and refocus public discourse on evidence based argumentation. Nothing is 100% certain at the moment, but we like to keep our hopes high.

Yes, we like to keep our hopes high ... although (in other news) I have discovered that I am the deathstar of wild hiking. Even Julian, who has been showing me the dried scat of bears and possibly, he thinks, a lone wolf, and explaining their diets, has been sucked into my orbit, and we are now lost on a path in a forest in Epirus, many kilometres off course from the route that had been mapped for us with such detail and concern by Pavlos, the co-owner of the enchanted Anemi guest house where we are staying in the village of Kato Pedina. Not that either of us cares. We are not really lost, we are just wandering in wonder through woods of oak and poplar and beech, following the banks of racing rivers, breathing the cool mountain air, clambering over rocks and scree, watching the small stones slide and tumble down the valley sides. Autumn has come to the high mountains, and the leaves on the trees are russet and brown and golden yellow, and we are scuffling through beech leaves, scrunching over acorns, looking for signs of bears. At one point we stop in the forest on a faint track on the top slopes of a gorge and listen to the sound of leaves falling, and that is all we can hear, there is no wind, just the dry scrape of a leaf twisting through the trees, and then another, until the robins start up again. There are ravens here, nesting in the cliffs, and down by the riverbanks the wild boar have been rootling in the sand and the mud. There is joy in every moment.

We walk across the famous looping stone bridges, and follow paths that lead nowhere, or take us past cemeteries and into empty villages. We see no one, until a man appears out of a doorway carrying a hammer and some lengths of wood and disappears into a church. Sometimes a dog barks from behind a wall, or shoves its muzzle through the bars of a metal gate and snarls. Our footsteps echo off the cobbles in the narrow streets. Thick green ivy has crept over the blank windows of an abandoned mansion, and in the village square scrub and brushwood lie in ragged piles, roped by living clematis, turning brown in the autumn air.

In Kato Pedina, walking through the quiet village before nightfall, Julian and I spoke to the owner of one of the inns, whose two large mountain dogs were the only other signs of life in the silent streets, apart from Pavlos listening to his jazz back at the Anemi guest house. The man who was standing in front of his immaculate inn was from Athens, he told us, but had grown up here in Epirus. When he was younger the village had a population of one thousand people, and now, in the winter, it is down to thirty. 'Maybe there are 125 of us here in the summer,' he said (the precision of it), 'and this pandemic has brought

some others back. But just look at the school,' he said, pointing
to a large, flat-grey, old stone building, its lovely frontage flaking
with decay, 'there is no use for it.'

And when I was back in London, in yet another Zoom call,
I spoke with Kalliopi Stara, a researcher at Ioannina University,
who writes about the culture and ecology of the forests of
Epirus, and she told me how she had moved back from Athens
to a village in Zagori with her young children, to the place
where her family had always lived, but they had to leave for
Ioannina because of the schools 'and who wants to live in a
car?' Her family used to own farmland around here, but it
reverted to forest and once that happens it belongs to the state.
'Emotionally it is really sad,' she said, 'to give up the land. But
we are not going to claim it. What is the point if you are not
going to farm?' We talked about the plans for oil and gas extraction, here in the forests and gorges of Epirus.

'It is like someone selling your eye,' she said. 'How can they?'

The innkeeper in Kato Pedina tells us that ever since people
stopped keeping goats, the trees have returned. And it is true.
There are trees growing from every untended scrap of land in
the village, even forcing their way through the pavements. Are
trees a problem now? It is an alien idea to a city-dweller. But
this is what it looks like, a population in decline, fading since the
1960s, people heading to the towns, birth rates on the way
down, the wild returning. Greece is being afforested. And it is
visceral, this fear, and the sadness, embedded deep in all of us,
the dread of abandonment and loss, of boarded-up shops and
shuttered homes, just the old people left, shuffling down the
same empty streets, prey to invaders.

The Romans, at the height of their Empire, fretted about depopulation. And Julian and I, on our way to Epirus, had visited all that is left of the immense city of Nicopolis, founded by Augustus to celebrate his victory over Antony and Cleopatra, once home to tens of thousands of people, and now it is just lizards and tree frogs and the little owl we found staring at us from the gloom above the mosaics. It is frightening, the idea that we might be moving backwards; no longer growing, but falling back. But we need to find a way to enjoy this reversal. To welcome back the trees and the wolves. Breathe the air. It should not be controversial to say that there are too many of us. Not here in Epirus, of course, at least not obviously (although the oil and gas concessions may soon show otherwise), but the truth is that our presence is felt everywhere. The cities where most of us live throw long and toxic shadows. We know it. To be clear, it is not necessarily true that there are too many of us (well, the arguments go on), it is just (just!) that there are too many of us doing the things that we do. And some of us are doing infinitely more than we should. Erysichthon on steroids. We need to take less. Learn to live with others. Share. Any ancient Greek could have warned us. 'Nothing in excess'. Not that they seem to have been very good at following their own advice.

I think that the answer to the question I asked the Oracle (brought to me by email from a surprising source) is straightforward, but hard. 'Know Yourself'. That is all. When we are in despair, and looking for hope (even Pandora's Hope), we probably already know what needs to be done. But to do it we also have to change ourselves, and do the right thing, and that is so much harder. We are going to have to learn restraint (but let the horses run!), and it is not easy. Most of us seem to be waiting for someone else to go first, or a final sign, although we were told long ago what to do. Honour the gods. (Revel in the beauty of the world.) And in the words of yet another Greek proverb, 'If you don't praise your house to the skies, it'll come tumbling about your ears.' Still, what do I know? It is famously difficult to interpret your own Oracle.

Even so, if you are in any doubt about the right way forward (and remember, we are meant to be looking to the skies for guidance), here is Socrates:

> Earth is a goddess and willingly teaches righteousness
> to those who can learn, for the better she is served, the
> more good things she gives in return.

It shouldn't be so hard.

But the anxiety must have got to me, because my dreams came back in the mountains, at least for one night only, the last one of all. I dreamed (#8) that I was in a bed wrapped in white sheets, and that I was dreaming (#9), and that I was even watching myself from the doorway as I dreamed (#10), my back turned, my legs tangled thrashingly in the white sheet. And – sorry – that was it. Hermes the messenger god (bringer of dreams, patron of writers, killer of dogs) waved me off to London with a bad joke.

The night before this lonely dream, after we had left the old innkeeper in Kato Pedina, Julian and I found ourselves sitting around a fire in a field in front of a farmyard, talking with Lila, the wife of Pavlos, and co-owner of the enchanted Anemi guest house. She had brought four friends, all of whom were involved in the protests against the development of oil and gas in Epirus. They were proud of what they had done, alerting other locals to the plans of the corporations, slowing the developers when they could. But also, said someone, 'Covid came to the rescue. Everything is on hold for now.' The laughter of women around the warm fire, the darkness at our backs.

Lila's friend, who owned the farm, brought us tomatoes and she toasted bread on the fire and we passed around flasks of tsipouro, the local grappa. Everyone was worried about the emptying villages and the closing schools. 'Let the refugees come,' said Lila, 'we need them here.' A young man agreed. 'We fight for this place,' he said, 'but it is dead. There is nothing to do after dark.'

It was a warm night, even away from the fire. The weather has been strange for the past few years, someone said, maybe the farmer. 'What do the other locals think?' I wanted to know, 'are they happy that you are protesting? Or do they welcome the developers?' 'They want their freedom to choose,' said Lila, 'they are sick of the lies of politicians.' A bull of a dog thrust its nose into the fire, looking for scraps, and sparks sprayed upwards.

I asked them all about hope, you can be sure I did, but they only laughed. 'Of course we have hope,' said Lila, 'what would we do without it?' The young man had heard Nietzsche's argument, that hope is the most debilitating punishment of all, but none of them were prepared to give the idea the time of day. 'Of course we have hope,' someone said again.

'We have to light our fires secretly,' Eleftheria Tsoyknaki had told me, who dances and fights to keep the oil in the ground and the beauty of Epirus alive.

Imagine looking down on our fire on this dark November night, as Zeus once did, fuming over Prometheus' act of theft, and seeing this tiny spark in the dark mountains of Epirus. And then further out, the lights of Ioannina and the roads to Athens and beyond, Italy and Europe, electric and neon, Saudi and the Gulf, the great cities of China, Malaysia and Japan, all burning so bright, India too, the flare of New York and the eastern states, the oil fields of west Africa, California and Siberia on fire, western Australia, the Amazon too, electricity and flames, no end to it, the blaze of humanity, Prometheus' gift and Zeus' curse. And here we are in a field in Epirus, lovingly tending our own embers, the sparks shooting up to heaven, nothing to sacrifice, just the dog nosing in the ashes, the tsipouro talking.

'Where shall we go tomorrow?' I say to Lila, coming back down to earth. 'Can we go and see the areas that are threatened?'

'Oh, just walk,' she said. 'See the beauty. Then you will understand. Don't worry about it. Find the bridges and the gorges and the woods. Follow the rivers. Go and see, it doesn't matter which villages or paths. The beauty is everywhere. You will see what we are fighting for. And then you will want to do the same.'

And that much is true, isn't it?

We have to hope.

Acknowledgements

In grateful memory of Tony Elliott (1947–2020), who fuelled my love of guidebooks.

And a heartfelt thank you to all of the following: Lila and Pavlos at the enchanted Anemi Guest House; Nadja Argyropoulou; Fiona Davison of the RHS; Richard Buxton; Natasha Carlish, Jay Griffiths and the 12 attendees of the Arvon Nature Writing course, who sat through the first readings of this book; Yiannis Chalkias; Lloyd Cole; Christy Constantakopoulou; Simon Critchley; Angeliki Kanelli, Eleni Tzachrista, Eleftheria Tsoyknaki and all the Dancing Women of Vrisoules; John Dimotsis; James Head; Julian Hoffman (travelling companion and sage of the wetlands); Kevin Ebbutt; Catharine Edwards; Sicily Fiennes; Dimitris Ibrahim; the eagle-eyed Kathleen McCully; Conor McCutcheon; Andrew McMillan; Gill Morgan; Kenny-the-mushroom-man; Malvina Panagiotidi; Dave Rimmer; Kalliopi Stara; Mark Saban; Penny Saban; Oliver Taplin; Elias Tziritis; Chris Vrettos; the very erudite Jonathan Williams; Sue Willetts at the Hellenic and Roman Library in London.

Thank you to Sam Carter, thoughtful and incisive editor and cricketer, and to all the hard-working staff at Oneworld Publications.

Thank you to my agent Rebecca Winfield of David Luxton Associates, for her enthusiasm and support (www.davidluxtonassociates.co.uk).

And thank you, and with love to, Anna and Alex, who set me on my way, and lovely Natalie and Esme for all their encouragement.

I made a donation to WWF Greece (www.wwf.gr/en) in an attempt to offset the impact (and guilt) of having flown from London to Athens and back again. But . . .

An A–Z of Gods, Goddesses, Heroes, Heroines, Mythical Beings and Some of the Mortals Mentioned in this Book

All of the following appear at least once in *A Thing of Beauty*. I am very aware how hard it is to keep track of these names (even if you've spent the last couple of years immersed in the myths), but this glossary is here to help. The names represent a fraction of the totality: if they're not in the book, they're not in this list.

A word on spelling: I have gritted my teeth and followed *Cassell's Dictionary of Classical Mythology*. So Dionysos is Dionysus and the river god Alpheius is Alpheius (and not Alfeios or Alpheios). Kallimachos is Callimachus. And so on. In the end, I chose consistency over my own random preferences.

Acheron One of the rivers of the underworld, over which **Charon** rowed his boat.

Achilles The greatest fighter in the Greek armies. Died in the war with Troy.

Actaeon Obsessive huntsman who saw the goddess **Artemis** bathing and was turned into a stag.

Aegeus King of Athens, father of **Theseus**.

Aegisthus Lover of **Clytemnestra** and co-murderer with her of **Agamemnon**.

Aeschylus Playwright. Author of the *Oresteia*. Fought at the Battle of Marathon.

Agamemnon The high king of Mycenae. Led the Greek armies to war against Troy.

Alcyone A beautiful princess who loved a man called **Ceyx** and was turned into a kingfisher.

Alpheius A river god who fell in love with the nymph **Arethusa** and pursued her to Syracuse.

Antiope Amazon queen, perhaps wife of **Theseus** and mother of **Hippolytus**.

Aphrodite The laughter-loving goddess of love and lust. Born out of the foam created by the severed genitals of **Uranus**. Married to **Hephaestus**; lover of **Ares**. Adored by nymphs.

Apollo The far-shooting and famously distant god of prophecy, harmony, music, healing, plagues and fresh starts. Lived at Delphi for most of the year. Twin brother of **Artemis**.

Archedemos The ancient world's most famous nympholept.

Ares The god of war.

Arethusa A nymph who was pursued to Syracuse by the river god **Alpheius**.

Ariadne Cretan princess, daughter of **Minos**, sister of **Phaedra**, lover of **Theseus**.

Aristotle Philosopher of the natural world, logic, politics, etc.

Artemis The goddess of wild places and animals, the moon and mountaintops, swamps, edgelands and the seashore. The virgin huntress. Oversaw moments of transition, adolescent girls and childbirth. Followed by nymphs. Murderous when angered. Twin sister of **Apollo**.

Asclepius The son of the mortal **Coronis** and probably **Apollo**. The greatest doctor who ever lived. Became a god.

Asopus River god who was told by **Sisyphus** that **Zeus** had abducted his daughter.

Athena The patron goddess of Athens, dedicated to war and crafts. Wise, like her symbol, the owl. Wore the severed Gorgon's head.

Bellerophon Hero who rode **Pegasus** and slew the dreadful **Chimaera**.

Biton Brother of **Cleobis**, very nearly the happiest people who ever lived.

Briareos A fifty-headed, hundred-handed monster who decided that **Helios** should be the patron god of Corinth.

Byron, Lord George Gordon Poet (1788–1824).

Cadmus Founded the city of Thebes. Married to **Harmonia**.

Callimachus Third-century BCE Greek poet. Gave us a version of the story of **Erysichthon**.

Calypso Beautiful island goddess and lover of **Odysseus**.

Cassandra Trojan princess, slave of **Agamemnon**. A prophetess who was cursed by **Apollo** to always tell the truth but never be believed.

Cecrops Early king of Athens, a man with the tail of a snake.

Celeus King of Eleusis, in the days when **Demeter** first came to visit.

centaurs Wild and untrustworthy creatures: half-man, half-horse.

Cercyon King of Eleusis, killed by **Theseus**.

Ceyx He loved **Alcyone** and died and was turned into a kingfisher.

Charon The ferryman who rowed the dead over the river **Acheron** to **Hades**.

Cheiron The wise **centaur**, teacher of heroes.

Chimaera A dreadful monster with three heads: a lion (front), goat (middle) and serpent (back). Killed by **Bellerophon**.

Circe A goddess and an enchantress. Sister of Pasiphae, the wife of **Minos**. Lover of **Odysseus**.

Cleobis Brother of **Biton**, very nearly the happiest people who ever lived.

Clytemnestra Wife and probable murderer of **Agamemnon**.

Croesus Legendarily wealthy king of Lydia.

Cronus Father of **Zeus** and other Olympians, son of **Uranus** (Heaven), whose genitals he sliced off with a sickle.

cyclopes One-eyed giants, sons of **Uranus** and **Gaia**, and/or maybe **Poseidon**, who forged **Zeus**' thunderbolts. They built the vast walls of Mycenae and Tiryns.

Daphne Nymph who fled from **Apollo** and was turned into a laurel tree.

Demeter The golden goddess of corn and the harvest. Mother of **Persephone**. Her secret Mysteries were celebrated at the sacred city of Eleusis.

Dionysus God of wine, danger and delight. Madness, metamorphosis and ecstasy. Wild animals and rebirth. Followed by **maenads** and **satyrs**.

dryads Long-lived and lovely nymphs, some say born and dying with their tree.

Dryope Woman who had a son with **Apollo**, and became a nymph.

Elpenor Odysseus' youngest crew member, who got drunk and died hungover, falling off the roof in **Circe**'s palace.

Endymion Legendarily beautiful king, lover of **Selene**, the goddess of the moon. Possibly asleep for all time ('a thing of beauty is a joy for ever').

Eos The goddess of the dawn, lover of (among others) **Tithonus**.

Epimetheus Slow-witted husband of **Pandora**; brother of **Prometheus**.

Erichtho A Thessalian witch.

Erichthonius One of the first kings of Athens, born from **Hephaestus**' semen-soaked rag. Possibly half-snake.

Erinyes Also known as **the Furies**, terrifying deities of vengeance. Pursued **Orestes** and became 'the Kindly Ones' (the 'Eumenides') when they were pacified by **Athena**. Born from the blood that flowed onto **Gaia** from **Uranus**' severed genitals, or perhaps from Nyx (Night).

Eros The god of irresistible desire and **Aphrodite**'s little helper.

Erysichthon A prince or king who chopped down a sacred grove and brought down the wrath of the goddess **Demeter**. He was punished with unassuageable hunger and ended up eating himself.

Eupolos The first athlete to cheat at the Olympic Games.

Euripides Playwright. Works include *The Bacchae*, *Medea* and *Hippolytus*.

Eurydice A **dryad**, wife of **Orpheus**, died when she was bitten by a snake.

Furies, the Also known as the **Erinyes**, terrifying deities of vengeance.

Gaia Mother Earth. The Great Goddess.

giants Children of **Gaia** and the blood from the severed genitals of **Uranus**. They tried to overthrow **Zeus** and the other Olympians, but were defeated with the help of **Heracles**.

Gorgons Three sisters with venomous snakes for hair and a look that could turn anything to stone. The most famous, **Medusa**, was killed by **Perseus**. The other two were immortal.

griffins Creatures with the body and tail of a lion, the head (and sometimes front legs) of an eagle.

Hades The king of the underworld. Brother of **Zeus**. Husband of **Persephone**.

Harmonia Married to **Cadmus**, with whom she founded the dynasty of Thebes.

Hekate Goddess of crossroads, flaming torches, howling dogs, witches, magic and night.

Helen Queen of Sparta, wife of **Menelaus**, lover of Paris, so beautiful.

Helios All-seeing god of the sun, patron of Corinth and Rhodes. Father of **Phaeton**.

Hephaestus The lame master craftsman, god of fire and anvils, son of **Hera**, married to **Aphrodite**.

Hera The queen of the gods, married to **Zeus**. Goddess of marriage and the happy home. Jealous.

Heracles The ultimate Greek hero. Had to complete twelve labours. Killed monsters, humans and his own children. Became a god. Hated by **Hera**.

Heraclitus Philosopher famous for telling us we can't step in the same river twice.

Hermes The messenger god, bringer of dreams and conductor of souls. The god of ghosts and magic, full of guile and craft. Shifts between heaven, earth and hell. Patron of writers, travellers and thieves. Dog-killer.

Herodotus Often called 'the father of history'.

Hesiod Author of *Theogony* and *Works and Days*. Brought us the myths in written form.

Hestia The goddess of the family and the happy home.

Hippolyte Lover of **Theseus**, perhaps the mother of **Hippolytus**.

Hippolytus Beautiful son of **Theseus**, torn apart by horses.

Hippothoon Grandson of **Cercyon**, king of Eleusis. Raised by wild horses.

Homer The eighth-century BCE poet(s) of *The Iliad* and *The Odyssey*. Blind.

Hope Was left in **Pandora**'s Jar when everything evil was released into the world. Or so we're told.

Hyacinthus The beautiful mortal loved by **Apollo** and **Zephyrus**. Killed by a discus. Transformed into a flower (*ai! ai!*).

Hydra Many-headed, venomous, swamp-dwelling monster killed by **Heracles**.

Iambe A servant in the court of King **Celeus** of Eleusis, when **Demeter** first came to call. Told the ancient world's most famous dirty joke.

Iasion Mortal lover of **Demeter**, father of the god of wealth.

Icarus He flew too close to the sun.

Iphigenia Daughter of **Agamemnon** and **Clytemnestra**, sacrificed by her father to speed him on his way to Troy.

Jason He led the Argonauts to steal the golden fleece, and fled with Medea, whom he later abandoned, with tragic consequences.

Julian the Apostate The last pagan emperor of Rome. Tried to reverse the tide of Christianity.

Kallippos The second athlete to cheat at the Olympic Games.

Leto A **Titan**, mother of **Apollo** and **Artemis**.

Lycurgus King of Nemea, whose son was killed by a snake.

maenads Female followers of the god **Dionysus**, sometimes prone to madness and violence.

Maia Nymph, mother of **Hermes**.

Medusa The only mortal **Gorgon**, with snakes for hair and a gaze that could turn any living thing to stone.

Meliai Ash tree nymphs, born from the severed genitals of **Uranus**.

Menelaus King of Sparta, brother of **Agamemnon**, husband of **Helen**.

Mestra The shape-shifting daughter of **Erysichthon**.

Metaneira Queen at Eleusis when **Demeter** first came to visit.

Metis The goddess of intelligence, mother of **Athena**, swallowed by **Zeus**.

Minos King of Crete, who became a judge in the underworld after his death.

Minotaur Grotesque, bull-headed son of Pasiphae, the wife of King **Minos**.

muses Nymphs, and the source of all our inspiration. Once there were three, now there are said to be nine.

Neda The eldest of the three nymphs that helped raise **Zeus**. A river in the Peloponnese.

Nestor Venerable, wise, honey-tongued king who went to Troy and returned safely to his home in Pylos.

nymphs Long-lived and lovely female spirits, associated with caves, springs, rivers, mountains, trees, glades and the sea. Followers especially of **Artemis** and **Aphrodite**.

Odysseus A cunning and valiant man, hero of the war with Troy, who spent ten years trying to get home. Lover of **Calypso**. Married to **Penelope**.

Oedipus As was foretold, he killed his father and married his mother. And then blinded himself when he discovered what he had done.

Orestes The son of **Agamemnon** and **Clytemnestra**. He murdered his mother to avenge his father and was pursued by the **Erinyes**.

Orion A great hunter, lover of **Eos**, killed by **Artemis** (or a giant scorpion), became a constellation.

Orpheus Created irresistibly beautiful music. Followed his wife into the underworld.

Pan The lusty, cloven-footed, fun-loving god of everything wild and wonderful. Spreads fear. Lived mostly in the mountains of Arcadia, playing his pipes.

Pandora She opened her box (it was really a jar) and released everything evil into the world and/or everything good. **Hope** remained trapped (but available?) in the jar – or perhaps it didn't.

Paul (Saint) First-century CE letter-writing Christian apostle.

Pausanias Second-century CE travel/guidebook writer, author of *A Guide to Greece*.

Pegasus A flying horse.

Peirene She died of grief when her son was killed by **Artemis**. Turned into a spring in the city of Corinth.

Pelops The first king of Pisa in the Peloponnese. Some say he founded the Olympic Games.

Penelope The famously patient and loyal wife of **Odysseus**. Mother of **Telemachus**, and perhaps also of **Pan**.

Pentheus King who got into a fight with **Dionysus** and was torn apart by his mother and aunts.

Pericles Revered leader of Athens at the onset of the Peloponnesian War.

Periphetes Brutal brigand, killed by **Theseus**.

Persephone aka The Girl, daughter of **Demeter**. Abducted by and married to **Hades**, with whom she spends a certain amount of time each year.

Perseus Hero who killed the Gorgon **Medusa** and founded the golden city of Mycenae.

Phaedra Cretan princess, daughter of King **Minos**, wife of **Theseus**, would-be lover of **Hippolytus**.

Phaeton A mortal son of **Helios** who insisted on driving the chariot of the sun, more fool him.

Pholus A friendly **centaur**, accidentally killed himself. Lived in the Forest of Foloi.

Phrontis The pilot of the ship that brought **Menelaus** home from Troy.

Pindar Theban poet.

Plato Greek philosopher (the purest form), author of *The Republic*, *Crito*, *Phaedo* and much more.

Pliny the Elder First-century CE Roman author and philosopher.

Poseidon Lord god of the sea, bulls and earthquakes; brother of **Zeus**.

Prometheus A **Titan**, humanity's friend (and creator?). Master craftsman, stealer of fire.

Proteus A fortune-telling sea god who could change shape at will.

Pythia The priestess who received and conveyed the oracles of **Apollo** at Delphi.

Rhea Daughter of **Uranus** and **Gaia**, mother of **Zeus**.

Sappho Female poet, based in Lesbos, wrote about her intense love for men and women. Only fragments remain.

Sarapion The only athlete ever to be fined for cowardice at the Olympic Games.

satyrs Shaggy-shanked, lustful and goatish followers of **Dionysus**.

Schliemann, Heinrich Nineteenth-century CE German businessman and archaeologist. Excavated 'Troy' and Mycenae.

Selene The lovely-armed goddess of the moon, lover of **Endymion**.

Semele Human lover of **Zeus**, mother of **Dionysus**; fried to a cinder.

Sirens Sang irresistibly and lured men to their deaths. Some say they were once the companions of **Persephone**.

Socrates Fifth-century BCE Athenian philosopher, left no writings of his own, but his teachings were immortalised by **Plato** and **Xenophon**.

Solon Statesman who explained happiness to **Croesus**.

Telemachus The son of **Odysseus** and **Penelope**. He went looking for his father and met **Nestor** and **Menelaus**.

Tellus According to the philosopher **Solon**, the happiest man who ever lived.

Theseus Heroic king of Athens, killer of the **Minotaur**, married to **Phaedra**, father of **Hippolytus**.

Thucydides Historian, soldier, plague survivor and author of *History of the Peloponnesian War*.

Tiresias He saw two snakes copulating and struck them with a stick and was turned into a woman, in which form he stayed for seven years, and then the same thing happened in reverse. Blinded. Became a prophet with the power to interpret the flight and song of birds.

Titans They were gods and ruled the world before the Olympians, and were then overthrown. Many lingered (**Prometheus**, **Rhea**). **Cronus** was one.

Tithonus Lover of **Eos**, the goddess of the dawn. Lived a very long time, before he was turned into a grasshopper.

Triptolemus Received gifts and knowledge from **Demeter** at the first Eleusinian Mysteries.

Uranus Heaven, Father Sky, son (and husband) of **Gaia**, the Mother Earth. Castrated and overthrown by his son **Cronus**.

Xenophon Athenian philosopher and soldier, wrote about **Socrates**.

Zephyrus The god of the West Wind. He arranged for the death of **Hyacinthus**.

Zeus The father and king of the gods.

Permissions

I have quoted from several classical sources in translation, and in general I have used the texts that can be found at the Perseus Digital Library (www.perseus.tufts.edu/hopper). They may be old (the translations, I mean), but they remain powerful and poetic. As for more recent material, I am grateful to the copyright holders who allowed me to use their words. I apologise if I have missed anything: please get in touch if you spot omissions or mistakes. You'll find the sources in the Select Bibliography, but I would also like to acknowledge the following:

Lines from *The Orchard Book of Greek Myths* © Geraldine McCaughrean, reproduced by permission from Orchard Books, London.

Line from 'The Muse of Happiness' © Copyright Louise Glück 2001, from *The Seven Ages*, published by Carcanet Press Limited, Manchester.

Thank you to Lloyd Cole and his management for allowing me to use a line from 'Forest Fire' by Lloyd Cole and the Commotions, which lodged in my brain over thirty-five years ago. (It's the title of chapter 7.)

Lines from 'Not Even Mythology' © Copyright Ritsos, Y. from *Repetitions, Testimonies, Parentheses*, trans. E. Keeley (Princeton, NJ: Princeton University Press, 1991).

Select Bibliography and Resources

The majority of everything that was written during the Greek Classical era has been lost, but fear not (or do. . .), plenty has survived. Instead of listing a great slew of books you can easily find elsewhere, I have only included the books that are mentioned in the text, along with a few that I found especially engrossing when I was researching and writing *A Thing of Beauty*.

GREEK (AND ROMAN) SOURCES

Where would I start, if I were starting afresh? With Claire Danes reading Emily Wilson's exhilarating translation of Homer's *The Odyssey*. It was written to be heard.

I cannot read ancient (or modern) Greek, but I have loved these translations.

Aeschylus, Sophocles, Euripides *The Greek Plays*, trans. M. Lefkowitz, J. Romm, E. Wilson, *et al.* (New York: Ballantine Books, 2017)

Apollodorus *The Library of Greek Mythology*, trans. R. Hard (Oxford: Oxford University Press, 1997)

Callimachus *The Hymns* (find them at the Perseus Digital Library, www.perseus.tufts.edu/hopper)

Herodotus *The Histories*, trans. T. Holland (London: Penguin Classics, 2014)

Hesiod *Theogony* and *Works and Days*, trans. M. L. West (Oxford: Oxford University Press, 1988)

Homer *The Homeric Hymns*, trans. P. McDonald (Manchester: Carcanet Press Ltd, 2016)

—*The Iliad*, trans. M. Hammond (London: Penguin Classics, 1987)

—*The Odyssey*, trans. E. Wilson (New York: W. W. Norton & Company, 2018)

Ovid *Metamorphoses*, trans. D. Raeburn (London: Penguin Classics, 2004)

Pausanias *Guide to Greece*, two vols, trans. P. Levi (London: Penguin Classics, 1971) My guiding light.

Pindar *The Complete Odes*, trans. A. Verity (Oxford: Oxford University Press, 2008)

Plato *The Republic*, *The Symposium*, *The Last Days of Socrates* and so on (all available at the Perseus Digital Library, www.perseus.tufts.edu/hopper)

Plutarch *Essays*, trans. R. Waterfield (London: Penguin Classics, 1992)

Sappho *Stung with Love: Poems and Fragments*, trans. A. Poochigian (London: Penguin Classics, 2009)

Trzaskoma, S. M., Smith, R. S. and Brunet, S. *Anthology of Classical Myth: Primary Sources in Translation* (Indianapolis, IN: Hackett Publishing, 2004) Indispensable!

MYTHS

What is a myth? No one agrees and no one knows. Perhaps
   sidestep the (sometimes enjoyable, often baffling) debate and
   enjoy the stories. Although if you are seeking rabbit holes,
   here is the entrance to a warren.

Burkert, W. *Greek Religion* (Cambridge, MA: Harvard University
   Press, 1985)

Buxton, R. *The Complete World of Greek Mythology* (London:
   Thames & Hudson, 2004) A thought-provoking and colourful introduction.

—*Forms of Astonishment: Greek Myths of Metamorphosis* (Oxford:
   Oxford University Press, 2018)

—*Imaginary Greece: the Contexts of Mythology* (Cambridge:
   Cambridge University Press, 2008)

Calasso, R. *The Celestial Hunter* (London: Allen Lane, 2020)

—*The Marriage of Cadmus and Harmony* (London: Penguin
   Classics, 2019)

Encyclopedia of World Mythology (London: Octopus Books, 1975)

Fry, S. *Mythos: The Greek Myths Retold* (London: Penguin Books,
   2018)

Graves, R. *The Greek Myths* (London: Penguin Books, 2017) First
   published 1955. Out of favour, more than a bit odd, obses-
   sional even, but worth dipping into.

Grimal, P. *Dictionary of Classical Mythology* (London: Penguin
   Books, 1991)

Hamilton, E. *Mythology: Timeless Tales of Gods and Heroes* (New
   York: Meridian, 1989) First published in 1940, still
   powerful.

Haynes, N. *Pandora's Jar: Women in the Greek Myths* (London: Picador, 2020)

Hughes, B. *Helen of Troy: Goddess, Princess, Whore* (London: Jonathan Cape, 2005)

Kerényi, C. *The Gods of the Greeks* (London: Thames & Hudson, 1951)

—*The Heroes of the Greeks* (London: Thames & Hudson, 1959) Written as though they really exist(ed).

Kershaw, S. P. *A Brief Guide to the Greek Myths* (London: Constable & Robinson, 2007)

Kirk, G. S. *The Nature of Greek Myths* (London: Penguin Books, 1974)

Lancelyn Green, R. *The Tale of Troy* (London: Puffin Books, 1958)

—*Tales of the Greek Heroes* (London: Puffin Books, 1958) I started here.

Marsh, J. *Dictionary of Classical Mythology* (London: Cassell & Co., 1998) Brilliantly concise retellings and reference work.

McCaughrean, G. *The Orchard Book of Greek Myths* (London: Orchard Books, 1992) For children.

Morales, H. *Classical Mythology: A Very Short Introduction* (Oxford: Oxford University Press, 2007)

Segal, R. A. *Myth: A Very Short Introduction* (Oxford: Oxford University Press, 2015)

TRAVEL

See also Pausanias *in Sources above.*

Cope, J. *The Megalithic European: The 21st Century Traveller in Prehistoric Europe* (London: HarperCollins, 2004)

Durrell, L. *The Greek Islands* (London: Penguin Books, 1978)

Leigh Fermor, P. *Mani* (London: John Murray, 1958)

—*Roumeli* (London: John Murray, 1966)

Miller, H. *The Colossus of Maroussi* (London: Penguin Books, 1950)

Stuttard, D. *Greek Mythology: A Traveller's Guide from Mount Olympus to Troy* (London: Thames & Hudson, 2016)

HISTORY

Beaton, R. *Byron's War: Romantic Rebellion, Greek Revolution* (Cambridge: Cambridge University Press, 2013)

—*Greece: Biography of a Modern Nation* (London: Penguin Books, 2020) Invaluable!

Byron, Lord. *Selected Letters and Journals*, ed. L. A. Marchand (London: John Murray, 1982)

Cartledge, P. *Ancient Greece: A Very Short Introduction* (Oxford: Oxford University Press, 2011)

Constantine, D. *In the Footsteps of the Gods: Travellers to Greece and the Quest for the Hellenic Ideal* (London: Tauris Parke Paperbacks, 2011)

Holland, T. *Dominion: The Making of the Western Mind* (London: Little, Brown, 2019)

—*Persian Fire: The First World Empire and the Battle for the West* (London: Little, Brown, 2005)

Meier, C. *Athens: A Portrait of the City in Its Golden Age* (London: Pimlico, 2000)

Morkot, R. *The Penguin Historical Atlas of Ancient Greece* (London: Penguin Books, 1996)

Peters, C. *Byron* (Stroud: Sutton Publishing, 2000)

Price, S. and Thonemann, P. *The Birth of Classical Europe: A History from Troy to Augustine* (London: Penguin Books, 2011)

Scott, M. *Delphi: A History of the Center of the Ancient World* (Princeton, NJ: Princeton University Press, 2014)

Stoneman, R. *Land of Lost Gods: The Search for Classical Greece* (London: Tauris Parke Paperbacks, 2010)

GENERAL

Baggini, J. *How the World Thinks: A Global History of Philosophy* (London: Granta Publications, 2018)

Cranaki, M. *Greece* (Paris: Vista, 1960)

Graeber, D. *Bullshit Jobs: The Rise of Pointless Work, and What We Can Do About It* (London: Penguin, 2019)

Hall, E. *The Ancient Greeks: Ten Ways They Shaped the Modern World* (London: Vintage, 2015)

Head, J. *Life Choice: Important Tips from Socrates, Plato and Aristotle* (CreateSpace Independent Publishing Platform, 2020)

Higgins, C. *It's All Greek to Me* (London: Short Books, 2008)

Nietzsche, F. *Human, All-Too-Human* (Ware: Wordsworth Editions, 2008)

Watson, L. C. *Magic in Ancient Greece and Rome* (London: Bloomsbury Academic, 2019)

THE EARTH

Bradshaw, C. J. A., Ehrlich, P. R., Beattie, A., *et al.*, 'Underestimating the challenges of avoiding a ghastly future', *Frontiers in Conservation Science*, 13 January 2021

Goodison, L. *Holy Trees and Other Ecological Surprises* (London: Just Press, 2010) Especially good on Minoan worship and trees.

Harari, Y. N. *Sapiens: A Brief History of Humankind* (London: Vintage Books, 2011) Some perspective.

Hoffman, J. *Irreplaceable: The Fight to Save Our Wild Places* (London: Penguin Books, 2019) 'Oh let them be left, wildness and wet'!

Hughes, D. J. *Environmental Problems of the Greeks and Romans: Ecology in the Ancient Mediterranean* (Baltimore, MD: Johns Hopkins University Press, 2014)

Hunt, A. and Marlow, H. (eds) *Ecology and Theology in the Ancient World: Cross-disciplinary Perspectives* (London: Bloomsbury Academic, 2019)

Klein, N. *This Changes Everything: Capitalism vs. the Climate* (London: Penguin Books, 2015)

Lewis, S. L. and Maslin, M. A. *The Human Planet: How We Created the Anthropocene* (London: Pelican Books, 2018)

Rackham, O. *Woodlands* (London: HarperCollins, 2010)

Schama, S. *Landscape & Memory* (London: HarperCollins, 1995)

Wallace-Wells, D. *The Uninhabitable Earth: A Story of the Future* (London: Penguin Books, 2019)

Wilson, E. O. *In Search of Nature* (London: Penguin Books, 1998)

FICTION

Barker, P. *The Silence of the Girls* (London: Penguin, 2019) The Trojan War, viscerally recounted by Achilles' sex slave.

Bunyan, J. *The Pilgrim's Progress* (London: Penguin Classics, 2008) I'm filing it under fiction, but not everyone would (nor me, once upon a time).

Haynes, N. *The Children of Jocasta* (London: Picador, 2018)
Imagine if your parents were Oedipus and Jocasta.

Ikonomou, C. *Something Will Happen, You'll See*, trans. K. Emmerich (New York: Archipelago Books, 2016) Contemporary Athenian short stories. Funny and sad.

Kazantzakis, N. *Zorba the Greek*, trans. C. Wildman (London: Faber & Faber, 2016) The sound of plates smashing . . .

Malouf, D. *An Imaginary Life* (London: Chatto & Windus, 1978) Ovid in exile, re-imagined.

Miller, M. *Circe* (London: Bloomsbury, 2019) What was she *really* like, the enchantress who turned Odysseus' men into swine?

O'Brian, P. *The Ionian Mission* (London: HarperCollins, 2003) Peerless, Byron-era shenanigans.

Renault, M. *The Bull from the Sea* (London: Virago, 2015)

—*Fire from Heaven* (London: Virago, 2018)

—*The King Must Die* (London: Virago, 2015) If you only have time for one book of fiction set in ancient Greece, make it something by Mary Renault. I'd start with *The King Must Die*.

—*The Persian Boy* (London: Virago, 2014)

Shelley, M. *Frankenstein; or, the Modern Prometheus* (London: Penguin Books, 2003) Captures the Romantic writers' excitement and dread. She was eighteen when she wrote it.

Stewart, M. *This Rough Magic* (London: Hodder & Stoughton, 1964) Gossamer escapist mystery set in Corfu.

Vann, D. *Bright Air Black* (London: William Heinemann, 2017) The story of Medea and Jason, as it might have been.

POETRY

Benson, F. *Vertigo & Ghost* (London: Penguin Books, 2019) Zeus
   unmasked.

Byron, Lord. *A Choice of Byron's Verse*, ed. D. Dunn (London:
   Faber & Faber, 1974)

Glück, L. *The Seven Ages* (Manchester: Carcanet Press Ltd, 2001)

Hughes, T. *Tales from Ovid* (London: Faber & Faber, 1997) I adore
   these retellings of *Metamorphoses*.

Oswald, A. *Memorial: An Excavation of the Iliad* (London: Faber &
   Faber, 2011) A mesmerising catalogue of the dead.

Ritsos, Y. *Repetitions, Testimonies, Parentheses*, trans. E. Keeley
   (Princeton, NJ: Princeton University Press, 1991)

RESOURCES

Perseus   Digital   Library   (www.perseus.tufts.edu/hopper):
   Classical texts in Greek, Roman and English, available for
   free online. Search or browse, just tuck in.

The Theoi Project (www.theoi.com): Clear, well-illustrated site
   for Greek mythology and gods in art and literature.

The Theoi Classical Texts Library (www.theoi.com/Library.html):
   The online library holds ancient Greek and Roman texts in
   English translation.

The Oracle at Delphi (oraclesfromdelphi@gmail.com): It looks
   rather stark written down like that, but this email address
   represents the endpoint of some haphazard but dedicated
   research. Other routes are available . . .

Hellenic Society (www.hellenicsociety.org.uk): Devoted to the study of Greece. Events, magazines and a stirring library in central London.

Romanticism Blog (www.wordsworth.org.uk/blog): Writings on Keats, Byron and the rest.

Hellenion (www.hellenion.org): A US 'church' dedicated to the revival and practice of Hellenic polytheism.

Newstead Abbey (www.newsteadabbey.org.uk): Once the home of Lord Byron, now open to the public.

Archelon: the Sea Turtle Protection Society of Greece (www.archelon.gr): Save the sea turtles! Volunteers needed.

WWF Greece (www.wwf.gr/en): Protect the seas and wild places of Greece!

The World Counts (www.theworldcounts.com): Track the number of earths we need to keep up with our annual levels of consumption and waste.

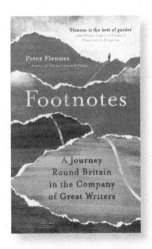

Footnotes

*A Journey Round Britain
in the Company of Great Writers*

A *Guardian* Travel Book of the Year

Shortlisted for the Edward Stanford
Travel Writing Awards

'Provocative and engaging'
Financial Times

Peter Fiennes follows in the footsteps of twelve inspirational writers, bringing modern Britain into focus by peering through the lens of the past.

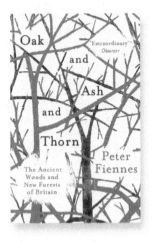

Oak and Ash and Thorn

*The Ancient Woods and
New Forests of Britain*

A *Guardian* Best Nature
Book of the Year

'Extraordinary' *Observer*

Immersing himself in the beauty of woodland Britain, Peter Fiennes explores our long relationship with the woods and the sad and violent story of how so many have been lost.

© Anna Fiennes

Peter Fiennes is the author of the critically acclaimed *Footnotes*, *Oak and Ash and Thorn* and *To War with God*. As the publisher for *Time Out*, he nurtured a lifelong obsession with old guidebooks, creating award-winning city guides, walking books and titles about Britain's countryside and seaside. He lives in south-west London.